The Rise and Fall
of New York City

The Rise and Fall

of

New York City

R O G E R   S T A R R

Basic Books, Inc., Publishers   *New York*

Library of Congress Cataloging in Publication Data
Starr, Roger.
  The rise and fall of New York City.
  Includes index.
    1. New York (N.Y.)—Economic conditions. 2. New
York (N.Y.)—Social conditions. 3. New York (N.Y.)—
Politics and government—1951-   I. Title.
HC108.N7S75   1985   330.9747'1043   83–46086
ISBN 0–465–07031–0

This book is for Jody

Contents

Acknowledgments   ix

Bibliographical Note   xi

Prologue
Cross-Town: Cross-Country   3

Chapter I
The View from the Bridge   9

Chapter II
Equal or Better   28

Chapter III
Repealing Geography   46

Chapter IV
The Unmaking of Manufacturing   68

Chapter V
For Better, For Worse, For an Apartment   84

Chapter VI
Paying for the Crime   105

Chapter VII
Counting on People   128

Contents

Chapter VIII
The Costs of Accomplishments   *147*

Chapter IX
A Little Learning   *167*

Chapter X
What's Government for, Anyway?   *185*

Chapter XI
A Wealth of Ideas   *204*

Chapter XII
Down for the Count   *223*

Epilogue
Cross-Country: Cross-Town   *242*

Index   *247*

Acknowledgments

MANY PEOPLE and institutions have helped give me access to information and data that have been useful in preparing this volume. Among the institutions are the Russell Sage Foundation and its library, the New York City Department of Health, the New York Public Library, the Citizens' Housing and Planning Council of New York, Inc., and its library, the Office of the Comptroller of the City of New York, and the Archives of the City of New York, known as the Municipal Reference Library when some of the research was done.

The Institute for Educational Affairs, and Philip Marcus, its Executive Director, generously made me a grant to cover certain research costs. Amy Carr worked intelligently and diligently to put the grant to use in collecting information about New York's immigration and the effect of the National Origins Immigration Act; I wish I had been able to use more of that information in this book. Steven Faust also helped immeasurably with other aspects of New York's history, mainly in housing. Eugene Bockman, now Archivist of the City of New York, was very helpful even though, at the time, he was the chief of the Municipal Reference Library. Marian Sameth, Associate Director of the Citizens' Housing and Planning Council, was a great help.

A special word for Jody Ward Starr, a close relative by marriage, who kept me at it when I needed spurring and urged me to relax a bit when I needed distraction. Being herself an editor, she had an eagle eye for errors and inconsistencies and a splendid tolerance of authors' whims. I must also thank my editor at the *New York Times*, Max Frankel, who allowed me to coagulate sufficient vacation time to get the work done. Finally, I must thank Sheila Friedling of Basic Books for her work on the manuscript. And Nina Gunzenhauser for her illuminating copy editing. And Martin Kessler, President of Basic Books, for the courtesy of listening with a straight face to my unworthy promises of completion dates.

If the facts herein referred to are correct, the credit belongs to those I have named. If facts have been abused, and inferences unfairly drawn, they have no share in the blame.

Bibliographical Note

I HAVE ENDEAVORED in the text to identify secondary source material whenever it is referred to.

The health statistics in chapter 8 are taken from the Summary of Vital Statistics issued year by year for the City of New York by its Department of Health, 125 Worth Street, New York, New York, 10013. The Bureau of Health Statistics and Analysis of the health department also issues an annual printed leaflet entitled *Vital Statistics by Health Areas and Health Center Districts*. This volume differs from the summary in that it breaks down the citywide totals by health center districts. The distortion that would be caused by the relatively high number of deaths that take place in areas in which hospitals are located has been corrected by the bureau through the establishment of a special area of "institutional" character in each borough. That practice has been followed since 1966.

In earlier years, similar records are provided by the annual reports of the city's Board of Health. Those reports are classified according to political jurisdictions, that is, by wards rather than by health districts. The disease classification is also somewhat different, but the data is roughly comparable, certainly for the purposes relevant here.

In chapter 12, data on New York City's financial status come from the Annual Reports of the comptroller of the city, in New York an official elected every four years. One beneficial result of the fiscal crisis was the institution of new auditing procedures; thus, the reports following 1976 are not precisely comparable with earlier reports, but they are considerably more accurate.

For the years immediately after the Second World War, financial data come from the annual reports of the Mayor of New York City. All of these documents may be examined in the city archives. The annual comptroller's reports can be found in the New York Public Library as well.

The Rise and Fall
of New York City

Prologue

Cross-Town: Cross-Country

FORTY-SECOND STREET crosses Manhattan at its waist, much as the 42nd parallel crosses the United States of America, from the middle of New England through the heartland of the older industrial states, the southern tips of the Great Lakes, the plains and prairies, the Rocky Mountains, and finally the western slope of the Cascades in southern Oregon. Taking the 42nd Street crosstown bus from the Hudson to the East River offers a compressed version of a flight along the 42nd parallel from ocean to ocean. Most observers describe the American continent as a succession of vertiginous contrasts between wealth and poverty, industry and agriculture, desert and fertile plain, mountains and mighty rivers like the Mississippi, which drops less in its course of 1,500 miles than a stream in the Rockies may drop in half a mile.

To ride the 42nd Street bus is to experience the continental contrasts within a tiny compass. The trip raises in the traveler's mind the unfinished question of the American experience: Shall it finally differ from the history of all other nations by achieving a relatively tranquil unity in which residents of widely different gifts and endowments manage to live peacefully with their disappointments? Or shall it repeat the long story of hatred and bloodshed that has soaked the soil of Europe and the rest of the world and that once, indeed, soaked the American land, only to be absorbed somehow as a distant memory, a promise not quite fulfilled?

The crosstown bus starts its trip at the edge of the Hudson River, where ocean vessels once docked. Now that pier is the terminus of the line that takes sightseers around Manhattan Island. The ocean vessels are gone and as far as one looks downstream, there's not a single working pier left in Manhattan. The bus glides easily across Twelfth Avenue, once clogged with trucks waiting to discharge or pick up transatlantic cargoes. Warehouses and factory buildings have disappeared from both sides of 42nd Street, along with waterfront bars and grills and the elevated roadway (now collapsed and removed), in the shadow of which stevedore gangs once shaped up to work the docks. The new, underwater highway, Westway, has not been started; it is tangled in the coils of environmental and administrative law, and its ultimate fate seems to hinge on how the Army Engineers, of all people, will appraise its possible effect on numbers of striped bass that have been spending a part of their lives in an adjacent stretch of the river.

On the sites of vanished industrial buildings two lonesome motels have arisen. We cross Eleventh Avenue, past the site of a former airline bus depot, and flash by a handsome towering apartment complex. Its construction was opposed by a number of local residents who did not know that many of them in time would be paid up to seven thousand dollars a year to live in it. On the right, now, new off-off-off Broadway theaters fill what were once empty storefronts, and the McGraw-Hill Building (no longer occupied by that company), a remarkable blue-tiled monument thirty or more stories high, celebrates a faded real estate dream that private enterprise would find tenants willing to pay a respectable rent to conduct their office business west of the worst block in the city.

The bus hesitates at the interstate bus terminal provided by the Port of New York Authority. As it crosses Eighth Avenue, one stops musing about the past to marvel at the vision of the future presented by 42nd Street's teeming sidewalks and theater marquees.

Anyone who wants to watch real people clawed by nine-foot beasts can satisfy this desire on the movie screens of the city's worst block. Or wants to rent a high school girl from the midwest, or buy a snort of cocaine mixed with heroin, or stage a brief romance with a consenting minor of the same sex, or see live nude (never naked) dancers, or make a deal for some allegedly stolen earrings, or watch three policemen take a knife from a man on his back on the sidewalk, or hear someone vomiting in the gutter, or try to imagine what's going on in a topless bar that one enters by navigating a sharp right-angle turn to keep street loafers from peering inside—here you can have your heart's desire, unless some demon pushes you on further. And so across Seventh Avenue, where the wind blows down Times Square as travelers wait for the bus, having stepped over or around the body of a woman sprawled, like a half-deflated balloon, on the Broadway sidewalk, her possessions, or most of them, stuffed in shopping bags ranged about her. The observer walks past three-card monte dealers, whose tables are corrugated boxes, while their stakes, incongruously, are twenty-dollar bills or even hundreds; walks by a woman, clearly demented, who sits on a stool at the keyboard of a portable electric organ in the middle of the sidewalk, singing with utter tunelessness and slashing angrily at the keys; passes secretaries and their bosses scurrying toward the bus terminal that offers them New Jersey sanctuary; passes gangs of toughs, each with its marching band, a stereophonic radio carried illegally on a strap over someone's shoulder; passes huddled groups of rubber-soled tourists from Dresden or Dubuque, waiting for the sightseeing bus that will take them around the city. The wind picks up old newssheets, ice cream wrappers, napkins from the souvlaki peddlers, brown bags that once held beer cans. Electric signs flash on and off in the darkening sky. Stores offer bargains in cameras, pipes for smoking unnamed substances, hats as broad as parasols, nude dancers, movies barred to anyone under sixteen, peep shows, and electronic games that give the curious a chance to battle invaders from another galaxy.

The bus passes dreary movie houses with triple adult features and "sexsational" acts on stage starting at 10 A.M. These melt into a stretch of sports stores, shoe stores, quick-lunch places filling the air with the smell of frying fat. The bus stops at a traffic light in front of the marble telephone company tower. Then, lumbering across Sixth Avenue, it passes the brilliant, parabolic façade of W.R. Grace's headquarters. On the other side of the street is Bryant Park, once the city's main reservoir and now a park named for the poet of Death and the former editor of the *New York Herald*. Death stalks the park, with needles, packages of drugs, and sudden outbursts of violence not to be understood by passersby. In the corner of the park at Sixth Avenue, on a set of marble benches honoring Latin America's statesmen poets, men doze, and women without stockings, their legs covered with oozing sores, sit and wait, wake and scream, and then sit and wait some more. All along the block between Sixth and Fifth avenues (where are we now, Chicago? St. Louis? Davenport, Iowa?), the north side of the street is dedicated to institutions, including the Graduate Center of the city's own university and the uptown so-called campus of New York University, a private institution. Across, in the park, the peddlers of food cache their unsold products for tomorrow's purchasers, police parade uneasily in pairs, a black man with a saxophone sends cheerless sounds into the gathering darkness, a crowd stands around a fallen body and waits for the ambulance. At the eastern end of the block looms the north façade of the New York Public Library, famous on its Fifth Avenue side for its pair of stone lions and bordered on 42nd Street by a handsome stone fence, desecrated by torn posters and smudges of extra-white on the stones, where graffiti have been etched away with acids and brooms.

As the bus crosses Fifth Avenue, the lucky traveler may get a quick look up its sweeping vertical lines still suggesting a Childe Hassam painting of the city, the venerable department stores (fewer each year) poking their flagpoles into the air above the street, the towering new office buildings and a few apartment houses soaring way above them, neo-Gothic arches celebrating the order, might, and majesty of the American economy. The sidewalks are jammed with shoppers, crowds from the office buildings, and peddlers who set forth their wares or hawk food-stuffs—nuts, dried fruits, roasted chestnuts, immense salted pretzels—from carts in the avenue. Then the vista disappears behind the banks of fast-food stores on the block between Fifth and Madison, briefly opening again as the bus crosses Madison Avenue. The bus soon arrives in front of Grand Central Station, once one of the city's most magnificent buildings, now defaced outside and in by cheap stores and stands tucked into its vacant spaces, selling cookies and brassieres, books and soft ice cream. Under the viaduct that carries Park Avenue across 42nd Street and then splits to encircle the terminal building, the strays gather. People mumble to themselves. A woman in white stock-ings with two dogs, carefully combed, pink bows in their long pearl-gray hair, screams that she loves the whole world; her eyes, as empty as discarded beer cans, roam her face. Three black men huddle, dividing something between them. Suddenly the bus arrives at (should we call it the equivalent of Denver?) the newly refurbished Grand Hyatt Hotel, for years the Commodore but now turned into a magic *trompe l'oeil,* inside and out, a set of curved mirrors so deceptive that you find yourself startled by your own strange image. Tables at which people take cocktails and munch on some special form of midday breakfast cereal hang over the 42nd Street sidewalk; squads of doormen wear squatty top hats and chase away loiterers who impinge too closely on the architectural marvels.

Across Lexington, the newly spruced-up Chrysler Building,

as full of the late 1920s as silk stockings rolled above the knee, calls to mind an ingenuous past, and on the south side of the street, the Chanin Building, another 1920s epic architectural production, Assyria with a steel framework, exudes confidence that age cannot stale. Then on to one of the city's major architectural disasters, the Mobil Building: its outer walls are made from a shiny version of the embossed tin used for the old barber shop ceiling that you would stare at (it was painted white in those days) when you had your early barber shaves knowing your neck would smart for a week after. The bus rises toward Second Avenue, like the transcontinental airplanes of an earlier day that climbed to clear the Rockies. The block starts off with a sanitized Automat, the handsome new Harley Hotel, and the classic *Daily News* skyscraper, and ends in a little open plaza at the corner of Second Avenue, where every weekend and on summer nights the local derelicts hang out, feet wrapped in odd pieces of plastic, mumbling to themselves or simply dozing with an empty wine flask on the stone bench.

One more block, under the tunnel over which Tudor City, an apartment complex from the 1920s, battles with its tenants, and the bus arrives at the far coast, where the United Nations complex rises just north of the busline. On the south side of the street, kids play roller-skate hockey in a playground. Perhaps the United Nations complex itself symbolizes the same question as the bus ride and the airplane trip it stands for: Will the United Nations be swallowed up in the endless bickering and conflicts of interest of its members, in a timeless battle of disorder against order? Will the United States be torn apart by the rising noise of factionalism, after centuries in which it seemed the nation had found possible the rough homogenization of a population drawn from a dozen warring European backgrounds? Will the streets of the city itself be restored to an order suggested by the buildings that continue to be built there, by the still existent but shredding social fabric of its population? Or will all three polities gradually crumble under the impact of technological changes that no one knows how to control?

Chapter I

The View from the Bridge

FEBRUARY 12, 1946, was an ordinary New York City winter day: seasonably cold, to use the jargon invented by weather forecasters years later, customarily damp, and monotonously gray. It was Lincoln's Birthday, a state holiday, and the first "shopping" holiday since the end of the Second World War. It was also the day on which it could be said fairly that New York stood at the very peak of its postwar power, a day never again to be matched in the view it seemed to provide of the undaunting future of a city as powerful in its spirit as it was in its markedly diversified economy. And on this day, Mayor William O'Dwyer, in office only a few weeks, ordered the city to forgo its holiday activities and close down.

People who remember the incident might argue even forty years later about whether the mayor acted properly in closing the city. He was responding to a strike by the tugboat workers who towed oil and coal barges from the mainland United States to the system of islands on which most of New York City's population lived and still lives. The strike had continued for nine days. The threat that New York City would be cut off from its fuel supplies was serious. In 1946 no pipelines brought natural gas from Texas oilfields to the city. There were no oil imports from foreign countries. Even had there been, many of the city's privately owned utility plants, its government-owned stations that generated power for its subways, and its apartment house boilers were equipped to handle no fuel but coal. Washington had decreed early in the Second World War that the oil that could power airplanes, tanks, and ships would not be wasted on generating municipal electricity or apartment house warmth. Oil in the form of gasoline was tightly rationed as well.

While the strike continued, the *New York Times* reported a warning from Albert Pleydell, the city's Commissioner of Purchase and Fuel Administrator, that New York had never faced a more serious disaster. Five days before the Lincoln's Birthday holiday, Mayor O'Dwyer had closed the schools, stopped fuel deliveries to places of amusement, and ordered homes to be kept no warmer than sixty degrees. Electric signs and street lights were dimmed or put out. On 9 February, city employees were sent home and asked to stay there.

All these conservation measures won applause from the *Times.* Its editorials praised the mayor's foresight and wisdom and the way in which he used his labor advisors in an effort— fruitless though it turned out to be—to produce a settlement. The workers remained adamant in their demands for release from the frozen wages of the war. The employers claimed they could not accept arbitration while prices for tugboat services were still under federal control.

When none of his efforts significantly slowed the drain on the city's fuel supplies, Mayor O'Dwyer decided to make a dramatic holiday gesture. Restaurants and theaters were forbidden to open their doors, although Lincoln's Birthday was a traditional Broadway matinee day. Thousands had expected to see Frank Fay in *Harvey,* a play about a genial alcoholic with an imaginary large rabbit for a pet, or Tennessee Williams' first great hit, *The Glass Menagerie,* with Laurette Taylor. Such exotica as nylon stockings and men's white shirts were only beginning to find their way back into the stores after a war-induced absence; many New Yorkers had been looking forward to a day free of work when they might look for them, but like all other places of public assembly, the stores were ordered closed. Public transportation was reduced to a minimum. The *Times* editorialists reversed their previous praise of the mayor and attacked him for acting too precipitously and drastically. Perhaps they had heard from the department stores that were the newspaper's most lucrative local advertisers and surely did not want the closure to be the first of many. It wasn't.

In his emergency proclamation, the mayor gave only the sketchiest justification for his action, probably because there was no balance sheet on which the saving of fuel could be quantified and related directly to the strike. He may have imposed the emergency decree not because he thought it would save a critical amount of fuel, but because he hoped that public indignation would focus on the strikers and their employers. Fear of adverse public reaction might soften both sides enough to make acceptable to them some form of accommodation. It could put the men back to work while the complex underlying issues raised by national price control could be worked out with Washington. The fact that the people of the city took the mayor's order in stride, obeyed it, and for the most part did not complain about its interference with their plans may have helped direct O'Dwyer's action to its target. The strike ended within a day.

The mayor's assumptions about the spirit of the people proved correct. The *New Yorker* caught that moment of high confidence a few days after it happened, in a few paragraphs in its "Notes and Comment" section of February 23, 1946. It wrote, "We were part of a smiling, idle crowd . . . which . . . seemed to fill every nook and dingle of Central Park. . . . It was indeed . . . a feast day . . . and we spent it as if we were under the equivalent not of Martial Law, but of the Mardi Gras."

In the years that have followed, other mayors have faced

emergencies that required similarly resolute action. The subway strike that began on January 1, 1966, John Lindsay's first day in office, brought him to the microphone to ask New Yorkers and suburbanites to stay away from work because driving to the city would jam its streets. In this talk the new mayor used the phrase "Fun City" to describe New York, setting a peculiarly inappropriate context for the request that working people give up their livelihood. The mayor's appeal had little apparent effect on the New Yorkers of 1966; they crowded in as best they could. Within a few years, the Lindsay administration had changed its philosophy drastically. The Lindsay who became a Democrat on August 11, 1971, and who was seeking to end the inequities suffered by the city's nonwhite population would surely not have used the term that he used in 1966. The fun had largely dissipated. In his first year, Lindsay and his closest associates still thought of themselves as bringing verve, style, and modernism to a City Hall encrusted with the habits and venalities of the "old pols." By 1969 they were themselves old pols.

Still later, during the transit strike of 1980, Mayor Edward Koch took precisely the opposite tack and rallied people to walk to work, defying the strikers. He was clearly much more successful in keeping up public morale than Mayor Lindsay had been in trying to keep people from working. His own account suggests that he felt that the people of the city had defied the transit workers so successfully that it might have been possible to impose a lean settlement on the strikers. Governor Hugh Carey, however, felt otherwise. He knew that labor union support was of great importance to his own political career and that he would be blamed by union leaders for the inevitable penalties the law would impose on them. Richard Ravitch, chairman of the Metropolitan Transportation Authority, an institution that did not exist in 1946, was reluctant to impose so draconian a settlement on the work force that he would have had a difficult morale problem afterward. In short, in 1980 the political crosscurrents in New York had become so much stronger than they had been in 1946 that not even Mayor Koch's dramatic and charismatic leadership at the moment of crisis could restore the sense of unified purpose that came naturally in 1946.

Transit crises were not the only disasters that tested the city in the years after 1946. Two in particular, both of them power blackouts, make a clear comment on the decline in New York's civility, the custom of treating other citizens with the minimal courtesy to which shared status as New Yorkers entitles them. In 1965, a major power failure darkened the entire Northeast on a November night. In the city it stopped subway trains between stations, stalled elevators between floors, and left streets and homes in total darkness, totally unprotected against lawlessness. In spite of the exposure, nothing much happened except, if rumors are right, a startling one-night increase in the fertilization rate, observable after a nine-month interval.

On 13 July 1977, a blackout limited to New York City's own power supply suddenly plunged the hot summer city into the same darkness as in 1965. The difference in public behavior was cataclysmic. Gangs of looters materialized almost immediately. They sacked stores in many parts of the city, fixing chains to the iron curtains that covered store windows and using automobiles to peel the curtains off as easily as one prepares to invade the meat of a seedless orange. Nearly 4,500 people were arrested for looting and other offenses and had to be detained temporarily, pending arraignment or dismissal, in makeshift accommodations in police headquarters and in overcrowded jails. Black leaders accused the administration of inhuman treatment. Civil rights leaders agreed. The incident heated racial strife.

New Yorkers in 1979 had clearly changed since the strike of 1946 had drawn them together into unified action, and so had the city of New York itself. To evaluate a city and its potential, professionals who rate municipal bonds have invented an elaborate set of standards. They talk about the total per-capita assessed value of privately owned real estate, the ratio between tax collections and debt service needs, the breadth of occupational variety in the city, the character and condition of the city's own facilities, including streets and pipes and transport systems. Then, of course, they leave numerical data behind and speculate about the quality of municipal leadership. They look at the participation of the elites of the city—leaders in business, education, and philanthropy—in the processes of government. They even, though they may not put it in writing, speculate about the spirit of the municipality, the willingness of people in general to make sacrifices for the common good and to support governmental reforms that, over a long period, will make the city a better place to live in, though not necessarily one with lower taxes.

New York in 1946 would have qualified extremely well under many of these criteria. It was certainly the world's strongest surviving city. The war had scarcely touched it at all. It had lost its share of men and women in the military. It had suffered the humiliation of drowning the S.S. *Normandie,* the largest passenger ship in the world, in the course of rehabilitating her for war duty, at a pier in the Hudson River. A welder's torch started a fire, and by the time the city fire department had finished off the blaze, the ship was so full of water that she simply rolled over at her pier. She was dragged off to the shipwreckers, bottoms up, a chilling reminder in the winter of 1942 that not even Pearl Harbor and the military disaster unfolding in the Philippines had yet awakened New Yorkers to the real threat of the war begun by the Axis powers.

Mayor O'Dwyer's Lincoln's Birthday proclamation offered New Yorkers a chance to know, without expending blood, sweat, or tears, the exalting experience that is a part of warfare, the sense of common purpose. Perhaps what made it seem so happy an occasion, an unexpected Mardi Gras, was that it gave citizens of that unscarred contributor to the war effort a sense of having participated in some small way in an experience that tested them. They felt they had passed the test.

In 1946, New York was the last survivor among the major world cities. London had been blitzed, its human and structural losses severe, its economy desperately wounded. There was no such city as Berlin; the nation it had led was split in two, and the city itself, divided into zones, was governed by occupying armies. Paris, liberated by alien armies despite the presence of a small symbolic French force, was exhausted by years of foreign occupation. As it pieced together what the Germans had left it, it faced severe political and economic problems in attempting to reconcile the bitter internal disputes growing out of the war. Tokyo was under an occupying army, its dreams of empire ruptured, facing the challenges of revamping its whole political and social system to the satisfaction of its western conquerors and of developing a competitive market economy. Moscow, never quite occupied and not grievously damaged by war, was an enigma, but surely the Russian losses in wealth and manpower, piled on top of the weaknesses in the Communist system exposed by the war, clouded its already mysterious future.

New York stood in sharp contrast. If one imagined the city as a ship of state, the view from its bridge was inspiring. Its economy had boomed during the war, yet it did not face major retooling problems because the products it had made for the war effort were very like those it made for civilians. In 1946 it was barely beginning to satisfy pent-up demands for homes, services, goods, office space. To be sure, the prewar years had left New Yorkers with many misgivings. Until war and rumors of war had created a demand for its manufactured products— clothing, books, prepared food, some nonferrous metals, ship repairs—unemployment had been high. Some of its biggest real estate investors—among them Vincent Astor—had publicly announced that they were getting rid of all their blue chip New York holdings; Astor was quoted in *Business Week* on 19 September 1942 as saying that in future there would be little interest in expensive Manhattan apartments, because of the socioeconomic changes imposed by the New Deal. The city's own capital plant had deteriorated. Its workers, among them the tugboat men, wanted urgently to make up for years of stagnant wages in the face of creeping prices. Memories of the depression that immediately followed the First World War were still fresh among the older people. And what was the future of the private economy, of which New York was the nation's capital, in the face of the immense growth of the public economy, headquartered on the Potomac? Who would be interested in common stocks in the Century of the Common Man?

Beyond these doubts, however, it should have been possible to discern the shape of the future. Europe desperately needed everything America could make and ship across the ocean, mostly through the port of New York. The greatest problem was the European nations' lack of money, but anyone with foresight could have imagined that America was rich enough to supply the money with which its own products could be bought. The accumulated purchasing power in the New York region alone would sustain immense levels of demand, big enough to turn Long Island's potato fields into much more valuable sites for mass-produced small houses. Wall Street would grow until it dwarfed the absurd dreams of 1929's optimists. The common man, it would turn out, did indeed want common stocks, and busy downtown brains were quick to find ways to let him have them. New methods of pooling money, through mutual funds and the pension and welfare funds of unions, greatly expanded the ownership of business enterprise. The innovations would create a need for unprecedented work forces in the financial districts of the city, especially as computers, new instruments for recording and transmitting data, would multiply the demand for facts. Banks shed their ancient policy of lending only to those who did not really need their funds. Wholly new credit enterprises would develop, employing thousands and raising questions about the nature of money that would not be resolved to everyone's satisfaction even fifty years later.

But beyond economic projections of established patterns of demand and supply were projections based on the prospect of new inventions like the television set and the transoceanic airplane. Beyond these economic projections, moral imperatives translated into political demands would stimulate another set of activities for New York. Mayor O'Dwyer began to voice these in his early messages to the voters. The city had to provide higher levels of pay for its work force; the city's employees must be given dignity. The city's buildings, already known to have been neglected during the war, urgently needed repair. The city's health services to its people had to be improved. A good city had to make adequate provision for those who could not support themselves and their children. The city had to intervene to supply housing for the returning veterans, who would surely marry and want homes of their own. The children who had been too young to participate in the war effort might become a special problem, feeling themselves forgotten and overlooked, and the city must prepare to spend money and invest time in dealing with the urgent problems of these youths. There were signs that as new housing was built on vacant land in some of the less dense sections of the city, those who moved would require new schools and other city services; they were citizens, too, and the city had to prepare itself to provide for them. At the same time, in the older sections of the city, some people were living in miserable, unsuitable housing, in rickety tenements, rural shacks, even in houses built on stilts at the edge of polluted Jamaica Bay.

These were the challenges that faced the mayor in 1946. They were challenges that would not only continue to confront mayors to come but would substantially reshape the nature of the mayoralty in future administrations. Let us look briefly at those mayors who presided over the dramatic changes that occurred in the city between 1946 and the fiscal crisis of 1975.

William O'Dwyer was an energetic and decent man who had studied law while a city policeman, worked as an assistant district attorney in Brooklyn, and risen through the political ranks of the Brooklyn Democratic organization. For him the challenges had to be met without gaudy rhetoric or an igniting vision of the future. He fought hard to maintain the subway fare at its traditional five cents. He was sympathetic to organized labor, and he accepted financial support from city employee organizations in his reelection campaign. He tried to modernize some of the processes of government, establishing voluntary boards that would help coordinate youth services. Since he did not visualize the immense wealth that would flow into New York City in the subsequent twenty years, he was careful to minimize the city's fiscal obligations by allowing the Port of New York Authority to take over assignments like the completion of what is now Kennedy International Airport.

O'Dwyer had been born in Ireland and was very much at home in the traditional ethnic politics of the city. His fiscal caution was balanced by a rather flamboyant manner; he had a taste for Florida vacations with Generoso Pope, the owner of a large building materials company and of *Il Progresso,* the biggest Italian-language newspaper in the city, as well as a radio station. A widower, O'Dwyer made newspaper readers happy by courting and marrying a handsome former model, Sloan Simpson, shortly after his 1949 reelection. A certain amount of gossip and suspicion of intimacy with organized crime hung about him, partly because he had come from the Brooklyn District Attorney's office. Among cognoscenti of New York's crime-and-politics, the mention of that office was always good for a wink; it was somehow implicated in the mysterious death of Abe Reles, a material witness in the "Murder Incorporated" investigation. And during Senator Estes Kefauver's later investigation of municipal corruption, one of the first great events of early television, it became known that while campaigning for election in 1945, O'Dwyer, then a brigadier general in the army, visited Frank Costello at his home. Costello was always described by the press as an underworld figure very influential in Tammany Hall, the Manhattan organization of the Democrats, a group whose support would be especially useful to an ambitious Brooklynite running for the city mayorality. If the rumors of unsavory connections ever had any factual substance, it was never fully revealed, although the city was left to guess why the mayor resigned from office eight months after his second term started in 1950 only to turn up as American ambassador to Mexico.

In an election to fill the balance of O'Dwyer's term, the president of the City Council—second only to the mayor in importance (at least on paper)—Vincent R. Impelliteri, won; he held office until the end of 1953. Although he certainly did not think of himself in that way, Impelliteri was a caretaker mayor, continuing the cautious O'Dwyer policies without the O'Dwyer flair for interesting the press. In 1983, thirty years after Impelliteri left office to become a judge, older New Yorkers liked to tell each other the Impelliteri elevator story. In one of the story's many forms, the narrator describes an elevator ride during which he notices a familiar face. He suddenly realizes that he has been riding with Vincent R. Impelliteri, a former mayor of the city. "I didn't recognize him at first because I didn't know he was still alive," the narrator ends his account. "As a matter of fact, I wasn't sure he ever had been."

With the election of Robert F. Wagner, Jr., in 1953, the nature of the city's mayoralty began to change. Private citizens, community leaders, and businessmen, as well as those responsible for civic institutions, began to demand that city government do more than simply keep city departments running. Despite its limited taxing powers, they wanted city government to assume new roles in solving social problems, assisting cultural growth, stimulating the development of important but neglected areas of the city, and offering higher education and better health care to a larger part of the population than had been served in the past.

Mayor Wagner, a well-schooled Democrat, trained in political theory and practice by his father, the distinguished liberal senator whose name was linked with national labor law and subsidized housing, was nevertheless viewed as something of a maverick by the Tammany Hall leadership. Unlike O'Dwyer, he was a Manhattan resident. (Nobody seems to recall where Impelliteri had lived before he moved into the mayor's official mansion immediately after O'Dwyer's unexpected departure.) Wagner was somewhat less tall than he looked, and a master of a great political *tour de force:* he made the average man think that

Wagner was barely his intellectual equal, more probably his inferior. The Tammany Hall people, however, had already begun to find out how wrong the average man could be. They recognized that as chairman of the City Planning Commission, an appointive office, and later as borough president of Manhattan, an elective office, Wagner had tuned his sensibilities to the feelings both of ordinary New Yorkers and the city's elite leadership. He had developed immense patience, which friends who were committed to the same political goals as his own frequently criticized as sloth or impassivity. They were quite wrong. Wagner instinctively distinguished those events that would shape themselves from those that required prompt intervention. He would store the deferrable matters in a closet, letting them decide for themselves whether they would turn into vintage Chateau d'Yquem or vinegar. He had strong connections to the city's ethnic groups, probably stronger with the German and, increasingly, with the Jewish groups than O'Dwyer, somewhat less strong with the Italians.

What Wagner had that no New York mayor had had in many years was a Big Three education (B.A. and L.L.B, Yale; graduate work, Harvard Business School) and the ability to get along with New York's social elites. Particularly through his first wife, Susan, who died near the end of his second term in City Hall, he was able to keep his ties to the business leadership while winning the support of traditional European ethnics and the labor movement. Simultaneously, he was admired by the social welfare establishment, one of the city's most powerful groups. In turn, the social welfare institutions had immense influence on the editorial writers and publishers of the *New York Times* and the *Herald Tribune*, the city's most influential newspapers.

Mayor Wagner set for New York City its first social policy goal since the war: to create a "slumless city," an "open city," in which no one would live in substandard housing, work at substandard wages, or suffer from substandard working conditions. The promise of the open city meant that no one would be discriminated against in finding work or a place to live by virtue of race, color, or any other invidious distinction. In Wagner's first term, the city passed legislation forbidding housing discrimination and set up a Commission on Human Rights. To meet the costs of the expanding social programs without having to impose higher tax levels on the city, Wagner invented a way to capitalize some of the city's operating costs. The Wagnerian improvisation legalized long-term borrowing to cover ordinary expenses of government, instead of limiting its use to paying for long-term capital investment. It was truly a new course for city government, and Wagner had to strain to keep up with the demands of the social welfare groups. To head off the growing power of the Democratic reformers, who generally claimed they were seeking advanced social goals and not simply the attainment of political power within the city, he sought reelection to a third term in 1961 by joining with them. The regular organization, against which Wagner declared war, put its own candidate, State Comptroller Arthur Levitt, in the race against him.

Mayor Wagner served out his third term considerably less successfully than his first two. The presence of reformers at City Hall tended to upset the rhythm that was a natural expression of his political timing. Though he was committed to the reformers' goals in social policy, he was enough of a realist to worry over the mounting costs. The reformers, on the other hand, having believed that Wagner had become one of them, despaired at his slow pace, mistaking its wisdom. By the time he completed his term in 1965, Wagner and the city had had enough of each other. He became ambassador to Spain, and John Lindsay took over a city whose government was now following headlong the course marked out for it by Wagner and the Manhattan elites.

John Lindsay came to office on January 1, 1966, having been elected as a Republican with the support of the Liberal party. His supporters celebrated his inauguration in an atmosphere that suggested the beginning of a new era in American urban life. Actually, the Lindsayites were committed to two courses that would be very hard to follow simultaneously. The first was a reformation of all the processes of municipal government, bringing to City Hall the benefits of modern management techniques, clarifying lines of responsibility, and imposing new views of how city departments should be arranged. In fact, none of this was quite as new or innovative as it seemed. Mayor Wagner had for years been relying on the advice of Luther Gulick, a noted student of public administration, to help reorganize the city government. The Mayor's Committee on Management Survey had made endless recommendations, and the city government had been reshaped to include an official called the deputy mayor–city administrator, who had paper responsibilities for seeing that all the city agencies ran well. At the same time, the city government had a budget director, responsible to the mayor for continuous auditing of the same agencies to make sure that they were living within their budgets. Since the budget director had control over the money, while the city administrator had control only over the people, there was no doubt that the budget director would prevail. Sometime after 1965, the city administrator disappeared.

The Lindsay administration's first step was to wipe out what its members and advisers took to be the vestiges of Wagnerism. Since Wagnerism was only a Democratic early version of their own reformist Republicanism, these changes were never as sweeping in reality as they could be made to look on paper. But the second set of changes that Lindsay hoped to bring about were far more important and eventually took precedence over the more formal changes in municipal structure. What the Lindsay administration wanted was an activist municipal government striking hard not merely to keep the manholes closed and the streets open but to raise the quality of life for everyone. Everyone in this case tended to mean the poor, especially the minority group poor, and the rich. The poor, aided also by the Great Society programs of the federal government (which incidentally aided the emergence of a temporary nonwhite middle class), were to be given easier access to welfare help, better

health care, and protection against police brutality or dis-
courtesy. The rich were to get a more interesting city, culturally
and architecturally, a city with a soul, an intellect, and style.
The small business people and many union workers and fore-
men, the people who lived in one- and two-family homes in
Brooklyn, Queens, the East Bronx, and Staten Island, felt themselves left out of all this. As someone said in comparing Wagner
and Lindsay: "If a letter carrier in Brooklyn awakened with sore
feet, Bob Wagner's arches hurt, and Lindsay wondered where
Brooklyn is."

Above all, however, the Lindsay years were those in which
the capabilities of the city seemed limitless. If parents complained that local schools were poorly managed, let the city
tap the potential of local citizens and give them more power
over their schools. Let public hospitals in the future give private rooms to their indigent patients, just as voluntary hospitals provided them for rich patients. Let the city take on the
costs of cultural institutions, because New York needs them.
And so it went. These were the days when guests at dinner
parties turned to the nearest government official and asked
why, in the richest city in the world, did the government say
we can't afford. . . . And there would follow a list of urgent
necessities ranging from comfort stations for dogs to better
taxicabs, preservation of more landmarks, and better education for the poor.

On August 11, 1971, Lindsay led a baptismal march of high
officials from City Hall to the Board of Elections, where they
changed their registration from Republican to Democrat. As an
independent, with Liberal support, Lindsay had won reelection
in 1969. The two subsequent mayors, Abraham Beame, who
held office from 1974 to 1978, and Edward Koch, who took
office in 1978, have been trying to retreat from enough of the
promises made and expectations raised to manage the city effi-
ciently without raising taxes, to encourage economic growth,
and to deal realistically with the city's human and social potentialities. It has not been easy so far, nor will it be.

The mayors and civic leaders who demanded that New York accomplish prodigious social policy gains may have been idealistic, even visionary, but they cannot be described as misguided in their assessment of the city's strengths. New York had them in profusion. In 1946, when it stood alone in contrast to the badly wounded world cities with which it traded, New York could measure its strengths not merely against other cities' weaknesses but on an absolute scale. If this had not been so, it would not have grown as swiftly as it did, even without being the nation's political capital, empowered to draw strength from many achievements that were actually made by other parts of the country. It developed its own economy, attracted a migrant population, and achieved a remarkably high standard of living because of the strengths that anyone standing beside Mayor O'Dwyer on the bridge in 1946 could have seen.

New York's first advantage, the natural cut of earth that seemed to have made it one of the world's finest harbors, was still its greatest asset in 1946. The harbor itself was huge and just about as perfectly protected as though it had been deliberately designed for the purpose. Its two large bays, the Lower Bay, open to the Atlantic, and the Upper Bay, reached from the ocean through a natural strait, the Narrows, offered a sheltered nexus for cargoes coming from North, South, and East. In the 1820s a canal had been built that linked the Hudson River and the Great Lakes. Once the harbor started to attract the flow of transatlantic cargoes and passengers, its water resources were supplemented by rail lines, connecting the city with all parts of the continent.

Inevitably, a city built around so many waterways would have to overcome internal problems of transportation: the ferries that connected the city's islands were grossly inadequate for modern life, and thus the city could not be unified politically as it is now until bridges had been built and rail transit tunnels were in contemplation. New York City solved its internal transport system with a superb subway network that could concentrate millions of workers in the central business district every day and get them home at night. No city could imitate this transportation system unless it constructed its own matching subway, whose cost, at a later date, would be many times greater than New York's had been.

Indirectly from the benefit of favorable geography flowed a second great asset of New York City, a remarkably strong manufacturing economy. Geography located the city close to both its national and its overseas markets. In addition, from the middle of the nineteenth century on, geography brought a steadily growing supply of semiskilled European workers. Their presence made possible the development of enterprises that made consumer goods for a growing market: garments, particularly those mass-produced for women, books, processed food, beer, and a host of small metal products. The manufacturing base supported more than a labor force. It also provided a market for service industries that maintained manufacturing equipment, stocked spare parts, and sold secondhand machinery. This chain of external suppliers made it easy for new enterprises to enter into the manufacture of new products with limited capital. The presence of so much manufacturing helped to insure the city against the risks of concentrating its labor force in the service sector. Spreading the risks increased the margin of safety. At the end of the war, New York added more value to manufactured products than any other American city, including Detroit and Pittsburgh.

A third asset of New York City in 1946 was its population, reasonably well educated by an effective school system backed by the most comprehensive city system of higher education in the country. The population provided a capable work force for the service and manufacturing trades, while large financial corporations were able to attract and keep immense staffs of qualified women as clerks in their office operations. The skills of the work force included highly specialized artisans, like diamond cutters. Such workers could be essential to the start-up or expansion of enterprises. Obviously, New York's myriad specialists attracted others from abroad or other parts of the country to join them. In this way they gave the city special advantages in fields in which other cities could not compete at all.

A fourth asset of immediate postwar New York was its immense housing supply, backed by an effective housing industry. While the national image of New York City was that of a place where only the very rich and the indigent were provided for, the fact is that New York had a large, well-housed middle class. Not only were many middle-class citizens living in one- and two-family homes outside Manhattan, but many others lived in new, modern apartment houses much closer to the city center and served well by mass transit lines. It was certainly true that many poorer families lived in deplorable housing, but that was a problem that could be handled. In any case, it would not discourage working families from coming to New York in search of employment, feeling that they would be able to find suitable housing after getting there.

A fifth asset of New York City was its lawfulness. At the end of 1945 the annual report of the Department of Correction noted that the city's prison population was below .1% of its total population. Its 20,000-member police force was quite professional by American standards, and its criminal justice system worked well. More important, even, was the extent to which the population voluntarily complied with the laws governing such minor offenses as smoking on public transportation facilities or committing nuisances on the streets. New York's population was not as docile and well-behaved as that of London, perhaps, and it had a serious and dangerous concentration of organized crime engaged in extortion from the commercial and manufacturing enterprises that needed services like trash collection or trucking, but its rates of pilferage were not prohibitively high, and interracial violence was rare indeed.

Another advantage possessed by the city in the immediate postwar years was its remarkable set of health facilities and institutions. No other city had a set of public hospitals that provided care to so large a part of the population as New York did. The municipal system was backed up by an intricate network of voluntary and proprietary hospitals. In a world that looked forward to an expansion of medical care for the entire population, New York had a significant head start. The hospitals and affiliated institutions also offered employment opportunities for a relatively low-skilled but ambitious work force. And behind the hospitals and other health institutions stood New York's own public health resources, a magnificent water supply system, a sanitation department that was as well equipped as any of its time, and a health department that ranked with the nation's best.

These last elements were part of a governmental system that must also be counted among the city's most important assets. New York had achieved, almost fifty years before the end of the war, a metropolitan government by incorporating suburban areas—some with a truly rural aspect—into a new, greater city. Its tax base was broader than that of most American cities, and its unused land resources were available for future population growth. If metropolitan government was as important to urban fiscal health as students of the subject insisted, New York was fortunate in its heritage of pioneering public administration.

Finally, no one can afford to overlook the assets that the city's rich cultural life provided. Its live theater had been left as a unique institution when theaters all over the nation closed down. Its privately owned opera company, supplemented by a city opera company, was one of the world's finest. Its museums, galleries, concert halls, universities, and specialized schools attracted talented people from all over the world as students and teachers. Given the difficulties faced by the war-torn cultural centers of the western world, New York's cultural life would surely be expected to flourish by contrast.

Those assets, at least, are what seemed to promise so much, to justify the gathering hopes of the people of the city on that gray February day when they took heart from the mayor and, as the *New Yorker* put it, turned their martial law into a Mardi Gras.

Chapter II

Equal or Better

FORTY YEARS after the end of the Second World War, it is possible to visit New York, or even to live there, and feel that little has changed since Mayor O'Dwyer closed down the city for a day and the postwar era began. One may even come to the conclusion that for many New Yorkers things are better than they ever were.

That conclusion may be easiest to reach in the proper circumstances on the upper East Side of Manhattan, though not only there. Imagine a room at the private, proprietary Doctors Hospital, overlooking Gracie Mansion, the mayor's official residence, Carl Schurz Park, and the East River. Hardly straining the imagination, let us conjure up a young mother in the bed, looking out toward Queens and the Hell Gate Bridge, enjoying a glass of champagne with visitors who have come to congratulate her on the birth of a daughter—her third and last child, as she assures her guests. Not remembering her own birth very clearly, she is not aware that her mother occupied the same hospital room thirty-five years earlier.

There are some slight changes in Doctors Hospital. Although the young woman now in bed had the very obstetrician that her mother had, her father had not been expected to be in the

delivery room at her birth; indeed, his presence there would
have been scandalous in 1949, the year of her birth. The nursing
staff, formerly of Irish and German extraction, is now largely
Hispanic and black. There was then no television set hanging
from a bracket in a corner of the room, and *quiche* was not on
the luncheon menu. The views of the river will seem the same
to the present occupant, who has no way of recalling that river
traffic has dropped to a small fraction of what it was when she
made her initial appearance.

The conversation between the new mother and her friends
can easily be superimposed on the words her mother and *her*
friends might have spoken in the same room; only a few topical
references would have to be eliminated from both. The truly
important matters of how one lives and what one's husband
does, and where one goes, and what organizations one spends
one's time with—these remain. Our young mother's husband is
a lawyer, product of the Harvard Law School, like his father.
The son has for several years now been a partner in what would
be called a Wall Street firm but for the fact that its offices are
no longer on Wall Street but in a new office building on Park
Avenue in midtown.

Just as her parents did, the couple with their three children
live in a cooperative apartment on the upper East Side. Her
father and mother, however, bought their apartment before the
Second World War because they thought it a good buy and
liked the idea that fellow-cooperators were carefully selected.
The younger couple bought their apartment because they had
to, when the apartment house they lived in was converted from
rental units to cooperative ownership. It has turned out to be
the best investment they ever made.

Their oldest child, a boy, goes to a school very like the one
that prepared his father for St. Paul's (Concord). Students still
wear blue caps with the school initial on them. Their elder
daughter is finishing her first year at nursery school. The children's mother had been cared for as a child by a live-in *mademoi-
selle,* but the dearth of live-in help is one of the major changes

of the postwar years. Naturally, for the first six months there will be a trained baby nurse for the new arrival. Selecting the right person is a traditional activity as important as selecting the right names for the infant.

If it were not for the new arrival, the woman in the bed and her husband would be getting ready to go to Shelter Island for the weekend in their Volvo station wagon. Her parents drove a Packard touring car for years, proving that even in these circles there have been some significant changes. Though she does not work for pay, many of her friends do, particularly after their divorces. Twice a week she plays tennis with other women at the River Club. Weekends she gets in a few sets of mixed doubles on Shelter Island. Now she will have to get back in shape; the last few months have been something of a drag.

Of course, she has been able to keep up with her other major interest, her memberships in the Carnegie Hill Association and the city-wide Landmarks Conservancy. The Carnegie Hill group is dedicated to preventing the wrong kinds of buildings from going up on Madison Avenue in the general area between 86th and 96th streets, or on the side streets between Fifth and Park avenues in the same part of the city. It keeps her busy writing letters to city departments, building owners, and other civic groups with similar interests. Sometimes the work, though generally interesting, begins to seem a little picky, and then she's glad she's equally involved with the Conservancy. Not only are the people a little more interesting—some of them very much more interesting—but they are concerned with the entire city. They are working hard to protect it from some of the crazy things that people will do in their endless search for the almighty dollar. Her mother was active in civic life, too; she was in the Junior League, as was her daughter for a time. Our young mother, however, did not find that quite as stimulating.

It is not necessary to be as rich as the owners of cooperatives on the upper East Side to feel at home in the city despite its many changes. The postwar world has been good to many New

Yorkers. In the East Bronx, just south of one of that borough's classic thoroughfares, Gun Hill Road, there is a development of modest but quite attractive red tapestry-brick detached houses on a bit of high ground to the west of the Thruway, across from Co-Op City, the largest cooperative development in New York and perhaps in the nation. These houses are prewar buildings, built long before the immense cooperative was conceived of. Originally they were sold mainly to families of Italian ancestry, who were moving up from the more urban environment of East Tremont Road, about a mile south of Gun Hill. The neighborhood still has some of the Italian families who first occupied the area. A remarkably good Italian restaurant stands at the corner where the side street meets Gun Hill Road. The present occupants of the third house from the intersection of two of the local streets are a black couple and their children.

The husband and father is a New Yorker, raised in one of the old row houses in a black neighborhood in Washington Heights. His father was a skilled mechanic who worked for one of the automobile dealerships on Broadway, about thirty blocks south of their home. The row house in which the son was raised was owned by another black, a retired post office worker who bought the house with his savings and a credit union loan and did most of the floor-through subdividing with his own hands after retirement.

The son, now a husband and father, moved to the East Bronx from one of the Housing Authority's projects for middle-income families not too far from where they now live. His wife, who trained to be a schoolteacher, now works as the director of one office of a Bronx community organization largely supported with government money and trying to deal with some of the acute social problems of the South Bronx. They have two children. Although they are not Catholic, the older child attends a parochial school on East Tremont Avenue.

The husband attended and graduated from George Washington High School in Manhattan. He was clever with numbers and decided to study accountancy at Baruch College, part of the

City University system, located on 23d Street in Manhattan. He worked in a drug store, selling and helping with some of the bookkeeping. In the late 1960s, after he had spent two years at Baruch, he went to work full time for a savings and loan institution not far from where he was living with his parents. Within a remarkably short time, he answered an advertisement in a New York black newspaper and qualified for a job at a major bank. This was the time of the Great Society, and the bank, like other major corporations, was not only opening its jobs to non-white minority employees but actively soliciting them.

Promotions came somewhat faster than might have been expected, and within a few years he had qualified as an Assistant Secretary, a promotion that put him on a rung, though a low one, of the executive ladder. His rise was hampered by his lack of a college diploma, but he made up for it with natural intelligence, mastery of accounting principles, a pleasant manner, and his race, which now, after all these years, turned out to be something of an advantage, at least at the lower managerial levels at which he was working. Buying a home after three years in the no-cash-subsidy project, as the Housing Authority called the development in which they were living, seemed like a giant step. His wife, who had graduated from the State University College at Albany, had lived down the block from where he had lived with his parents, and they were both excited at the prospect of having a free-standing home of their own, in a neighborhood in which neither auto nor drug traffic would menace their children, and, it must be admitted, at the sense that they were to live in a neighborhood in which both whites and blacks had homes.

Although it was perfectly clear to both of them that race would continue to play a dominant role not only in their lives but in their children's future, and their children's children's, a window had been opened in their lifetimes that his own father had warned him would never be opened. At first, whenever he and his wife had dinner at the Italian restaurant on the corner, that warning kept coming back into his mind. But as time passed, it came back only when some white person looked at him in the restaurant with an expression that said only too clearly, what are *they* doing here? Instead of dropping his eyes, as he had done at first, he simply stared back.

If he got another promotion at the bank or his wife changed jobs again with a real increase in salary, they would move on, probably out of the city. But the city had been good to them.

Perhaps the most remarkable of all transitions in the status of the city's working people was the change that came in the postwar years to the people who worked for the city government or one of its dependent agencies like the Board of Education, which runs the whole public education system up to and including high school. In 1945, when the war ended, garbage collectors and "white wings," as they were called, who swept the streets, were the lowest paid and least dignified of all city employees, earning between $1,801 and $4,800 a year, according to the *New York Times* of September 21, 1945. Those who retired with that amount as their final annual wage, and whose pensions were governed by it, were in real trouble for the rest of their lives, and so were their widows. But the people who went to work in the late 1950s and the 1960s found themselves and their way of life remarkably transformed.

By 1980, the starting salary for a sanitation worker was more than $18,000 a year, and counting in the last year's overtime earnings, their retirement pay after twenty-five years' service could well exceed $20,000 a year, more than six times the working salary earned by their predecessors.

In true purchasing power, their income was probably closer to double what their predecessors earned, but that somewhat understates the magnitude of the change. The high wages paid during the working years made it possible for the sanitation workers, like other city employees, to acquire homes, which were at least partially amortized as they approached or reached retirement, and sometimes even second or vacation homes, autos, trailers, and boats. These accumulated possessions meant that after retirement the former city employees could maintain a significantly higher standard of living than the bare figures of their retirement pay suggest. Even more important to many of these workers was the sense of dignity and personal worth that higher pay brought with it. They began to think of themselves as something more professional than "garbage collectors," and even their own children talked of them with a measure of respect.

It is easy enough to visualize the difference between the 1980 home and the early postwar childhood home of a sanitation worker, perhaps brought up in one of the tenement houses along Mulberry Street in lower Manhattan, or on First or Second Avenue in East Harlem. Six-story walk-up buildings these were, and those in lower Manhattan often did not have toilets within the apartment, but out in the common hallway on each floor. They dated back to the 1870s and 1880s and were as anachronistic alongside typical homes in postwar America as ice boxes and telephones with cranks.

By 1980, a sanitation worker could expect to live in Benson-hurst, a section of Brooklyn that borders the Lower Bay. From the promenade that runs between an automobile parkway and the waters of the bay (here called Gravesend Bay), one can see the Atlantic Highlands behind Sandy Hook in New Jersey and watch the ocean vessels coming across the bay from the Atlantic and threading their way through Ambrose Channel and the Narrows into the Upper Bay.

Homes in Bensonhurst are generally semidetached, brick-veneered two-family houses. The stoops that lead up from the private concrete sidewalks to the front doors have brick posts and balustrades on both sides, and the posts are topped with white cast-stone caps. Statues ornament the small front gardens, sometimes set off by mirrored globes atop gray pedestals. The houses cannot possibly be compared to the tenement houses left behind in Manhattan, or even the smaller houses of Red Hook along the Brooklyn waterfront. Yet the people who live here, including the contemporary sanitation workers and their families, are leaving for Staten Island, where the homes are even nicer, the atmosphere is more rural, and the schools have fewer disruptive children. By this, of course, some mean disruptive and some mean black.

It is important to remember that the sanitation workers take pride in more than just their new standard of living (none of them think of it today as new, but as the natural order of things). They take pride in the fact that they have won the new standard for themselves, by the militance of their municipal union and the strength and courage with which they have fought to get what they have. They take no less pride in their accomplishment at the bargaining table than a businessman might take in the negotiation of a profitable contract that no one had thought could be won.

The unexpected power of the municipal labor unions is certainly not the only unanticipated difference between the post-war world in New York City and the world that had preceded it. Another immense change has been the increased importance of professionals to the urban economy and the role that this army of young, highly trained, and well-paid people has played in the resuscitation of what had been perceived to be moribund parts of the city.

Jane Jacobs, publishing her observations of her Greenwich Village neighborhood in 1961, was the first to note the emergence of a new class of New Yorkers that chose not to live in apartment houses. Until then, even those who wrote about the city and its architecture had taken apartment houses for granted. What Mrs. Jacobs described, and in the process helped to give it a great boost, was the movement now known as gentrification. She did not put a name on it, nor, in her enthusiasm for its results and her impatience with government efforts to clear and rebuild large sections of the city, did she realize that purely private reconstruction would also cause immense hardship for relocated people. The gentrification of the West Village in lower Manhattan has been followed by recapture of large sections of Brooklyn, and now some parts of the Bronx are also being recaptured for use by families of young professionals. In this sense, these areas are being returned to the condition they had been in before the extensive decay of the earlier postwar and even the prewar years when the move to the suburbs began.

There is no such thing as a typical gentrifying couple, and yet it seems clear that for the most part they are young, professionally trained, and both working. Often at least one member of the family is busy in a profession not widely known before the Second World War: city planning, business counseling, market analysis, design consultancy, hospital administration—the list of new professions is a long one.

The sections of New York City into which these couples move were originally developed with the row or terrace housing familiar both in British cities and in many of the other older American cities like Baltimore, Philadelphia, and Boston. The families that originally moved into them sold them long before the outbreak of the Second World War, usually because it was impossible to get help and because the attractions of suburban living outweighed the difficulties of commuting. Subsequent owners turned them into rooming houses or cut the floors into tiny but self-contained apartments. Depending on the convenience or glamour of the area in which they were located, they filled up either with black and Hispanic families or with young white single persons. Sometimes they were taken by older people, often of foreign birth, who had worked as domestic servants all their lives and had never married.

When an area becomes ripe for gentrification, a condition that cannot be rigorously identified in advance but seems to depend on the inscrutable whims of an invisible hand, the new purchasers face monumental tasks. First the building must be emptied. Then layers of paint must be scraped from fine paneling; improvised partitions must be removed; plumbing must be installed and heating ripped out and replaced. Sometimes the new buyers spend years under pioneering conditions. Ultimately, however, they find they have changed not only the house they own (often they rent out one or two of the upper floors) but themselves as well. They now live not so much in the big city but in a neighborhood. They have become interested in neighborhood matters, are active in the neighborhood association, and perhaps even belong to a block association affiliated with the neighborhood association. They occasionally contribute articles to a small journal circulated among brownstoners, as these young professionals (some are not so young any more) call themselves. To their astonishment, they sometimes realize that they have become not only homeowners but investors in New York City real estate. That is slowly changing their point of view about such things as real property taxes and municipal expenditures, a process so slow that they are almost able to ignore it as it happens.

No matter where they happen to live in the city, the full-time working members of these families (except for the wife who works for the Bronx community organization) must find their way to the central business district of Manhattan almost every working day. The bank Assistant Secretary goes in a privately owned express bus; the gentrifying couple go by subway; the sanitation worker goes by truck. It's quite conceivable that they all find themselves on the same block of Park Avenue at some time during their working day. If so, they find themselves surrounded by others clearly part of the emergent, modern city: a new city of glass-clad office buildings with novel communications methods and record-keeping machines, a city with new highly mechanized sanitation trucks. (There's still a lot of hoisting and physical work in the Sanitation Department, but trucks are coming in with side-mounted loaders. In a few years, solid waste will no longer be dumped in landfills but burned to produce useful steam.)

The parade of smartly dressed people along the Park Avenue sidewalk seems almost completely homogeneous. Yet when one looks at the edges of the human stream, eddying along the plazas that modern zoning encourages builders to create around office structures, stray bits of human flotsam can be singled out. Sometimes the first look is deceiving.

There's a man in a tee shirt, a bit out of place at this time of a spring weekday, just when the morning rush hour starts to taper off. A second look discloses that the man is unshaven and probably hasn't washed in several days. His legs are bound in what seem to be the remnants of army puttees of a kind not seen in a half century. Below them he wears an old pair of hiking boots. Obviously the man is one of the homeless, perhaps dismissed from a mental institution, left to wander in his new freedom up and down the avenue, his possessions in a shopping bag, a bruise on his left cheekbone. Once the eyes of the passersby have trained themselves to pick him out, they find a half dozen or so like him, men and women wandering the streets, sometimes camping on the stone seats in the plaza that was meant to offer a moment of sunlight to office workers, allowing their eyes to recover from constant attention to the cathode ray tubes in the word processors on their desks.

Nor are the homeless the only incongruous sidewalk sights on Park Avenue. Why are those three young blacks—the ones walking down the side street carrying a loud stereophonic radio that must be at least as heavy as an accordion with piano keyboard—not in school? The beat is disco, and as the visitor watches them walk, he imagines that they think of themselves as more real than real people. They are like figures in a movie, and the music, like a sound track, brings them to life. Without it, they have no purpose at all.

New York has always been the city of the disappearing middle. The rich and poor share the same sidewalk, while the middle class seems to have been abolished. That might be the impression of a visitor from a remote land, who does not understand that the people who look affluent and who have available to them all the expensive instruments of high technology are not, in fact, rich themselves in the traditional sense. The contrast between the classes in New York is no longer the contrast imagined by Sidney Kingsley in his depression-time play about the city's juxtaposition of rich and poor, *Dead End*.

In that play, the rich, unseeing and insensitive to the plight of the worthy poor, live in an immense luxurious apartment house over the river, at the very end of a crosstown street. On the other side of the same street, a bare twenty yards away, the poor live in an old tenement house. The play's purpose was to explain how contact with the poor—a partially disabled young man in particular—changes and improves the rich, a haughty but handsome young woman in particular. The poor are of course good, deserving people whose lives have been blighted by the injustices and inhumanity of an industrialized society.

In the more sophisticated world of postwar New York, the rich have grown to understand—or more correctly to believe—that it is not necessary for the poor to be deserving. To insist that they merit compassion by trying to help themselves is considered to be a deplorable effort to impose one's own standards on people who have their own culture with its own values. It is demeaning to suggest that the poor should help themselves; that is blaming the victim for his victimization. The crucial institution in improving the condition of the poor is no longer the religious or the economic institution, or even the social welfare institution, but the government.

That view encompasses the idea that the middle class no longer exists. The view is wrong; the middle class may have become invisible, but it's still in the city, though differently employed. Its members are more likely to be operating taxicabs than dry cleaning stores, or working in semiprofessional unions, like the American Federation of Teachers, rather than trying to establish new businesses making brass parts of lamps. Even that set of contrasts somewhat overstates the disappearance of small, individually owned stores. Small, individually owned stores are still just that even though the sign in the window calls them boutiques or bodegas and even if they are owned by Koreans instead of Italians.

What the middle class has lost, however, is confidence in the future of the city. Its members are no longer convinced that change is synonymous with progress or that their children will be able to compete with better educated and perhaps smarter people, or with people who are currently being given advantages in hiring and seniority in order to make up for disadvantages that other black or Hispanic or Oriental people undoubtedly suffered from in the past. The uncertainty with which the middle class in the city—particularly the white ethnic middle class—views the future is one of the major changes in the spirit of New York life. Even when the city wallowed in the trough of the Depression, those who were gloomiest about the future took up the causes of revolutionary change in the economic system and exuded a sense of their certainty about the future. Everything would be fine when the workers owned the means of production or, alternatively, when a strong man took over control of America and put the destructive unions in their proper place.

The lack of middle-class confidence continues despite the assertions of economists and students of public policy to the effect that the middle class gets all the tax breaks. These assertions refer to the deductibility of mortgage interest and real estate taxes from income before calculating income tax liability. But since interest is a deductible expense for businesses, it does not seem unreasonable that home owners should be allowed the same rights (though there certainly should be a top limit on the amount of mortgage interest that is deductible; it becomes a wholly regressive deduction for those very rich homeowners who carry mortgages of several hundred thousand dollars). The tax breaks that middle-class homeowners get, whether justified or not, are not enough to make them feel that they are now living as they expected that middle-class people would live. That is true of New York's middle-class population no matter what their race. It may, in part, account for two extraordinary phenomena. It may explain why middle-class black people tend to think of themselves more as blacks, and therefore closer to low-income blacks, than as middle-class Americans, and thus closer to middle-class Americans of other races. It may also account for Mayor Koch's extraordinary popularity with middle-class voters during his first two terms. His frequently re-

peated support of the middle class appeals to more than their
natural desire for a bigger slice of the municipal pie, even if it
lacks pie filling. It also appeals to their sense of being badly
abused. When Mayor Koch announced that he would treat
everyone the same, middle-class people, particularly white
middle-class people, understood his words to mean that poor
people would no longer be favored over them, as they were sure
had been the case under his predecessors.

One of the curious lessons that middle-class New Yorkers
have derived from their experience of the postwar years, however many they can remember, is that government never fulfills
its promises. That does not mean only that officials say they will
do one thing and then do the opposite. It also means that even
when government officials try to do what they say they are
going to do—build "middle-income housing," for example—
they don't succeed. The housing, once built, turns out to be
more expensive than the residents expected it would be. Programs never work as they were intended to work, and the
bigger the program, the wider the variance from expectations.
After long years in which they were led to believe that social
security was the perfect middle-class subsidization program,
middle-class people are hearing that the system is going broke
because too many Christmas tree baubles are being hung from
it. Medicare gets smaller as health costs go up. And, of course,
what people think of as the biggest program of all—welfare—
seems to be doing the opposite of what it was intended to do.
Instead of temporarily supporting worthy people through crises
over which they have no control, it has created a special class
that does not work, never heard of working, and is not expected
to work.

Perhaps the most curious of these gaps between promise and
performance developed in the aftermath of the Supreme
Court's decision that separate but equal education had no further place in the United States. What the court was striking
down was the legal segregation of black and white educational
systems, whether by direct mandate of state laws, as in the

South, or as a result of deliberate but unstated policy, as in the North. The Court did not promise that all the children in the nation would go to schools that would be effectively integrated on a numerical basis congruent with the population statistics. It did promise that the deliberate and willful segregation system, whether or not legally required by state law, would be dismantled. The two promises are very different. Not unnaturally, most of the black leadership came to believe in the promise that the Supreme Court did not make. And legislators, recognizing that they would win praise from neither side by insisting that the Court had not gone as far as the first promise, passed statutes that the Court later could interpret to mean that the first promise was the law of the land.

The so-called civil rights revolution that started slowly but gradually attained speed in the 1960s changed more than the relations between the races. It opened new vistas of change in the way of life in the nation that could be effected by changes in the law. The vistas, as it turned out, were largely mirages. Changes in laws could be and were very effective in striking down legal obstacles to the attainment of civil rights. They were most effective in getting black people the right to vote throughout the country. They were of material help in striking down laws requiring separate accommodations in states and cities that had such laws. But they were noticeably less effective—and much more controversial and disturbing to those who worry about the future—when they sought to replace or even to supplement individual and group efforts with governmental edicts.

An example of the way in which laws sometimes frustrate the very purposes of their passage was provided by the Voting Rights Act of 1965. Its purpose was to give blacks (and other minorities) access to the ballot, a fundamental right often denied by states that imposed discriminatory literacy tests and registration procedures, and permitted outright threats of violence or reprisal against blacks who exercised their franchise. So far, so good. But it was not good enough to achieve the results some imagined could be achieved instantly by the passage of a law.

The law was amended to provide that the Department of Justice would assist, not simply in assuring that blacks could vote, but in trying to assure that they would actually vote for, and have a good chance of electing, black representatives. Governments in all parts of the nation were then subject to a set of criteria with respect to literacy tests and the percentage of potential voters who actually went to the polls in certain years. If the criteria were not met, the department had the right to rearrange the lines of future voting districts if they seemed detrimental to the election of minority group representatives.

New York City failed to meet the criteria, a fact that allowed the department to supervise the reapportionment of City Council districts following the 1980 census. After rejecting two plans submitted to it, the Department finally approved a plan under which it expected that at least three additional black or Puerto Rican candidates would be elected. The result was the election of only one. It appears that the act of designating a district as a probable minority district makes it harder, not easier, to elect a minority candidate. Knowing that a minority representative is likely to be elected, those in the district with ambitions for office find it harder to abandon their own hopes in order to produce united support of a single minority candidate. The result in the designated districts in New York was—and continues to be—that several minority candidates would enter the race, enabling a white candidate, though lacking a majority of all the votes, to win with a plurality over each of the others. Meanwhile, blacks who aspired to win offices that represented much larger constituencies, such as the presidency of the entire Borough of Manhattan (to which blacks had frequently been elected), found that whites were far more reluctant to vote for them than they had been; possibly they—or at least some of them—considered that blacks were already enjoying special voting rights and deserved no special favors from those who did not share them. Like many others, this effort by lawmakers to pass beyond a negative process (unfair literacy tests, for example) to a positive process of effectuating desired actions by non-official citizens (voters and candidates, in this case) is to step from the realm of the possible to the kingdom of the wishful.

Looking at the areas in which blacks have been extraordinarily successful since the civil rights revolution, one would find that the greatest successes have been in fields in which government assistance has been minimal; sports and the arts come to mind. Yet black leadership keeps demanding greater government intercession, not to strike down bad laws that interfere with black economic and social progress but to substitute for individual and group effort.

Taking a leaf from the black political initiative, other groups are demanding similar legal intervention on their behalf. In New York, women and homosexuals demand, and in some cases have received, legal help in overcoming what the courts have sometimes seen as unfair barriers to their progress. The decisions seem, at a minimum, misguided and confusing.

Women were in 1977 allowed to apply for the job of firefighter, but none of the first women applicants passed the Fire Department's physical tests; their conclusion was that the tests were sex-biased. The tests they complained of were tests of strength and agility. The court ruled that the tests had to be changed until women could pass them, pointing out that many firefighters actually on duty could no longer pass the tests. That argument is stunning. Obviously, older firefighters who passed the tests originally may no longer be able to pass the same physical tests after years of service. That is an argument not against, but in favor of, rigorous tests for newcomers. A fire company is a team in which each member has a different assignment. The younger members must be relied on for their strength; the older ones, for their experience. It is an assault on the people of the city to put men, women, or children on the firefighting team if they cannot pass the physical tests.

Society has a strong interest in reducing the differences between the races, and most assuredly in eliminating invidious distinctions that impair the earning capacity of minority ethnic group members. It should draw no distinctions between people on the basis of race. Matters are different with respect to sex. A society that is interested in its posterity has a consequent interest in distinguishing between the sexes; to remind its members of that distinction, every society customarily classifies some jobs as primarily feminine, others as masculine. New York should not be so rigid as to deprive either sex of the opportunity to fill a job slot that is customarily filled by a member of the other sex, but neither should it be so indifferent to the significance of heterosexuality that it overlooks substantive differences in the pursuit of theoretical interchangeability. Surely, with respect to homosexuals, society has a strong interest in preferring heterosexuality. That does not mean that homosexuals should be denied employment or housing solely because they are homosexuals. Neither should it mean that homosexuals have an *a priori* right to employment in schools or other settings in which what some of them describe as the tyranny of heterosexuality is vulnerable to attack.

Discomfort over homosexuality is but one cause of middle-class uneasiness. Families that achieve middle-class status soon find that society tries to remove what they have won. Taxes and prices rise quickly. Worse, taxes are spent to damage their new status by helping those who scorn it: the rich and the poor. Middle-class neighborhoods organize resistance—to the garbage incinerator, the jail, the bus garage that threaten their homes and status. They resent tax-subsidized penthouses on top of museums and welfare families moving in around the corner.

Discovering the strength of middle-class feelings, politicians propose new schools, special housing programs, health benefits, day care centers that may—or may not—fulfill crucial demands. To keep their distance, richer elites acquiesce. The more benefits middle-class neighborhoods get, the more they demand. And while those who pay taxes directly to the city are more cost-conscious than apartment dwellers, few worry about cost. The poor pay no taxes. The rich shelter themselves. Should the middle class worry alone?

Chapter III

Repealing Geography

IN ANY LIST of New York's assets tabulated in 1946 or earlier, its natural harbor would come first. What else, after all, made possible the growth of the world city but the divine gift of a port protected against winds from any direction? The port of New York is entered through a strait called, with some lack of imagination, The Narrows. The Upper Bay, which laps against the shores of Brooklyn and New Jersey, is almost always calm whatever the season of the year. When an occasional hurricane misses its normal path and darts up the coastline from Florida, not even its great high tides make much of a difference to the Upper Bay.

It is only after a truly careful look at the harbor, and after the sobering experience of some of the postwar years, that one comes to understand that the harbor on which New York depended for its rise to world dominance was not entirely a natural phenomenon but merely a natural opportunity. It may have begun as a logical stopping place for Dutchmen looking for fresh water and beaver pelts, and for British freebooters looking for Dutchmen. But it required a political system and a political personality to enable the city to turn the opportunity into the mechanism for its dominance of the Atlantic coast of North America. That dominance, by another set of circumstances that combined opportunity with energy, intelligence, and will, made it the dominating port of the world.

New York harbor was not merely the meeting place of the Hudson River and the Atlantic Ocean. By way of the Hudson River, it was linked to a tiny settlement called Troy, New York. Not only technological imagination but political sapience and tremendous determination were required to turn that connection into the key that unlocked for New York City the center of the North American continent. But it was that vision, and the talents to make it a reality, that confirmed New York's rise to world eminence as a seaport. And without similar imagination and energy, the city cannot maintain the position that its leading citizen in the early nineteenth century put within its grasp.

In 1810, a survey party tramped the 300–mile stretch between Troy and Lake Erie and made plans for the construction of a canal that would join the lake and the Hudson. It would make road-building unnecessary (a blessing) by opening the newly settled lands of what is now the Middle West, the heartland of the modern nation, to barges and freight coming from or going to the ocean. In 1810, railroads were as primitive as the airplane at Kitty Hawk. The canal route followed the line of the Mohawk River through the one real gap in the Appalachian Mountains, the chain that, before the development of the railroads, kept America's East and West from meeting.

The building of the canal was delayed for years by the War of 1812 and by the difficulty of financing it. A member of the original survey team, DeWitt Clinton, who had previously served terms as United States senator and as mayor of New York City (temporarily removing the mayoralty from the list of "dead-end" jobs), induced the state to establish a commission on the canal proposal. He promptly became its inspired and inspiring president. As recorded in Columbia University's *Con-*

quering the Wilderness, Volume V of its history of New York State, DeWitt Clinton's brilliant work on the canal contributed to his becoming governor, and in that office between 1817 and 1823 he devoted most of his political and executive energies to getting the canal built. When the Erie Canal was finally opened in 1825, it confirmed New York City's position as premier port. New York's harbor was thus the product of a fruitful partnership among DeWitt Clinton, Nature herself, and thousands of immigrant farriers who dug the ditch for a pittance and, as the farmers said, drank and brawled their way across New York State. Geography, in short, is not simply a set of natural phenomena, but a product of the marriage of the natural with practical political vision.

All over the nascent republic in the late eighteenth and early nineteenth centuries, canal proposals were igniting public imagination. Only a few of the visionary schemes ever reached the point of carrying water. In the 1780s, according to biographer James Thomas Flexner, a semiretired general named George Washington, resting from his military chores and not yet called to chair the constitutional convention at Philadelphia, was considering ways to push freight from the seaboard ports to what is now West Virginia, on the inland slope of the Alleghenies. His was no idle speculation about the future of America. In fact, he owned vast tracts of land near the Kanawha River and, like any other land developer before or since, sought ways to make his spread more valuable.

In *George Washington and The New Nation,* Flexner reports that a proposal of James Rumsey intrigued Washington. An intricate hydraulic system would have poled barges up the Potomac, letting them down gently on the far side of the Alleghenies. Ultimately this scheme, which would have avoided locks and dredging, proved impractical. While the Father of His Country waited in Philadelphia for a constitution to emerge from the squabblings of the convention, the poling scheme foundered. That was just the sort of thing that did not happen to DeWitt Clinton's plan. The Erie Canal required locks, but the climbs and descents were much gentler than what the Alleghenies required. Clinton imposed his leadership by selecting a plan related very practically to the real needs and potentialities of the region he was trying to help.

The proof is that the Erie Canal confirmed New York's growth, already well under way, as the Atlantic port of choice. Although Newburyport, Massachusetts, was nearer to Europe, or at least to Britain, on the great circle route, and although Boston and Philadelphia had escaped the blight of the British occupation during the Revolutionary War, New York carried an increasing amount of commerce. When Manhattan, which constituted practically the whole of New York City until 1898, was given its first survey and street plan in 1811, the designers drew many crosstown streets connecting the East River and the Hudson, to accommodate the drayage needed to carry cargoes from ocean vessels docked on the East River waterfront to canal barges on the Hudson River. Clinton's achievement stimulated New York businessmen to establish all the services needed in a great harbor. Banks grew to handle letters of credit and all the documentation required to make payments. The Customs House needed brokers to clear cargoes for distant owners. Ships' agents were needed to provide ships' captains with equipment and stores for the next voyage. Crews had to be paid. Insurance brokers and the underwriters gathered in the port to solicit business and settle claims. There can be no shipping without a flock of admiralty lawyers, screeching after ships as persistently as gulls, to negotiate settlements or litigate claims. And, of course, the port offered opportunities to ship builders and ship repairers.

Some of America's greatest clipper ships were built in New York in the nineteenth century. The first federal ironclad, the *Monitor,* came from an East River shipyard. So did the heavy wood caissons under which immigrant navvies worked in compressed air to dig the footings for the two towers that still support the Brooklyn Bridge. The caissons, one of which caught fire in the course of construction, are still there, filled with concrete and pressed against compacted sand and bedrock below, a tribute not only to the Roeblings' daring but to the skill of the shipyard workers who assembled them. Later, the New York Naval Shipyard built aircraft carriers and battleships through the Second World War; Bethlehem and Todd, and many lesser firms, have run shipyards in the harbor.

The development of New York's ocean commerce conveyed another economic advantage to the city. It became the natural terminus of the railroads that by the middle of the nineteenth century were displacing the eastern canals in carrying freight inland. It was natural to base the railroad operations where the heaviest freight traffic was already being put down: New York, of course. There, manufacturers and dealers in agricultural products and minerals knew they would find ships competing for their cargoes.

The New York Central Railroad was built by Commodore Vanderbilt, a New Yorker by birth and heritage, to run roughly parallel to the Hudson River and the Erie Canal—the "water level" route, as it was called. Although other lines found different passageways through the mountains to the west, few early observers noted that railroads were far more flexible than canals. But it's easier to lay rails than dig ditches, and once the railroad designers learned that steam was powerful enough to pull heavy loads up mountain grades, they began to take advantage of shorter routes that were also more convenient to the ports that competed with New York: Baltimore, Norfolk, Philadelphia. And when government later entered the picture to regulate freight rates, it generally ruled that the shorter the route, the lower should be the rate. By the end of the Second World War, New York was at a disadvantage on rail freight costs compared with Philadelphia, Baltimore, and Norfolk.

Nor was that the harbor's only postwar problem. New York's piers had been laid out in the nineteenth century, when long-distance trucking was unknown. Narrow Manhattan Island was built up so densely that little space remained for direct access by rail to the piers where the cargoes were. Even when, as was sometimes the case, special dockside rail lines were installed, they could not connect directly with the trunk lines, most of which stopped at the New Jersey side of the harbor. In New York harbor, therefore, the railroads had to establish and maintain elaborate and quite expensive water transportation systems to carry cargoes back and forth between the New Jersey terminals and the ships wharved at piers in Brooklyn and Manhattan. They designed and used special barges that had railroad tracks installed on their decks. All of these systems added to the expense of operating through New York harbor, making the port less competitive. Nowadays, most rail freight from the South and West destined for New England and Long Island avoids the lighterage link by crossing the river on a bridge near Albany, far upstream from the city.

Naturally, the water-borne railroad services were costly to the railroads for the same reason that they were welcome to New Yorkers: they were labor intensive. Armies of longshoremen, bargees, tugboat crewmen, and specialized engineers and firemen or oilers operated the tugboats, floating derricks, steam-powered lighters, and a myriad other harbor craft. Most were relatively unskilled. You don't need algebra to throw a six-inch Manila hawser around a bitt; that job could be handled readily by a man with a prison record as long as he was willing to work. A criminal past was tolerantly, perhaps even proudly, assumed to be a qualification of many dock workers. Their union was regularly denounced in the press and on the screen. Losses on the docks by pilferage in New York harbor rose in the postwar period until they exceeded what shipping lines and their insurance underwriters wanted to pay for. But the city was such a good place to find or drop cargoes that for years the shippers muffled their complaints.

Within a few years of the end of the war, the Marshall Plan had begun to stimulate the export of large quantities of general cargo to Europe (general cargo is separately packaged freight that, before the development of containerization, was best handled with cargo nets lowered into vessels' holds by gangs of longshoremen). The lines of trucks waiting at the piers of Manhattan to unload their individually packaged freight stretched for blocks. The delays were poisonous to the trucking and stevedoring interests. Cheaper rail rates at other ports made the high costs of stevedoring in New York more galling. New York harbor, though it was still the nation's busiest, was not growing as fast as its competitors; instead, its share of the nation's oceanic freight was getting smaller, although the tonnage moving through the port actually increased somewhat from year to year.

The natural advantage of New York's geography, even when augmented by DeWitt Clinton's political wit, was being wiped out by external forces over which New York City itself had little control. It could do little to hold them back. It could not even prevent the construction of the St. Lawrence Seaway, which finished off the Erie Canal except as a historic curio for pleasure boaters. The story of the decline of the port of New York is closely linked with that of the rise of the Port of New York Authority. The Port of New York Authority, established in 1921 by the states of New York and New Jersey with congressional ratification, had been intended to bring its extraordinary powers of borrowing and construction to bear on improving port facilities, including transportation. On October 25, 1946, the Authority's executive director, Austin J. Tobin, was quoted in the *Times* as explaining that its Board of Commissioners and executives wanted to save the harbor from further relative decline. They were therefore offering to take over New York City's piers (in February 1948) and, where advisable, to modernize them.

The Authority was negotiating an agreement to expand Port Newark, on the New Jersey side of the harbor, when, in September 1947, it offered to do the same for the port of Hoboken. Both of these New Jersey port projects were designed for areas that had been little developed. It was physically possible here to build modern berthing and unloading facilities: large storage space upland of the piers, railroad tracks at dockside, and heavy

cranes that would supplement the loading and unloading capacity of ships' gear.

The Authority's purpose in developing the New Jersey ports
was to make part of New York harbor more competitive with
the other, more modern ports that were beginning to undermine
the city's relative position in cargo handling. Yet to New Yorkers, particularly to the union leaders on Manhattan's West Side,
the Authority seemed to be threatening to use its governmental
powers on behalf of New Jersey at New York's expense, and to
encourage a way of loading and unloading cargo that would
result in a reduction in jobs. Fear of job loss was enough to
persuade New York City to keep the Port Authority's hands off
its piers in the early 1950s.

After the city had turned down the Port Authority, it had an
opportunity to test its own wisdom in waterfront matters. In
1947, a fire destroyed Pier 57, a Grace Line pier on Manhattan's
Hudson River waterfront. Like many or most of New York's
piers, this one, which was owned by the city and leased to the
shipping company, had a wooden sub deck and stood on
wooden piles driven well into the river bottom. The accident
seemed to require New York officials to restore the city's dignity
by replacing the old wooden pier with high technology. Having
rebuffed the Authority's previous offers of help, and paying
little attention to the question of how transatlantic air travel
would affect the demand for passenger ships, the city decided to
display its own capabilities by designing a magnificent pier.
Engineers proposed that in place of a wooden deck supported on
wooden piles, the pier be constructed as a hollow concrete box of
gigantic size. The box would be built about thirty miles upriver
from New York City, in an unused excavated clay pit that once
supplied raw materials for a nearby brick manufacturing plant.
When completed, the hollow, uncovered box would be towed,
afloat, to the prepared site of the burned-out pier and deliberately lowered until its own bottom rested on the prepared foundation; a deck would be made of prestressed concrete beams, in
what was then up-to-the-minute technology, hardly tested in

New York City. The enterprise was carried out, and all the engineering aspects went off without a hitch. When the box was completed, in the clay pit, whose bottom was below sea level, the narrow earthen dam that kept out the waters of the Hudson was demolished. The box floated, and it was brought down to its final resting place without incident.

The only disappointment in the entire story rests on the shoulders of the shipping line. Within a short time after the final installation of the new pier, passenger-ship travel had dwindled to the point where the line no longer operated scheduled service requiring the permanent and exclusive use of a pier. The innovative prestressed concrete box is now used as a parking lot. Since it was financed with city bonds, the revenues from its operations need not be distinguished from those of the city as a whole, but it seems unlikely that the parking fees come close to covering the debt service on the money borrowed to build the pier.

Perhaps this experience made the city somewhat more receptive to further assistance from the Port Authority. It accepted the Authority's offer to construct the Brooklyn Marine Terminal near the northern end of the Brooklyn waterfront, providing enough upland space for the storage of some containers. Until 1982, the area was surely busier than the west side of Manhattan, which no longer has even one working cargo pier. After this rather favorable experience, the city found it possible, under Mayor Lindsay's leadership, to seek the cooperation of the Port Authority in developing a passenger-ship terminal on the Hudson side of Manhattan and a containerport in the Red Hook section of Brooklyn. The passenger-ship terminal has been badly hit by the rise in oil prices since 1973 and no longer operates in the winter, when more cruise ships leave from Florida ports than from New York to save oil by staying in warm southern waters. The containerport is operating successfully and will probably be expanded.

The net effect of the repeal of New York harbor's geography has been to turn the primary asset of the city, the foundation of its greatness, into a liability. The waterfront jobs have dropped precipitously, even though thousands of longshoremen who do not work continue to be paid for an entire year's work each year under a union contract that opened the port to the use of containerized cargo. A flock of industries ancillary to shipping has been diminished to a small, uncertain number.

In place of the harbor, the city has its two major airports, both maintained by the Port Authority, which is now officially the Port Authority of New York and New Jersey. Between them, Kennedy, handling the bulk of the international travel, and LaGuardia employ about 100,000 people. The new jobs in air transportation make up for a great part of the loss from the decay of the city's stevedoring and other waterfront activities. There is a difference, however, in the jobs provided. The airports do require a certain amount of baggage handling, but it is trivial in comparison with the tonnages that had to be lifted and moved by the longshoreman gangs of the past. The low-skilled jobs at the airports consist of cleaning and other service jobs. They can be performed as easily by women as by men, and they are. If part of New York's difficulty in absorbing its newest young male residents stems from the disappearance of jobs for which they are capable and which they do not feel shamed by taking, the loss of the harbor has been even more a human than an economic disappointment.

The loss of the waterfront industries has also disappointed the city because it has not stimulated the kind of practical political vision that DeWitt Clinton displayed 170 years ago. The obvious decline of the harbor has exacerbated the long-standing resentment of municipal and state legislators toward the Port Authority, although that resentment was not caused by the decline alone. The legislators resent the fact that some Authority officials are paid salaries that exceed their own. They also resent the fact that the Authority is generally exempt from local real estate taxes and that local governments must always bargain with the Authority over a formula for determining taxes that commercial enterprises in an Authority airport or bus terminal would pay if they were not on Authority property. Another natural source of resentment flows from the bi-state parentage of the Authority. Officials of both states, from governors down to the lower ranks, sincerely believe that the Authority is always partial to the other state.

To these lamentably human resentments against the Authority must be added other, more ideological objections to its constitution and its program. First of these is the issue of accountability. This word, which may have a distinguished ancestry but has come into common use only recently, in this case is used to denote the control that legislators wish they had over the Authority. The legislators argue that the Authority is "accountable" to none but its own staff. In fact, the commissioners who run the Authority cannot embark on any major project without special legislation from both states, unless the project was authorized in the basic interstate charter. Further, the governors of the two states, elected by the people, have the right to veto the minutes of its Board of Commissioners, whom the governors appoint. Moreover, there's nothing to prove that such accountability, whatever it is, is good. Brendan Byrne, as governor of New Jersey, used the mere threat of one veto to keep the Authority from raising fares on the PATH trains, the old Hudson Tubes that it had rescued from bankruptcy. While PATH's fare was fixed at thirty cents to carry a passenger all the way from midtown Manhattan to Newark, a New York subway rider was paying seventy-five cents for a much shorter ride in less savory surroundings. Not only is the Authority thus subject to both state legislatures and their governors; it is very much accountable to the marketplace. It has no taxing power and must raise its capital funds entirely by selling bonds. If its projects do not cover the total debt service requirements of all its outstanding obligations, it is out of business. In effect, it has the accountability of both a privately owned enterprise and a government agency.

In passing, let it be said that no political system in the world today can possibly include a provision by which a specific person can actually be made to answer for a specific governmental act. In theory, the governor of a state is responsible for the acts of his or her appointees. But if the voting public decides it does not like the performance of one of those appointees, what, exactly, can it do about the matter? Not vote for the Governor for re-election? Then it is disregarding all the events of his administration which, we may assume, the voters liked. The only way in which a government could be made explicitly "accountable" would be by subjecting each agency or department head to election, so fragmenting the governmental process that universal accountability would lead to universal inaction.

A second more specific source of local government friction with the Port Authority is based on the assumption that the Authority should have done more to help rail transportation in the region. The critics, who have included a long succession of New York and New Jersey state legislators, tend to argue the negative side of their proposition. They claim that the Authority has done too much to help the automobile, an instrument that Manhattanites, in particular, have been carefully taught to hate. It dirties the air, it crowds the streets, it is imperious—whatever that means—and, one suspects, it smacks far too much of American industrial might for the comfort of those who are dedicated to higher, more cultural or humane values. The rise of the imported car has done nothing to mitigate this feeling; indeed, the resentment against American automobiles has become all the more intense since it has been proven that the industry is not only more arrogant but less clever than it should be. Since few critics own or operate autos, they cannot be expected to understand how convenient autos are for those who do not live on Manhattan's crowded West Side.

On the positive side, the arguments for more intensive participation in railroad development drift into non sequiturs or absurdity. Bella Abzug, a former congressional representative from Manhattan, has advocated a cross-harbor tunnel to provide rail freight service to Brooklyn, Queens, and the rest of Long Island. The cost would be formidable; such a tunnel would be longer than any of the tunnels that connect Manhattan Island with the continental mainland. Moreover, the demand for rail freight service on Long Island is not nearly strong enough to keep such a tunnel busy. It is doubtful that the railroads would want to incur the costs of building up a new rail freight service on the Long Island side of the harbor. They can now deliver by truck from wherever their lines terminate in New Jersey, or ship directly to the customers' sidings by using the land bridge at Selkirk, near Albany.

Jerrold Nadler, a state assemblyman from Manhattan, has made increased rail freight service the alleged key to a rebirth of New York's faded industries. He claims that the Port Authority could resurrect New York harbor by building new piers equipped to handle containerized cargo. The cargo would be transported on flatbed trucks to railheads in an effort to reverse the obvious verdict of the past forty years.

Nadler faults the Authority for offering to assist New York and New Jersey to redevelop their currently useless waterfronts to residential and light industrial use. This criticism, echoed elsewhere within New York City, is troublesome because it stands in the way of making productive use of land that is potentially very valuable for housing purposes. Some critics argue that if waterfront land is redeveloped for housing purposes, the increase in land value will spread to inland areas in which some industrial jobs are still to be found. The assumption is that there is an endless demand for luxury housing in New York City. Nadler contends that the rich are so hungry for it that their demand is independent of the attractiveness of the area in which housing is erected. But while land on the waterfront with a view of midtown Manhattan across the river is surely desirable, there is no evidence to support the belief that rich renters will want to live a mile or more from the water, in an area now dotted with reinforced concrete industrial buildings and adjoining an elevated transit line.

It seems that these bitter arguments against redeveloping the waterfront for the only use to which it now lends itself are based primarily on a will to be obstructive. In this case, the opponents are fighting "real estate developers," arguing that they are not interested in building for the poor (any more than automobile manufacturers are). It has been proven that legislators are on strong political ground when they attack people in the real estate business. Their attacks have become so ritualistic that they may at some time lose force, but not until they have elected more squadrons of legislators. In the meantime, the antipathy to the real estate interests seems well calculated to prevent the city from taking full advantage of their possible help in retrieving some new value from the wasteland of the city's waterfront.

The Port Authority, an institution with some imperfections like all others, has despite these imperfections progressed far beyond its original mandate of helping the two states jointly to improve facilities related to the harbor and its watercourses. Without official taxing power, it has succeeded in building facilities—automotive bridges and tunnels, airports, and an immense world trade center and office building—for which customers are willing to pay user fees that have, in effect, become partially voluntary taxes. As Peter Goldmark, executive director of the Authority, has pointed out, its revenue stream would support a sizable issue of bonds that could provide the money for major capital reinvestment on both sides of the harbor. The staff of the Authority has developed technical knowhow in fields rarely touched by government. Put to work by the municipalities on the harbor, the Authority could produce substitute uses for the geographical assets whose value was repealed by the invention of new transportation technologies. It is one of the perversities of postwar New York that the faith in progress that once lay at the heart of the city's political system was repealed at about the same time as its geography.

The city's growth would have been impossible if its politicians and entrepreneurs during the latter part of the nineteenth century had not found a way to overcome some of the negative implications of its geography.

New York's harbor was a remarkably well-protected body of water linking three islands and the North American land mass. Its 650-mile waterfront was created by the bays and rivers that lapped all sides of Manhattan and Staten Island and parts of the Bronx, Queens, and Brooklyn. The same water that made the city so hospitable to ocean and inland transportation also made movement by land vehicles between its parts impossible through the nineteenth century. The need to overcome fierce tidal currents that separated the then-city of Brooklyn from the nineteenth-century city of New York was the mother of the Roeblings' famous invention, the world's longest suspension bridge.

By the time the Brooklyn Bridge was completed, the city had recognized that unless it could place some of its transportation system on a level other than street level, it would have to give over an intolerable portion of Manhattan's narrow surface to vehicles. To find another level, one can go up or down. In the 1880s, down was impossible. Electric motors had scarcely proved themselves workable outside the laboratory, and covered tunnels would fill with the smoke and vapor of steam engines. The alternative—open cuts for the tracks—would not answer the city's need; since by definition they could not be decked over, they would reduce the available street as sharply as building in it. So the city went up. The steam locomotives of the elevated railroad on which construction was started in 1876 blighted the north–south avenues with smoke, noise, and soot. Even when the trains were not passing, the latticed steelwork of the structure that held up the tracks was of value only to impressionistic photographers who liked light and shade.

With improvements in electrical motors specifically, and electricity-generating technology generally, it became possible to think of putting the trains in tunnels underground and underwater. The New York subway system was born. The mere hint that its first line, in Manhattan, would be in operation by 1904 made possible the unification in 1898 of Brooklyn and

New York with Staten Island, Queens, and parts of the northern Bronx.

The subway was for many years an even greater source of New York pride than the Brooklyn Bridge. For five cents, the price of a glass of beer, the subway would take a New Yorker from Riverdale, in the northern Bronx, to Coney Island, on the ocean beach—a distance of about twenty-five miles. It made interborough romance feasible. By accumulating crowds of office workers in Wall Street before the invention of high-speed electronic communications, it made possible the Coolidge bull market and the 1929 bust. By bringing couples or whole families to Times Square, it lit the lights of the Great White Way, or at least it helped pay for them.

In a sense, the subway extracted an awesome price from New Yorkers. It became a symbol of the city's democratic spirit, and as a symbol, it left economics in its wake. Cheap transit was so important to New York that the city fell hostage to it. When the private companies that had built the subway with city financing seemed on the verge of dropping the whole system because it could not pay for itself on the five-cent fare, Mayor LaGuardia arranged to take it over. The city, having built its own line connecting the Grand Concourse with the garment manufacturing district, then had a unified system reaching deep into four of the five boroughs. But while the subway was built to make possible the assembly of a work force at important office and industrial locations, it was not without inequities. What it gave to the areas that were connected to it, like the German and Irish sections of the upper East Side and the lower Bronx (ethnically very different from what it is today), it effectively took away from areas that were not, like the Jewish sections of the lower East Side, Alphabet City (where the Avenues are dismally identified as A, B, C, and D), and Little Italy.

The subway continued to torture the political process by making retention of the five-cent fare an essential issue. From early 1946 on, Mayor O'Dwyer had to twist logic into a pretzel at special hearings of the Board of Estimate. He was attempting to defend the clearly uneconomic fare against its critics (who never ran for public office) by demonstrating that eliminating the city's deficits in subway operations would not, as a matter of law, benefit the city's general financial position. Finally, in 1947, cooler heads prevailed, and the fare became ten cents.

In 1953, the ten-cent fare went the way of the nickel cigar and the free lunch and became fifteen cents. The turnstiles were converted to accept tokens. In a valiant effort to protect all future mayors from the opprobrium of another fare increase, the subway and elevated systems were taken out of the hands of the city Board of Transportation and put in an authority whose job it was to run a combined system that would lose no money in operations. The authority would be allegedly independent, but it would be dependent on city capital budget support when it needed new cars or major expenditures on maintenance of way and stations. On November 5, 1951, the voters had approved a constitutional amendment exempting from the city's debt limit a $500 million bond issue for starting the construction of a Second Avenue line in Manhattan and for such other capital needs as the city decided on. The Second Avenue line was never started with the money. Many years later, during the Lindsay administration, some holes for it were dug along the avenue, but as the city ran out of money they were covered over without being connected.

The theory that the new Transit Authority would be able to raise fares as needed to cover operating costs without embarrassing the mayor was quickly shown to be absurd. Fares went up too slowly for sound bookkeeping but too fast for the mayors. During Governor Rockefeller's terms, it became clear that governors did not like fare raises either; nor did governors, dependent on labor union support for their political strength, like to have the city bargaining too hard with the transit workers and using the state's Taylor Law to show the unions their place. The Taylor Law forbids strikes by government employees. It imposes a fine equal to one day's pay for every day of work missed by striking, and it can penalize a union of government employees by annulling the right to a check-off of union dues.

When Governor Rockefeller found that he was embarrassed by the poor performance of the Long Island Rail Road, which had been taken over by the state from the bankruptcy courts, he established a new, more or less independent authority, the Metropolitan Transportation Authority, into which were poured two other suburban rail lines, already deeply in trouble, and the New York City Transit Authority. The city by this time had also taken over most of the private bus lines that had specific franchised routes in the city.

The first chairman of the M.T.A. was a former Rockefeller secretary, William J. Ronan, who carried the handicap of being generally recognized as a brilliant man with outstanding academic credentials in public administration. Ronan would show them what railroads could do, the governor suggested, and Ronan showed them, all right. He invested in hyper-modern lightweight cars for the subway system. Shortly after the cars were put in operation, their innovative trucks—the assemblies from which the axles and wheels are suspended—started to crack dangerously. Ultimately the authority discarded them all, replaced them with traditional trucks, and successfully sued the manufacturer for $94 million.

Ronan left the Metropolitan Transportation Authority to become executive director of the Port Authority. He was followed by David Yunich, a former chief executive of Macy's department store who left little mark on the Authority, and then by Harold Fisher, a lawyer with impeccable Democratic connections. By that time, Hugh Carey had replaced Rockefeller as governor.

We have now reached 1975 and the New York City fiscal crisis, threatening the city's ability to pay its notes and meet its payroll which quickly became the only New York subject worth talking about. Abraham Beame, who was then mayor, got permission from Washington for a fiscal maneuver called the "Beame shuffle." It permitted him to use federal transit grants originally sequestered for capital improvements for operating subsidies instead, keeping the fare from rising precipitously at a time when neither the state nor the city could afford to increase subsidization. Nothing could have been less helpful in the long run for a system that desperately needed new capital in places like repair shops for buses and subway cars. The public, alas, never sees such places, although they are crucial to sound and economical maintenance. Nothing has demonstrated more clearly than the Beame shuffle that no matter what agency technically owns the transit system, the mayor of New York feels responsible for the size of the fare. So much for accountability. It has nothing to do with organization charts and everything to do with public perceptions and attitudes.

Until Governor Hugh Carey appointed Richard Ravitch, a New York builder and developer with a clear understanding of governmental process and a fine record in combining public finance and public subsidies, to the chairmanship of the Metropolitan Transportation Authority in November 1979, the Authority lacked any serious long-term plan for self-improvement. Its subway ridership had dropped by about forty percent between the immediate postwar years and 1977. Its maintenance procedures were inefficient and costly. Its tunnels leaked. Its signal systems urgently needed replacement. Its labor relations were extraordinarily difficult because the union leaders were of Irish extraction while the newest—and many of the most militant—workers were black and Hispanic. It lost its best trained workers as an indirect result of the city's 1975 fiscal crisis. With all these serious systemic troubles, the Authority had spent its new funds primarily on new cars, which passengers see, while skimping on the more basic reconstruction of shops and tunnels and tracks, which the public notices only when there has been a calamity.

Ravitch continued to give priority to the replacement of inadequate cars, but for the first time in the history of the M.T.A. he gave the organization a comprehensive long-range capital program. By raising tolls on its bridge and tunnel subsidiary serving automobilists, by using sale and lease-back techniques with private financial institutions, and by persuading the state to impose special transportation taxes, he developed a $10 billion capital program. It was a remarkable achievement, intellectually and politically. But his successor—Robert Kiley, who took office in November 1983—pointed out what Ravitch knew all too well: it would not be enough to restore the transit system to its former standing in New Yorkers' esteem. And visible improvement would take much longer than the public —or the politicians—wanted to wait.

New York's subway system can conveniently be compared to the circulation system of the human body. Its functioning is crucial to life itself. In New York, however, the transit system, like too many people, suffers from life-threatening circulatory problems. Without the transit system, much of the city's midtown and Wall Street economic expansion would be imperiled. But the decay of the subway system has already deprived it of practically all passengers but those who must use it to go to work. Virtually no one uses the subway any more to visit Times Square in the evening or to go on shopping expeditions. The loss in ridership makes reconstruction of the system more difficult, because the operating losses mount with reduced ridership.

As the city has lost manufacturing jobs, its basic work-related subway load has diminished. It could cut its losses by rationalizing its route structure, eliminating lines and stations that are underutilized. It can't do that, however, for political reasons. The stations and lines it would eliminate turn out to be the stations in black and Hispanic neighborhoods. Even the mere suggestion of closing them down brings the local politicians out in force, with the cry that the management of the system is deliberately refusing to transport minority group members because they might compete with whites for jobs in the central business district. Though the charge is, on its face, false, it has undeniable psychological impact and makes a certain "objective" sense. Closing down stations and lines that connect minority-occupied areas with central Manhattan would effectively cut down possible minority group access to employment opportunities, no matter what its motive. And in the predominately white borough of Queens there is resistance to the opening of new subway lines, although the line that now serves Forest Hills, Kew Gardens, and Jamaica is grossly overloaded. While white Queens officials of twenty-five years ago were demanding new subway service to relieve rush-hour congestion that has since gotten worse, present Queens politicians seem more interested in establishing medical schools or making the already overcrowded trains accessible to people in wheelchairs, at considerable capital and operating costs. In franker, off-the-record moments, some—not necessarily the same officials who favor the disabled—hint that their constituents fear that more subway lines will bring more nonwhites into the borough.

Fear is, obviously, the crucial word. And fear, in the subway, refers not to the fear of an accident because the tracks have been undermined by rising groundwater (though that has actually been happening in Brooklyn and Queens since the city has closed down pumping stations that had supplied some of their residents with water). The fear that discourages subway ridership is the fear of violence. The transit system has its own police force (paid by the city's general taxpayers, not the subway riders). It has 3,600 members to patrol the trains and the stations, both below and above ground. Clearly the force has its hands full, and the only eventuality that might reduce the need for police would be a great increase in the number of riders. But the number of riders will not increase until passengers feel safe. That's known as a vicious circle.

The vicious circle of reduced passenger loads increasing the fear that leads to still further reductions of ridership is only one of several in which the subway system is snarled. Capital spending will be unproductive unless it is accompanied by improved maintenance procedures. They require that large capital sums be spent on improving maintenance shops. But the public never sees the maintenance shops, so their high technological priority is not matched by a high political priority. Failure to improve repair facilities, however, stiffens the resistance of those who work in them to accept managerial changes that would speed their productivity. Failure to maintain properly the rolling stock and right of way increases the risk of accidents that will further reduce ridership.

As these concentric circles of despair and inconsistency tighten around the subway system, it will become increasingly difficult for the subway's managers to improve matters. Fewer and fewer talented people will assume the responsibility of directing major sectors of the Authority's work force and administration. The resulting vacuum will make the subways increasingly attractive to the young vandals and criminals, the vagrants and the sleepers whose growing numbers will still further reduce the acceptability of the subways to its potential, work-bound riders. Thus, in the subways, the two worlds of New York collide: the working world that seems normal and the never-working world of the criminals and the utterly helpless. In an older New York, these were kept separate. When they meet in the subway, it raises the possibility that the entire system will come, bit by bit, to a stop.

Chapter IV

The Unmaking
of Manufacturing

ONE OF New York's best-kept secrets in 1946 was its status as the nation's largest manufacturing town. Bemusing other cities with its symbolic office skyscrapers and the penthouses serenaded by songwriters, New York did not let the rest of the nation know that in fact a very large fraction of its population worked at factory jobs. And rather grubby factory jobs at that. Until the end of the Second World War, the city's mayors and business and political leaders did whatever they could to encourage manufacturing and to reduce the factory workers' cost of living by maintaining the low subway fare and providing subsidies to housing. After the end of the war, however, growing interest in the "quality of life" and in the sociological problems of race relations, advanced health care, juvenile delinquency, and substandard housing overshadowed the attention that leadership had given to the cultivation of manufacturing.

It was not until thirty years after the end of the war, when the Federal Bureau of Labor Statistics announced that the city had lost 600,000 manufacturing jobs in ten years, that New

Yorkers who had never set foot in a factory learned that they had been living in a factory town. The rest of the country never had known. New York, in fact, was the only factory town in the nation that could lose 600,000 factory jobs and still retain 600,000 people working in factories.

Of course, New York's factories did not always look like factories, at least not like modern factories—one-story boxes floating in a parking-lot sea. New York had some multistory reinforced concrete buildings, designed to carry heavy machinery on their extra-large floors and clearly labeled by design as buildings within which objects were produced. But the busiest factory district in the city was incongruously located in central Manhattan, just south of 42nd Street and the theater district. Here, sometimes in new brick-faced elevator buildings that looked like extraordinarily solid office buildings and sometimes in older structures on the choking side streets, the women's garment industry made its headquarters. Adjacent were the furriers.

In the early postwar years, imaginative real estate people were chagrined that dress factories kept such valuable real estate from attaining its "highest and best use"—meaning office buildings, whose tenants could pay much higher rents per square foot. Samuel J. Lefrak suggested moving the whole garment industry to a site over the vast Sunnyside rail freight yards in Queens and offered to build new, modern factories if the city would only lend him the money. The city was properly afraid that the industry was already too fragile to move. If we let them disconnect their electric cutting machines, they won't stop moving until they get to Alabama, officials said, probably correctly (within a few years they would not have stopped before reaching Korea). Even today, what's left of the dress business fears that the proposed reconstruction of 42nd Street and Times Square will raise the value of the land under the remaining dress factories. Ultimately, they fear, the industrial buildings will be demolished by their owners (the dress manufacturers usually rent their space from others) to make room for high-rise offices.

If the general public was unaware of the extent to which the city economy was based on manufacturing, the dependency was noted by the city planners. A multivolume study of New York's economy, headed by Raymond Vernon of Harvard, predicted in 1960 the decline of New York's manufacturing sector, but concluded that expanding service enterprises would put an equivalent number of New Yorkers to work. It was clear to careful observers that the traffic congestion, the dependence on elevators to handle goods for a number of unconnected manufacturers in the same building, and other expenses of midcity operation would inevitably make New York's multistory factory buildings obsolete. The problem of factory obsolescence was not limited to New York. By 1970, when environmentalists in the Middle West were beginning to celebrate the disappearance of chimneys and black smoke from their midst, their fellow citizens had their first chance to breathe clean air. They discovered, unhappily, that it smelled of unemployment.

New York's manufacturing businesses included some that did produce obnoxious noises and smoke. Its power stations burned coal until the 1970s. Despite sophisticated electrostatic devices that removed most gritty particles from their smoke, the dust and fly ash that remained seemed to be irresistibly attracted to the human eye and to the hamburgers that penthouse dwellers were grilling on their terraces downwind of Consolidated Edison's stacks. Everyone, including the rulers of the Middle East, celebrated the conversion of its coal-burning plants to oil. Chemical plants that produced synthetic tiles and rendering plants that made tallow and fats produced horrible smells in parts of the city. No one except their employees and suppliers regretted their departure. But the city was genuinely sorry to see the garment manufacturers disappear; they made no smoke, except what came from cigars smoked on Seventh Avenue during the postprandial noontime "schmooze." The smell they exuded was the salty smell of herring, and the only danger they presented to passing pedestrians was that of being bumped by one of the handcarts in which unfinished dresses were rolled from the buttonhole-maker to the hemstitcher.

Nor did other typical New York manufacturers present worse problems. They put ink on paper, stamped out small pieces of metal to make electrical fittings, prepared food, and brewed beer. What made them leave New York was not the environmental problem in its simple physical sense.

The garment industry flourished in New York because its fairly skilled workers from Europe provided the entrepreneurial skill to organize a mass-production clothing business. First they raised home production to its uttermost limits of inhumane efficiency. The immigrant families worked in their tenement homes, disturbing domestic tranquillity, raising dust, and exposing children to adult language and behavior that greatly disturbed some of the settlement house reformers. Many garment workers contracted tuberculosis in the airless rooms in which they both lived and worked.

Housing reform laws pushed industrial production from the tenement houses. After the catastrophic event of the Triangle Shirtwaist fire in 1911 killed 146 workers, mostly women, factory reform laws were passed as well, and the union, The International Ladies' Garment Workers, grew enormously in power and importance.

Control of factories for the safety of the workers was only a short step from governmental control of factories for the protection of nearby buildings and the neighborhood. Many pieces of land in New York were subject to ownership covenants that prevented their use for obnoxious purposes like glue factories, but that was not enough protection. In 1916 the city adopted the first true zoning ordinance. This law in its original form permitted industrial uses only in areas that were classified as "unrestricted," a deprecatory label that few landowners wanted to attach to areas that might sometime respond to residential demands. The ordinance was comprehensively revised in the early 1960s; one of the major changes was an attempt to classify industries by performance standards so that innocuous manufacturing processes could be located much nearer to homes.

In practice, it has turned out that New York neighborhood groups have become unsympathetic to the need to retain jobs and will do whatever they can to prevent nearby factories from expanding, whether or not the factories are causing nuisances. Homeowners do not seem to care that a factory may even be forced to close its doors or leave the city if it is not permitted to expand. Sometimes neighbors will find a legal technicality that can be used to prevent an expansion whose purpose is to comply with new regulations designed to improve air quality. It was inconceivable, when the city was growing rapidly, that its taxpayers would try so hard to impede economic and job growth. But that is how it has been since the Second World War, and particularly since the phrase "quality of life" has come into common speech.

One of the most poignant aspects of conflict between local residents and the industrial enterprises in their midst is the amount of political and civic energy that must be expended in the New York style to resolve it. A dispute may ultimately be compromised in a way that would have kept the factory alive, but only after such a long period of uncertainty that it either kills off the enterprise or leaves the company so angry that it moves the factory anyway. Local residents always enjoy favorable political odds over industrial enterprises. Elected representatives are well aware of the residents' interest in the quality of life because the representatives themselves live in the same area. Factory workers do vote, but they generally live far from their work places. Scattered in other parts of the city, and perhaps even outside it, they lack the means of stimulating local officials to support their case in the Board of Estimate, the city's executive governing body.

One of the most drawn-out of these matters involved the S. & S. Corrugated Box Machinery Manufacturing Company, an enterprise located in the Greenpoint section of Brooklyn. The company was the world's leading manufacturer of the machinery used to fabricate corrugated cardboard boxes. In the mid-1960s, the company purchased a large tract of land in New

Jersey. It had to expand to meet current demand, and it had found that it could not do so in Greenpoint because the land it had to acquire was occupied by eighty-eight houses, whose owners refused to sell. Naturally the owners didn't care that the city government considered retaining the plant's jobs and adding 200 new ones more important to New York City than replaceable private homes.

Under the state's urban renewal statutes, it was possible for the city to acquire the homes by right of eminent domain, pay fair market value for them, and resell the land to the S. & S. company at cost. When such plans were announced in 1969 and approved by the Board of Estimate, however, the local residents organized into a very sophisticated opposition that began by trying to stop the use of the power of eminent domain altogether and then insisted that substitute housing had to be provided for those who were to be forced to sell their homes. The dispute took years to settle. In the intervening period, the S. & S. Company changed its mind about the need to expand. The new jobs did not materialize, but the city was still stuck with many of the costs of the new housing. By that time, the local people were so well organized to fight City Hall that no one dared to propose changes in Greenpoint.

In 1984, a similar situation arose in Queens. A company called the Quick Roll Leaf Manufacturing Company had for fifty years been operating a plant in Queens, adjacent to the tracks of the Long Island Rail Road. The company manufactured the rolled labels with adhesive backing that supermarkets use to put prices and advertising materials on cans and boxes. Over the years, residential neighbors moved in alongside the factory. Then in 1983, the federal Environmental Protection Agency found that the factory violated federal clean air standards, a condition that could be corrected only by extending the factory smokestacks to a height of seventy feet and installing special exhaust-filtering equipment. The owners decided to do this on a section of the property alongside the railroad and as far as possible from residential neighbors. Then they learned that the city had mapped a possible future street in that part of the property.

Under New York City law, when the city puts such an imaginary street on the official map, it need not pay for the land until it actually moves to build the street, an event that may never take place. The owners, however, may not build at any time on the demarcated street site without special permission from the Board of Estimate following a public hearing. Although the zoning law permitted enlargement of the building, the residential neighbors thought that they would be able to stop the expansion by urging the Board of Estimate to refuse permission to build in the mapped street. They were right. The Queens elected officials were persuaded that the opposition was too strong politically to resist, even though it seemed likely to cost seventy-five jobs. The local people did not care whether the factory was closed down or not. Although they had lived alongside it for many years, most of them having moved in with full knowledge of its presence, they persuaded the Queens borough president that their "quality of life" would be imperiled. They also feared that seventy-foot factory stacks would make their houses less salable.

A third and more complicated form of interference between residential and industrial land involves another New York City law, J-51. The law permits the city to forgive existing taxes on substandard buildings that need rehabilitation and to exempt from taxation the value of improvements to render it modern. Originally passed to encourage the installation of heating systems in tenement houses that had previously lacked them, it proved to be flexible enough to make economically feasible the restoration of thousands of old buildings. The law increasingly aroused the indignation of so-called progressives on the City Council, who argued that rehabilitation would have occurred without the two tax concessions. Neither the truth nor the falsity of that claim can be proved. The critics then aimed at the use of these tax concessions to turn an industrial building into a residential building. That activity, they claimed, resulted in

the loss of badly needed industrial jobs for relatively poor people in order to pile up profits for those who constructed less
badly needed housing for the wealthy.

The argument has some validity, but it is more persuasive at
first hearing than after serious examination. It should be obvious that a city that has lost 600,000 manufacturing jobs in a
single decade must have lost many manufacturing enterprises.
Their former factory floors have not been refilled by other
manufacturers. It is not usually practical to fill a building with
both manufacturing and residential tenants. Codes concerning
safety regulations differentiate between the two different kinds
of tenancy. Practical questions like elevator size and speed as
well as staffing on weekends make a happy combination of
workers and residents utopian nonsense. As we have seen, most
people do not want to live near a factory.

As a practical matter, many industrial buildings in New York
City are partially empty. The owners of two loft buildings on
the same street may be struggling to make ends meet, each with
one half-empty building. If their tenants were consolidated in
one of the two, it would survive. Then it would certainly be a
useful conservation of resources to use the other industrial
building's shell as part of a new residential building, for which
there is a market demand if the building is centrally located in
a desirable section of Manhattan. If, on the other hand, the
owners are forced to maintain their buildings for one or two
industrial tenants, who may at any time move out anyhow, the
chances that the buildings will remain in tolerable condition are
minimal.

The critics of the law that gives tax concessions for the conversion of buildings from industrial to residential use surely
know that cutting out the concessions will not do anything to
improve the prospects of manufacturing companies in New
York. Manufacturers are beset with a variety of difficulties, and
space is perhaps the least of them. The critics also know that
laws taxing owners of real property on the capital value of the
improvements they make to their property tend to discourage

them from making such improvements, truly the last thing that intelligent tax policy should aim to do. Critics are, it seems, bemused by the specter of profits, an economic term that has been tarred with a certain opprobrium in New York since the end of the Second World War. The public policy question is not whether it is bad to permit builders and owners of buildings to make profits on their investments but rather, who would invest and operate buildings if there were no profits to be made from them? When government provides housing that the private market cannot profitably provide, it must charge rents that, together with the subsidies it dedicates to housing, cover not only the immediate costs of the housing operations but all the elaborate governmental superstructure needed to run them. The cost to the economy might, if someone bothered to analyze it rigorously, be greater than the normal profits on privately owned housing. And, even if it covers its costs, government housing does not directly help accumulate new funds in the hands of entrepreneurs who then invest in new projects.

Yet the taint on the word *profits* never seems to fade any more, whether the speakers are discussing the hard-won small percentage of turnover made by highly competitive supermarkets or the regulated profits of natural monopolies. To decry profits at the same time that one seeks to restore or at least maintain the city's industrial employment is obviously futile. It makes the sympathetic observer of the city's economic problems wish that the leaves cut from the calendar could be reaffixed to it, so that modern New York could enjoy the same enthusiastic innocence with which the city greeted economic activity back in the nineteenth century.

The problems New York faces in restoring its industrial base are far more intractable than they were when the original industries were established. In the garment industry, there are still thousands of workers employed at union scale in New York City. There are also thousands of new arrivals, some of them undocumented aliens, who are willing to work below the regular union scale. The ILGWU has agreed to establish a special secondary wage scale, recognizing that the new workers are competing not with the regular union members but with off-shore labor working at even lower rates. But there's always fear that relaxing the wage standard will have a depressing effect on future contract negotiations with the employers of the union's scale-paid members. Organizing the workers in the ladies' garment industry was difficult enough before the passage of the Wagner Act, in the days when the workers were immigrants, unsure of their rights, and fearful of their future if they alienated their employers. Under present circumstances, a new difficulty has arisen. When the union permits employers to pay some workers a much lower wage than others doing similar work, it creates a division between its own members, making the better-paid members worry that their own pay scale will be imperiled by the union's acceptance of a lower scale. It also makes the lesser paid workers feel that the union is not truly solicitous of their welfare. The alternative, however, of dropping the lesser paid workers from the union altogether is equally dangerous. It may mean a loss of jobs to overseas production centers, or the growth of non-union employment practices that will even more seriously threaten the pay standards of the union's older members.

It is a fact that new garment shops are springing up on the edge of Chinatown in lower Manhattan, perhaps even in the houses in which Jewish immigrants once sewed overcoats a hundred years ago. No one wants to recreate the conditions that existed before the Triangle fire, but if cheap factory space cannot be found in which to use the cheap labor, how are the new arrivals to support themselves?

The city is unprepared in the 1980s to accept working conditions that were made illegal, bit by bit, over years of reform legislation. And yet it cannot do the opposite. It cannot build modern, highly subsidized manufacturing space for enterprises paying subnormal wages without running into opposition from those who claim that it is subsidizing management but not labor. Nor can it be too generous in its assistance to businesses that pay normal wages and that threaten to leave the city because of its high costs. When it assists a strong, prosperous enterprise, it opens itself to the accusation that it is simply wasting valuable resources, perhaps for corrupt reasons. When it assists a weak enterprise, it often stands accused of making the survival of the strong more difficult, perhaps impossible.

The difficulty of stimulating economic growth, or of even so modest a goal as simply hanging on to what the city already has in business and jobs, is best understood by reviewing the reasons why businesses leave. First must come the high wages prevalent in New York City, pushed up by the high cost of housing, transportation, and practically everything less that goes into the standard of living. High wages can be offset by high productivity, but in the relatively primitive industries left in New York today, there seems to be no clear way in which productivity can be improved and jobs simultaneously be made more plentiful. The cost of manufacturing space is high because land cost is high and so is construction. The costs of handling goods are high because of urban congestion as well as the inconveniences of multistory buildings. Taxes are high because both local and state governments pay high wages, though not uniquely so, and then supplement them with unusually high pension and other fringe benefits. The state and local governments also conduct programs that other cities avoid, including paying a significant share of Medicaid and Aid to Families with Dependent Children. Finally, power costs are higher than just about anywhere else.

The simplest stimulant that city and state governments might apply to business is tax reduction, but that would reduce the city's ability to spend on other problems; the prospect of doing so seems remote, especially under the pressure of the municipal unions that feel they have been underpaid since the fiscal crisis of 1975. Moreover, the city needs all the money it can lay its hands on to restore its own weary capital plant. The manifold services it provides—and that bulk so large in its expenses— seem to the New York mind more essential than cutting taxes.

In a city in which 70 percent of the people live in rented apartments and do not know that they pay real estate taxes to the city every time they pay rent to their landlords, that spirit of largesse is practically invulnerable to the wiles of sober selfishness.

The city's inability to establish principles to guide its economic development policy leave it trying to bargain with each business separately. It tries to give as few concessions on taxes and regulations as it can get away with. Business bargaining is not what city government does best. The official responsible for handling the negotiations, now called the deputy mayor for economic development, has to bargain in full view of the public, while corporate negotiations are carried on with all the discretion of wartime meetings between enemies.

If the deputy mayor is perceived as being too generous with such items as low-cost electricity from hydropower generated upstate, or too harsh in terminating previously negotiated promises, he or she will be criticized. Since the deputy mayor's income, or position with the city, is not dependent on the size of the city's "profit"—there is none—critics can always argue that too much generosity was shown for reasons at which they can only hint darkly. The consequences of this exposure to criticism—threats to livelihood and reputation—lead the deputy mayor to believe himself exempt from ordinary ethical rules of business conduct. It's rare indeed to find a public official who has enough experience in the private sector to carry on these negotiations successfully and yet understands the ways of government well enough to know how to modify business practice sufficiently to mollify critics.

Not so surprisingly, therefore, the Koch administration has not succeeded in actually putting together, to the point of signing papers and getting the work under way, any of the large industrial development deals on which it has announced it was working. The same can be said of previous administrations. Matters that seem quite simple—the erection of bus shelters by private concessionaires who would sell advertising space and share the revenue with the city is one—have so far baffled the best efforts of the Beame and Koch administrations. Instead of getting shelters in all the boroughs that would keep passengers warm and dry while they wait for a bus, the city has gotten lawsuits and bad publicity. Manhattan residents have been legally entitled to purchase cable TV since 1970, but it has not been possible to get cable TV operators to sign final contracts covering the other boroughs. Whenever the city negotiators offer terms acceptable to the entrepreneurs, they are criticized for giving too much and asking too little.

This inability to get matters finally pinned down hints broadly that a city as large as New York, whose leaders represent so many groups of people with different interests and goals, simply cannot conduct negotiations with business firms in the way that a business firm can. The reason is fundamental. Though stockholders and directors may disagree over the best course for their company to follow, there's little disagreement about the ultimate goal: to maximize the financial return to everyone connected with the enterprise. For a city, even so banal a goal is impossible to frame universally. In the case of cable TV, for instance, some believe the city should seek maximum franchise fees. Others ask for maximum employment for minorities. Others demand priority for community broadcast facilities. Others think nothing is so important as the number of channels accessible to citizens who want to enlighten or shock their friends. By contrast, the negotiators on the business side simply want profit. Their job is easier to define, but in view of the uncertainty across the table, their goal is difficult to attain.

The British long ago recognized the difficulty that local governments face in trying to mobilize their inadequate resources to stimulate industrial development. Peter Hall, a geographer at Reading University, suggested that the national government could help by creating what he called Enterprise Zones. Within specially designated areas that were suffering from high unemployment rates and showing other signs of economic stagnation, Hall suggested, the government could provide sanctuary against the taxes and intrusive rules and regulations of welfare statism. Washington under the Reagan Administration has been proposing a similar set of zones for the United States. Several states had already established them within their borders, but since the states generally impose fewer restrictions on industry than does the federal government, mere exemption from state regulation is a rather small stimulus.

So far, Congress has been unable to decide whether to make Enterprise Zones national policy. Nor, assuming that Congress decides in the affirmative, is there agreement on just which taxes or labor and environmental rules should be waived, or exactly how many zones there should be. Obviously, every state with economic woes wants its enterprise zones, or a fair share of them. But the more zones there are, the less attractive their benefits become; competition will tend to obscure their charm.

An even deeper set of questions underlies the problem of selecting a proper number of zones that will strike the right balance between effectiveness and political practicability. One question raises the fundamental national policy question: do Americans want their industrial development investments to be made in the cities that have always had their share of industries, at least until lately, or in those places that are most likely to be able to use the zones effectively? A second question asks: if it is necessary and desirable to exempt industries in some locations from regulatory restraints, why should it not be advisable to lift those restraints everywhere? A third question is: if the restraints are lifted only temporarily, until new enterprises establish themselves, will the same industries be able to withstand the shock of the reimposition of normal regulations? Puerto Rico's Operation Bootstrap offered tax concessions to mainland companies that opened plants on the island. Employment soared, but only as long as the special tax benefits lasted.

The Enterprise Zones may prove helpful, even in New York, but they would be more helpful yet if the nation and particularly the city bothered to understand why such legislation came up for discussion in the first place. The zones would not be necessary if the leadership of city and nation had not for years been taking for granted that the spirit of enterprise would always be loose in the United States. The question of why exemption from regulation—including environmental regulation—should be necessary to eliminate unemployment, balance the budget, and balance overseas trade is hidden under the proposal for the zones. Why should exemption be available only for the benefit of the weakest enterprises? Are special zones not more likely to encourage familiar types of enterprise that compete with other companies outside the zones? Are the zones needed by new enterprises in which highly motivated innovators are likely to run big risks in the hope of earning very substantial rewards?

One of the telling indices of city attitudes toward entrepreneurship is the way the cities treat their public utilities. New York City has an interesting relationship with Consolidated Edison, the privately owned utility that keeps the city and its people supplied with most of their electricity and gas. Consolidated Edison has been required to bury its cables and distribution lines throughout the central parts of the city at formidable original expense and high expenditures for upkeep. The company is the city's most effective tax farmer; it pay taxes on the value of its equipment as well as on its real estate and franchises and collects them in concealed form from its customers. At almost regular intervals, the city imposes new restrictions on the company's right to cut off service from customers who fail to pay their bills. And now the city encourages large users of electricity to install their own generating equipment and forces Con Ed to buy any surplus current they produce, although the air quality effects of cogeneration, as the process is called, are in basic conflict with the city's goals of cleaner air, free of diesel oil residues. Then, as though to add insult to injury, Mayor Koch, without any justification other than imperfectly understood figures prepared by the city, has accused the utility company of overcharging the city by more than $100 million.

Of course, when electricity was new, and when the city for the first time was able to see the advantage of using electricity to replace gaslight, power its transportation, and run a magnificent invention—the elevator—that made New York's high buildings possible, utility companies were treated with great respect. The difference in the treatment accorded utility officials today may explain why so few young people start off in life with a burning desire to run an electric power company.

In the present climate, it is hardly surprising that New York City's efforts to stimulate business with government intervention has produced so little. Perhaps if the national economy continues to reduce inflation and increase employment, the cultural attitude toward enterprise will soften. Taste-makers may look at entrepreneurs with respect in place of scorn.

It is not inconceivable that someone somewhere will invent something that can do for the city what the ski did for Vermont. That was an economically forlorn state resting on little more than its maple sugar until Europeans pointed out that skiing was fun and that Vermont was quite a convenient place for it. The ski revitalized overgrown farms and deserted villages with remarkable efficiency. If New York creates the right atmosphere, the city might be tempting to any number of daring entrepreneurs who have in the backs of their heads ideas for an urban equivalent of the ski. Until that equivalent arrives, the best thing the city can do to prepare a proper welcome for it is to cultivate a hospitable attitude toward the people who risk obloquy and scorn for devoting their lives to getting rich by finding a way to make what people want.

Chapter V

For Better,
For Worse,
For an Apartment

AT THE BEGINNING of the Second World War, New York City had a far larger number of rental apartments than any other city in the United States. Seventy percent or more of its people lived in homes they did not own. Its housing construction industry, though badly hit by the depression, was one of the more efficient in the country, capable not only of throwing up apartment houses quickly and inexpensively but also of managing and operating them very well on the whole. For example, the Metropolitan Life Insurance Company was so pleased with its Parkchester development in the Bronx, erected during the 1930s, that it laid plans long before the end of the war to build the 9,000-unit Stuyvesant Town and Peter Cooper Village projects. The city's building laws permitted apartment houses of up to six stories to be erected with wooden floor beams, an inexpensive form of multistory construction that has proven to be quite safe from fires, thanks to its concrete first-floor slab, exit requirements, heavier scantlings, fire-stopped cocklofts (space between roof and ceilings of top-floor apartments), and ampler courtyards. The cruder tenement houses of an earlier day, which had also been built with wooden floor beams, were dangerous firetraps. At the beginning of the war, the city had a substantial surplus of housing and a comfortable vacancy rate, comfortable at least to tenants and prospective tenants who, on the whole, were able to find apartments with ease. Competition for tenants kept rents below what many building owners thought was a reasonably profitable level.

At the end of the war, the apartment situation—and the supply of homes for purchase—was very different. Prior to the war, effective demand for housing, thanks to the Depression, had dropped even more sharply than the supply; when the veterans came back and the economy improved, there was a shortage. That shortage was written large in the want ads of each of the city's many daily newspapers. A small symbol that came to be called "the ruptured duck," though it actually depicted an eagle, denoted the veteran's status of any qualified person who inserted a want ad in the newspaper. The ruptured ducks studded the advertising pages, as veterans returning to the city, or moving there, desperately pleaded for apartments. Mothers grew frantic, fearing that their sons and perhaps even their daughters would entangle themselves with someone unacceptable, simply to avoid sleeping on ma's and pa's living room couch.

It seemed easy to understand why there was a housing shortage. In wartime, there had been almost no private construction anywhere. Construction workers who were not in the armed forces were busy on projects connected with the war effort: housing for shipyard workers and their families; army camps and barracks; naval installations, shipways, and airfields; hospitals; camps for war prisoners and for the Japanese-Americans who were forcibly evacuated from the Pacific Coast; and a wholly new town called Oak Ridge, Tennessee. All these endeavors consumed large quantities of construction materials as well as labor.

The war-induced stoppage of private construction followed years of depression during which housing starts had dropped in 1932 to little more than 100,000 for the year, much less than 10 percent of the annual total required to keep abreast of the nation's prewar housing needs. These two impediments to the supply of housing—the war and the depression that preceded it—were made calamitous by a sharp increase in demand. As in many other sections of the country the demand in New York was increased by a sharp rise in the number of families and individual people who were looking for their own homes. The prosperity that came with war, and government programs to make mortgage money for homes flow more easily and more cheaply into construction, went hand in hand with the increased desire of many young people to be on their own. Young people had naturally grown up during the war and had come to feel more independent, even if they had not married. They could not imagine returning meekly to parental discipline, worse than a sergeant's.

The organization of New York's housing and construction industry, and the city's importance as a financial center capable of providing an almost limitless amount of construction and permanent mortgage money, inspired confidence that, properly unleashed, these forces would sooner or later eliminate the postwar shortage and remedy the city's other housing problems. But forty years after the war the city continued to suffer from a severe shortage, perhaps not so acute as it had been in 1945 but with a vacancy rate that was far too low for tenant protection and comfort.

Solving the immediate postwar housing shortage was the highest priority problem for New York City government and the construction industry. It was, however, by no means the only housing problem that the city's leadership faced and to which it was sensitive. The city's second major housing problem was the challenge of raising the very low quality of many of the apartment houses in which a million or more of its citizens had to live because nothing better was available at prices they could afford.

Much of this bad housing had been the object of reformers' attention for decades. The houses were built in the last part of the nineteenth century, when New York's population was growing very rapidly, fed by an astonishing influx of poor European immigrants. Tenement houses for the poor tended to be higher and more densely designed in Manhattan, where land values were high, than in those sections of Brooklyn, still an independent city, or the South Bronx, where poor families settled. A few buildings were seven stories high, many were six. None had elevators. All such buildings were erected on lots twenty-five feet across, often a hundred feet deep. The size and shape of the lots made light and air difficult to attain in the apartments. On the most valuable downtown sites, four apartments were fitted into a single floor. None had bathrooms. The tub for bathing was located in the kitchen, and toilets were located in the common hall. There was no heating system unless it had been installed long after the building was erected and occupied.

Over the years since their erection, such tenement buildings have been the subject of many new laws, passed by both state and city governments, which have had the effect of bringing conditions in them nearer to modern housing standards. Heating became a requirement in all New York apartments twenty years after the Second World War, and the J-51 law was passed allowing the owners of these old unheated buildings to recoup most of the cost of installing heating systems by a deduction from real property taxes.

After 1901, buildings that lacked bathrooms in each apartment and provided inadequate light and air and fire escapes could not be built in New York City. The ban on such new buildings, however, did not do anything to improve the old ones. Nor did piecemeal improvements, like the requirement for heating, make any change in the inadequate light and air, the room sizes, or the overcrowding.

In the years before the Second World War, agitation for clearing the slums of New York City had been almost continuous. Among the immense problems in the way were the people who lived in the buildings that would have been demolished or rebuilt. Where would they find new places that they could afford? In the postwar housing shortage, any change that involved changing room sizes and reducing overcrowding meant displacing people. Not only was it difficult to move them elsewhere, but the reduction in occupancy combined with the need to recoup the cost of improvements meant that the rents would be sure to go up unless some government or other—or all of them together—subsidized the changes.

The third major long-range housing problem that faced New York at the end of the war was improvement in the peculiarly bad conditions under which nonwhite New Yorkers lived. Their incomes were lower than those of white families, and they suffered from the same disadvantage that all poor people suffer from in buying or renting anything as expensive as a sound home. But in their case, the disadvantage was made worse by the reluctance of white families to live beside them in apartment houses or neighborhoods. Prejudice narrowed their prospects for decent housing and confined them to generally undesirable areas of the city in which, because of softness in the local housing market, they were able to establish a toehold. As the number of nonwhite New Yorkers grew after the end of the war, on a scale that no one foresaw, the areas occupied by nonwhites expanded in size and number, also to an extent that no one foresaw. But in comparison with the growth in numbers, the enlarged space was certainly not enough to simplify their housing problem. The areas they occupied continued to be for the most part inferior in quality, and more expensive per square foot, than the areas occupied by whites. That does not mean, however, that no black families occupied good housing, and that there were not some areas in the city in which black families could live as well as white families with similarly good incomes.

These two problems required long-range solutions, and the local, state, and federal governments all developed programs intended to deal with them. In 1949, Washington made a major contribution to the solution of housing problems of low-income families by adopting a public housing program that was an extension of the principle established by Congress in 1937: public housing was based on the theory that if the federal government pays for the development of housing for poor people, the people can afford to pay its maintenance and upkeep costs. This theory worked well for many years, until in the 1970s operating costs—especially fuel and power costs—rose so steeply that operating subsidies became necessary. The 1949 act provided that public housing was to be built and owned by an agency of local government, though funded by the federal government. No state was to be given more than 15 percent of the total allotment of subsidies for the nation as a whole, but since some states did not use their full share, others that asked for more might inherit some unexpended allocations. New York State, including New York City, always used up its 15 percent and managed to get part of the unallocated excess.

The federal program, a state-subsidized public housing program, and a more lightly subsidized city program enabled the New York City Housing Authority to build and operate apartments in which more than 600,000 people were living by the beginning of the 1980s. Generally conceded to be one of the best managed housing agencies in the nation, the Authority, in effect, was in 1980 providing good, sound, solid homes for at least half the number of people who had been living in old tenement housing when the postwar era began. What is disturbing about that statement is that the number of people living in grossly improper housing—improper at least by generally accepted American standards—did not seem to have been reduced by anything like the number of people who had moved into public housing. That means that the number of people who cannot afford decent housing has increased in the city. It also means that the number of poorly maintained apartments has risen sharply. Many thousands of apartments that were built after 1901 and were acceptable as standard American housing when the war ended had deteriorated into unacceptably bad housing in the following forty years.

The census of housing conducted as part of the national head count in 1960, 1970, and 1980 does not indicate that the deterioration of housing quality in the city has been that serious. But the census measures only the existence of stipulated equipment and facilities, such as a heating system and a bathroom within each apartment. It also counts the number of units that are described by its enumerators as "dilapidated," a somewhat subjective category. The trouble with New York's housing in the 1980s is that though there are heating systems and bathrooms in a much higher percentage of units than ever before, a very discouraging percentage of them are not working properly.

The impression of the deterioration of good housing into substandard housing is reinforced by anyone who takes the pains to explore once-good neighborhoods in all five of the city's boroughs. One of the city's most impressive avenues is in the Bronx. The Grand Concourse, modeled after the grand boulevards of Paris, is a very wide street, separated into through-lanes and local lanes by islands planted with trees. It is lined with apartment houses that were built in the 1920s, some of them striking examples of Art Deco architecture. A casual inspection reveals that many have been abandoned by their owners, while a larger number are grossly disfigured with graffiti, broken windows, cracked panes on their doors, boarded-up windows, and other signs of decay. Some of the abandoned buildings have been rehabilitated at government expense, but some of those that have been rehabilitated have deteriorated all over again and are practically indistinguishable from buildings that have never been touched up at all.

There are further evidences of the housing shortage and the shift of basically sound housing into the categories of deterioration that stop just short of blatant dilapidation. One bit of evidence is the many people receiving public assistance whom the city must put up in temporary hotel quarters because their houses have burned down or because they have been evicted for nonpayment of rent. Ostensibly, assignment to a hotel is a temporary expedient. The facts are, however, that the stay of the typical hotel family has become more and more extended because it is increasingly difficult to find standard apartments (the "standard" used is not excessively high, incidentally) to which these families can be sent. A second bit of evidence of rapid deterioration of sound housing is the amount of money the city must spend, much of it taken from community development grants given by the federal government, on the repair of occupied apartment houses that the city has taken over because the owners failed to pay their real estate taxes. Only the most crucially needed repairs are made in these buildings, and yet the city must spend millions more than it receives in rentals to make them minimally habitable. Another bit of evidence of a serious housing shortage is to be found in the growing number of people who have no home at all. The city has had to open shelters for them. There have, of course, always been some homeless people in the city, sleeping at the municipally owned lodging houses for men or women, but the number has grown, while their age has dropped.

Many of these people are former inmates of mental institutions, released because under court rulings they cannot be held against their will unless they are found to constitute a danger to themselves or others. Some formerly lived in apartment houses that long ago had been cut up into one-room apartments whose occupants shared common toilet and bathing facilities. These so-called Single-Room Occupancy (S.R.O.) buildings were among the city's worst housing accommodations. Whole families lived in one-room units in the early postwar days, until the city forbade the practice. Recently, the housing shortage has become so acute that S.R.O. buildings in reasonably good neighborhoods have become attractive for remodeling into standard apartments. Although the remodeling improves the quality of the building, its immediate consequence is to displace the people living in it.

The deterioration of basically sound housing has helped stimulate the city to encourage remedial measures. Its public housing program was supplemented some years ago by a Washington program administered by the Housing Authority that offers cash subsidies to specially selected tenants who live in privately owned apartments and whose rent is greater than 30 percent of their income. The city has taken over many buildings that were delinquent in taxes, and as noted has spent federal money to fix them up; some have been fixed up to the point at which they become "standard." Some of the apartments are sold to their occupants at bargain prices, though the buyers must agree that if they resell they will turn over a major portion of their profits to the city. Finally, in the housing projects themselves, a new and rather frightening phenomenon has appeared to which the Housing Authority now turns a reluctant blind eye: doubling up. Families have moved into already occupied apartments, creating illicit overcrowding. The Authority does not like the overcrowding, knowing that it speeds housing deterioration and raises maintenance costs, but there is no other place for the doubling-uppers to go.

All of these are expedients. None has been as successful or satisfactory in New York as the federally funded public housing program. And even that program has its problems in the city, mainly the question of where to put the projects, assuming that the federal government were willing to finance a new flock of them. If projects are to be racially integrated, or at least to have a reasonable chance of becoming and remaining racially integrated, they must be placed in areas where white families are willing to live and, later, to stay. But the residents in such areas are not likely to welcome low-income neighbors in a publicly owned project. In part they resist the very race of their new neighbors, but more significant are the considerations of social class and economic status that are deeply entwined with locational choice. Location is one of the explanations of the most depressing of all New York's postwar housing problems, the galloping deterioration of the city's most solid, middle-class apartment house sections. Single-family home sections of the city have also deteriorated, but many of these have staged and are staging a remarkable comeback in the process we have described as "gentrification."

To understand the matter more clearly, locational problems should be separated into several categories. The Grand Concourse can be taken as an example of one kind. The very reason why it developed so well in the prewar years became a major defect in the postwar years. The Concourse had been built up in the expectation—soon realized—that a new, city-owned subway line would connect it to the ladies' garment manufacturing district in Manhattan. The "D" express train daily took workers from the Concourse and the side streets off it down to Sixth Avenue in Manhattan, a short distance from the Seventh Avenue Center of the garment manufacturing district. When, after the war, most garment manufacturing left New York City, and the children of aging garment workers left the garment trades to become psychoanalysts, electrical engineers, lawyers, and accountants, the Concourse was in fact doomed. Its ailment was a lingering one, because rent control, of which much more must be said, offered great inducements to those who lived in bearable apartments in the city to remain there. Ultimately, however, many of the people of the Concourse no longer had to travel to the places where their subway stubbornly took them, and they moved. That left many of the remaining people afraid that they were now an aging minority in a tougher world than any they had ever known. The newcomers, some of them black but most of them Hispanic, earned less money than the departing tenants. To pay the rent, they were forced to double up and overcrowd the buildings, which consequently deteriorated faster than they might have otherwise.

A second type of locational problem was almost purely racial in character. As the sections open to black and dark-skinned

Hispanics expanded, both the white and nonwhite groups were aware of traditional boundary lines. Usually these were natural or man-made geographical features—railway lines, highways, parks, rivers—that demarcated the sections that were open to nonwhites from those that were not. These facts of life, despite their unpleasantness, gave whites a sense of safety and encouraged them to live near nonwhite neighborhoods, relying on the familiar dividing lines to keep their own immediate surroundings from "turning." When these dividing lines were breached, as they inevitably were with the growth of the nonwhite population, white families left the changing area, speeding the change in what the sociologist Robert Merton would call a "self-fulfilling prophesy."

A third type of locational problem is related to the other two but involves an issue so crucial to apartment-house owners that it deserves a category of its own. That is the effect on bank lending that is exerted by the bank's perception of the importance of other locational problems. Unless they are insured under government programs, most apartment-house mortgages are not what the industry calls *self-amortizing.* That is to say, they are written for terms like ten years—a much shorter period than the expected life of the buildings they finance. While they require the borrower to reduce the principal outstanding at the start of the mortgage term, they do not require the loan to be paid off. Both lender and borrower expect that when a mortgage term expires, the original lender, or another thrift institution, will renew the mortgage, changing its interest rate to reflect current money market conditions and perhaps demanding a reduction in the principal at the very beginning of the new mortgage term. In recent years, because of unprecedented fluctuations in interest rates, new mortgages sometimes require readjustment of the interest rate even while the mortgages continue outstanding.

One of the factors that influence savings institutions when they are asked to renew or replace a maturing mortgage is the bank's perception of the condition of the neighborhood. Obviously, if the neighborhood is going down—if buildings are being abandoned by their owners, if tax arrearages are piling up, if repairs are being postponed indefinitely, if the condition of the streets suggests that municipal government finds the burdens the neighborhood imposes on the Sanitation, Fire, and Police Departments too heavy to bear—a bank will consider the investment as entailing greater risk than if it were in a more stable area. It may either refuse to make a new or replacement mortgage on property in such an area, or it may require both a substantial reduction in the mortgage principal and a hefty increase in the interest rate. The downright refusal to write a mortgage in a given area—a practice known as "redlining"—is catastrophic, a *coup de grace* to a mortally wounded section of the city. Some banks, incidentally, deny that they ever redline an area. Their denial usually means that if a specific borrower has an extraordinarily good past record, or a long history of satisfactory credit dealings with the bank, they will consider a mortgage request in an area in which the normal borrower would not even be considered. Redlining arouses passions because it not only dooms an area but casts aspersions on it; but in candor, the thrift institutions of New York City cannot be accused of eschewing risk: their mortgage losses on apartment-house loans in once-sound areas are wounds suffered in action. But people who want to save their area from final devastation cannot be expected to view the banks' instinct for survival with equanimity when it means their own demise.

Another economic locational problem is the redlining of areas for fire insurance because of a bad record of arson or fires of mysterious origin. New York has sought to circumvent this practice by developing a system of assigned-risk insurance. That system may have helped to keep buildings alive, for without fire insurance mortgage renewals would be impossible. Yet the assigned-risk pool is full of the most severely deteriorated housing in the city. Guarding the insured properties against arson is as difficult for the assigned-risk pool as it had been for the normal insurance companies whose refusal to write policies on endangered properties produced the pool in the first place. The issuance of a fire insurance policy on a grossly deficient and unprofitable building is an invitation to the torch.

In addition to locational problems, a second set of problems that have contributed to the deterioration of once-good housing relates to the welfare system. In a provocative and penetrating book, *The Ecology of Housing Destruction* (1980), Peter Salins of Hunter College, part of the City University system, has analyzed the effect of welfare families on the condition of housing. It is unfair to summarize the work in a few brief paragraphs, and yet what Salins has to say is important enough to justify the effort. New York, to begin with, is one of the states that divide the cash payments to qualified welfare recipients in two parts. One part covers all the living expenses of the family except rent. Because of the wide disparity between rents that may be paid by different families, a separate check is sent covering the family's precise rent bill up to a maximum of $230. Federal regulations specify that the recipient of public assistance must have sole possession of the rent check; it must be sent to the recipient, not to the owner of the property. The check must be made out to the recipient alone, in order to encourage the development of thrifty habits. It cannot be made out jointly to the welfare recipient and the landlord unless the recipient has piled up a record of misapplication of the rental payment. Even then, the Federal Government imposes a percentage ceiling on the number of welfare recipients to whom a joint check may be sent; it cannot exceed 10 percent of the total number of families getting welfare. The welfare families are subject to the temptation to use the rent check for their personal expenses, knowing that rather than allowing them to be evicted for nonpayment of rent, the welfare officials will give them a second rent check so that they can stay in their apartments. Finding other apartments for them would be a most difficult task.

Salins points out that the New York system of providing a separate check for rent implants in the family the idea that they can either spend all of the check for rent or none of it; there is no possibility of their deciding to economize on rent and use the saving to increase their consumption of other goods. Those tenants who spend it all on other goods expect the welfare officials to bail them out, a waste of government money. Perhaps worse than the waste, Salins feels, is the increased mobility that is given to welfare tenants by killing whatever incentive they may have to economize. The welfare family is motivated to move into the best housing accommodation it can find, carrying with it, according to Salins, the omen of deterioration. That argument seems somewhat less convincing than the argument that the welfare family is likely to spend its rent allotment on other goods. If a welfare family does take the trouble to find the best possible housing for its money, it is likely to be more caring of its environment than others and might have a less adverse effect on the house into which it moves.

The arrival of welfare tenants in an apartment house is a signal to all other tenants that the owner has abandoned hope in the future of the building. Salins points out that the presence of a welfare class of tenants in apartment houses changes owners' views of their own financial interest. Once owners find that they have difficulty attracting tenants who pay their own rent, their future expectations are reduced to a very short span. There is no hope of a change for the better that will enable them to select tenants again, and so their financial interest is reduced simply to spending as little money as possible while collecting rent from the welfare tenants. What the welfare family does to the rental housing market is, as Salins points out, to provide a tenant of last resort. And in the end such a tenant also brings on a landlord of last resort. That landlord is probably inexperienced but sufficiently cynical about human behavior to be ready to extract whatever residual values remain in an apartment house that has been buffeted by locational changes and by years of rent control (a subject to be examined momentarily). The landlord of last resort picks up an apartment house at a very low price, spends as little as possible, and expects to recoup the investment in a very short time. Any additional income is profit, but experience in the city suggests that it is not an easy profit to earn. One of the saddest features of this aspect of the story is that the welfare tenancies and the years of rent control have interfered with the longstanding practice of making real estate entrepreneurs from members of the first wave of each new immigration into the city. Many of New York's most dignified real estate dynasties are the descendants of the people who were first to own tenement houses of the type in which they first lived when they arrived in New York City. Yet no landlord class has emerged among the recent mainland black migrants.

By all odds, the factor that has contributed most to the decay of once-good apartment houses and apartment-house neighborhoods in New York City has been rent control. First imposed during the Second World War, it was later continued as the proposed solution to what everyone expected would be a short-range problem, the immediate postwar shortage of housing. No one, of course—even its most enthusiastic supporters—expected that rent control would increase the supply of housing. What its advocates did expect was that rent control would shield tenants, the consumers of rental housing, from the exorbitant rent increases that might be expected to follow naturally from the acute shortage that suddenly appeared at the end of the Second World War. While in theory this principle seems fair enough, in practice there is no way of defining what constitutes a "fair" rent and what an "exorbitant" rent. It is difficult enough for a utility commission to decide what constitutes a fair price for electric power per kilowatt hour; would that shelter were as easy to measure as current.

The quality of electricity scarcely varies from user to user, and the quantity can be determined by instruments that cheaply measure the power used by each consumer. Utility companies all pay roughly the same price for the money they must borrow to construct the capital-intensive plants in which they transform other forms of energy into electric power. Nothing could be in sharper contrast than rental housing. Its quality varies from the most glorious penthouse on the most exclusive corner of the city to the dreariest windowless tenement room on a street that all fear to tread. The interest rates at which the providers of housing must borrow vary from the moderate rates enjoyed by the biggest developers with the soundest properties to the demands of loan sharks who provide temporary financing for the credit-less borrowers who buy worn-out buildings for a quick turnover. The regulators of utility rates have but a few companies to audit, all of them big enough to keep their books in accordance with the utility commission's regulations and procedures, while the rental stock of New York City is provided by thousands of individual entrepreneurs. Some can hire the city's finest accountants and shrewdest lawyers. Others keep what records they have in the backs of old school copybooks.

Nevertheless, New York City got rent control in 1943, as one of the last group of cities to be brought under control by the Office of Price Administration. Rent control, like all American price controls, was a wartime measure, intended to keep the price level, and hence the wage level, and hence the money supply, from exploding as everyone went to work but not at making consumer goods for the general population. When the war ended, New York was still under rent control, and federal regulation was not abolished until 1947. The federal controls were immediately replaced by city controls, then by state controls, then again by city controls, and most recently, in 1984, by state controls once again. Except for a brief period during which apartments were freed from controls when they became vacant, rent regulation has continued uninterrupted, either in the form of a rigid control system with no provision for increases, or in a modified system adopted under the Lindsay Administration, or in a related form of regulation called rent stabilization, adopted in 1969 and continuing to the present day.

No other major American city has had rent control continuously since the Second World War. Since other major cities have experienced some of the housing problems that are familiar in New York, friends of rent control argue that the presence of those problems in cities without rent control proves that rent control cannot be responsible for them.

The trouble with that argument is that no other city has tried to house so large a proportion of its population—nearly 70 percent—in rental housing. No other city had so large a percentage of its middle-class population living in rental apartments that met accepted standards. No other city had so well-developed a rental housing industry, such a complex of laws concerning aids to housing construction, so valiant an effort to build housing for low-income families with federal and other subsidies. No other city has developed its own middle-income housing programs. And despite all this, construction of rental housing in the city has virtually come to a stop, conversions of rental apartments to condominiums and cooperatives continue apace, older buildings are deteriorating rapidly, a chronic shortage exists, and public funds, for which taxpayers are ultimately responsible, have had to replace the private financing market in order to create whatever moderate-priced rehabilitation is actually taking place.

A persuasive case for rent regulation can always be made on humanitarian grounds. It is true that when the vacancy rate is below five or six percent, the market does not act as a brake on the soaring level of rents. It is true, furthermore, that a tenant whose lease expires when vacancies are few is at the mercy of the owner of his building. Moving is expensive, and to save moving costs a tenant-in-occupancy often accedes to a rental demand that a prospective tenant on the outside would reject. Housing is, after all, a necessity of life, the argument goes; people are more important than profits. Landlords are business people who have to accept the risk of regulation as part of their enterprise. They have no serious grounds for complaint if their failure to build enough housing forces the government to control the prices of rental apartments.

Everyone in New York has heard these arguments over the

years. The main trouble with them is not that they are wrong, but simply that they do not work.

New York government has accepted the notion, as the federal government has done on a national level, that it must do what it can to offer to every New Yorker a clean, safe, and sanitary dwelling unit in a suitable living environment. But if the government is to depend on private industry to produce these accommodations, it must expect the providers to charge rents that will cover costs and offer enough of a yield to attract capital. It is simply impossible to audit housing suppliers as suppliers of electricity are monitored, to establish rental rates that, like electricity rates, will cover all costs and offer an attractive yield. In fact, even electricity rates are becoming harder and harder to regulate to the public satisfaction. In the absence of an agreed-on definition of what constitutes the reasonable rent for every apartment in the city, rent control must operate on something that is hardly more than a superstition: that the rents charged on a certain historic day were reasonable. If that assumption is made, the rent control authorities must determine, at the very least, how much costs have risen since that time, and at respectable intervals they must increase rental ceilings to cover the increased costs.

The trouble is that not even that oversimplified statement is capable of realization. What are the costs of rental housing? Do they include mortgage interest? a return on the owner's capital? mortgage amortization? a provision for depreciation of the building? reserves for replacements of fixtures that are certain to wear out? And even if these questions could be decided to everyone's satisfaction, all that they would provide if they could be worked out with precision is a return (or a loss) exactly equal to the yield or loss on the building on the day when rents were frozen.

It should be obvious that such a fixed return is not satisfactory in producing investment in residential real estate. To develop a workable rent regulation system, its advocates would have to apply to rental housing the same complex calculations that regulatory bodies now apply to the infinitely simpler utility industry. First comes the establishment of a "rate base," the true value of property on which the owner is entitled to a fair return. What an army of housing economists, accountants, bookkeepers, investigators, and statisticians would be required to modulate the "rate base" of every apartment house in New York City and to determine, once an agreed-upon rate of return had been established, the true current value of the building on which the return should be calculated.

It is easy enough to say that it doesn't matter what the housing rate base is, because the value is going up all the time and the owner should be happy over the increase in capital value. But that's only true of the best-located properties in the city, especially when the income is controlled by law. And even in the best-located property the owner can obtain the real value of his buildings only by selling them to the tenants who are living in the buildings rather than to another landlord. They, for the most part, do not really want to buy the buildings, and as more are sold in less desirable areas, the profits that tenants have made in such transactions in the past become less certain. Tenant leaders and their sympathizers in the state legislature and the City Council would dearly love to forbid apartment-house owners from selling their buildings to tenants, but they seem to understand that the constitutionality of such a ban would be questionable. And so the supply of rental apartments dwindles, along with the quality.

Nor is that the only price the city pays for trying to regulate rents. The taxable value of rental real estate in all but the best neighborhoods is reduced by the ceilings on rents. The costs of administering rent regulation, together with the complexities of adjudicating disputes between landlords and tenants, rise constantly. It was only a small step from regulating rents to regulating evictions for nonpayment of rent, causing serious losses to owners. Ultimately these losses are imposed on the municipality through defaults in real property taxes. A seldom-discussed price of rent regulation is the competition that rent-regulated private housing offers to non-rent-regulated publicly assisted housing. The city's tremendous investment in the mortgages on so-called middle-income housing has been reduced to a fraction of its cost because residents in those buildings balked at having their rents raised at a faster rate than the rents in private apartment houses.

New York's rent regulation has, therefore, broken up the rental housing market; it has speeded the deterioration of fundamentally good buildings; and it has forced tenants to buy cooperative apartments, so far with no visible ill-effects but with a threat to the future and a high cost to the metropolis. Above all, it has not succeeded in accomplishing what sanguine legislators promised: it has not provided moderate-cost housing for New Yorkers.

The irritating feature of all this is that much of the trouble with rent control might have been averted if the politicians had recognized from the beginning what rent regulation could and could not do. It could not provide a moderate-cost apartment for every New York family, and it surely could not guarantee an apartment at any price in the specific neighborhood in which the family wanted to live. It could not guarantee the continuing quality of an apartment unless the income of the apartment house was sufficient to cover all its operating and capital costs. It could not guarantee that every New York family could have sufficient income to pay such a rent, nor could it make up the shortfall from municipal resources.

What it could have done was to develop a system in which the tenant in an apartment house would be treated as though he were not under the threat of having to move when his lease expired, by allowing him to meet and match the rent asked of anyone else for the apartment he occupied. It could have provided limited financial help in finding apartments to classes of tenants in need of special help for reasonably serious reasons. It could have developed a tax system that would encourage new construction and rehabilitation of deteriorated buildings by taxing the improvements to buildings at a lower rate than it taxes land. It could have explained to the people that after rent controls had been in effect for a few years, there would have to be not one but two kinds of adjustments to rents: one, a catch-up adjustment allowing owners of buildings to cover the accumulated shortfall due to the fact that rents were frozen while costs rose, and a keep-up provision that would have given owners reasonable coverage for the continuing rise, though a very uneven one, in all costs. And above all, the city government could have avoided arousing in its citizens false hopes of frozen rents, and the false belief that government can accomplish miracles of egalitarianism through governmental repeal of economic reality. That's the final price of rent regulation.

Chapter VI

Paying for the Crime

AT THE END of the Second World War, it seemed highly unlikely that New York would find crime to be one of its major problems. Indeed, those who gave the city its leadership—not in politics so much as in education, cultural affairs, business leadership, and civic good works—seemed to believe that the city, along with the rest of the world, was entering a new era in which intelligence, education, and the insights of psychology and other social sciences would overcome most behavior problems. This optimism seemed to stem from beliefs that evil had been vanquished in war; that the United Nations was an organization dedicated to lasting peace; that full employment would eliminate crime; and that the mysteries of political economy had been unraveled.

This view did not necessarily overlook the fact that New York, in the period of its greatest growth, had been a lawless and violent city. Most educated New Yorkers had heard of the draft riots of 11 July 1863, subsequently described in all their gory detail by Edward Banfield in an article in *New York Magazine* (July 29, 1968). His dour and chilly views of the difficulties that faced those who established order and peace in major cities became well known—though not welcome—twenty-five years after the Second World War ended.

The 1863 draft riots were not, Banfield theorized, a protest against the law that permitted Unionists to hire substitutes to enter the army in their place. They were an outpouring of venom against blacks, who were a convenient scapegoat for the hardships of urban life among the very poor, for the threat of cheaper labor that would compete with the immigrant working class, and for the rigid class structure and nativist prejudice encountered by Catholic Irish immigrants. In the course of the riots, 500 to 2,000 New Yorkers, mostly blacks, were killed, including helpless orphans from an asylum sacked by the mobs; perhaps 10,000 people were injured.

The draft riots spawned a new group of organizations dedicated to civic good works. The city already had a number of organizations trying to improve the conditions under which poor New Yorkers lived, such as the Prison Association, which sought to improve sanitation and foster humane treatment of inmates in the jails and prisons of the city and to mitigate the hardships of families left behind by those convicted of crime. The post–Civil War years produced settlement houses to aid immigrants, housing associations, visiting nurse societies, and committees that investigated and wrote voluminous reports on health, housing, vice, and municipal corruption. Some of these reports laid the groundwork for subsequent changes in government and private institutions that offered services to those in need.

The associations dedicated to good works did not hesitate to condemn government officials and laws that they found corrupt, vicious, and destructive. They offered help in the form of alms, education, special services, religious uplift, and personal counseling to those who needed help and who, no matter how reticent initially, ultimately showed themselves capable of benefiting from it. But they did not assume that everyone was capable of being helped by what they offered; they did not believe that psychological insights would enable antisocial characters to reform themselves, except by an immense effort of will, aided and abetted, in most cases, by religious help. In short, they distinguished between the worthy and the unworthy poor. If they faced a choice between several who needed help, they were more likely to spend their time and energy on those who, they thought, could best benefit from it.

The specter of the lower-class violence and anger that had burst upon the commercial and trading gentry in 1863 stimulated the activities of all these and many other organizations. But they would not have achieved a gain in civic order without the assistance of other forces.

The attack on violence in the streets became an attack on crooked politicians who sold appointments to the police force and who participated in the profits of saloonkeepers and prostitutes. Crime was decried, not so much because it threatened the immediate security of the gentry but because it promised an increasingly unlawful and uncivil society. As the population continued to swell with the arrival of new immigrants, the latest group to arrive always bore the onus for the increase in gang violence and other crimes. The Germans, the Irish, the Jews, and the Italians were in turn denounced as responsible for crimes that were seen to be typical of their race—the word *race* was used rather loosely in those days—and descriptions of the nature of these new foreigners were freely associated with the crimes they were said (often correctly) to be committing. The Irish were called drinkers and violent; the Germans were considered clever and somewhat unscrupulous; the Jews were seen as less than honorable in their business dealings, while their women were said to constitute a large percentage of the prostitutes in the city, whose numbers were immense in the last fifteen or twenty years of the nineteenth century and the beginning of the twentieth.

To stop crime and to impose order on the new arrivals were regarded as monumental but essential tasks by the gentry, particularly by the religious and reformist elements among them. In his book *Urban Masses and Moral Order in America, 1820–1920,* Paul Boyer of the University of Massachusetts describes the interest of urban gentlefolk in taming the new poor in cities throughout the United States. He makes clear that they were particularly concerned with the long-range threat of disorder. They sought to impose moral order through various means: religion, what would now be called social work, special education and vocational projects, trips to the country, uplifting sports and recreational activities, and a number of other remedial social programs, not the least of which was urban design. It is clear from the writings of Frederick Law Olmsted, the superintendent of Central Park during most of its construction, that he was not only an urban designer but a practical humanist. A principal object of the urban parks that he designed was to uplift the masses by putting them in immediate contact with an orderly reproduction of nature; against the backdrop of nature, however counterfeit, they could observe how the leadership classes of the city comported themselves and be enlightened as a result.

Certainly, by the 1900s an unprecedented level of civil order seemed to have been achieved for the first time since immigration began. It was far from perfect; any city of the size of New York was certain to produce enough people with criminal dispositions and propensities to create an underworld. New York certainly did, but the criminal element kept violence on its own turf. Burglars stole, usually without violence, from the homes of the wealthy, even from those who were only relatively wealthy. There was the usual run of confidence men playing on the gullibility of the aged and the greedy, and street gangs with primitive extortion schemes preyed on small merchants. In the early days of the labor movement, there were enough paper unions threatening strikes, particularly in the construction trades, to make legitimate unions allow employers' representatives to decide for them which craft would handle what kinds of work. And, of course, there were gamblers, honest and otherwise, cops who protected them, bucket shop operators in Wall Street selling spurious or valueless securities, swindlers, and simple violent thugs who used their knives (guns were rare) on

Saturday nights, usually to settle quarrels among their own kind. But there were no muggers invading relatively secure sections of the city to commit armed robberies; that invention of eighteenth-century London was to come to New York much later. There were sections of the city that decent people did not frequent, and those who did invade such areas in search of adventure of one kind or another accepted the risk as part of the fun of slumming.

In this period of urban life, the social distance between the classes of society was formidable. The gap between the so-called criminal classes and the elite gentry was surely greatest of all. This was the period during which many accepted Cesare Lombroso's theory that the criminal is a distinctly different type of man from the noncriminal. The natural consequence of this theory was development of a penal system that wasted little energy on efforts to reform or rehabilitate criminals; since they were distinct at birth for physical reasons, there was little incentive to invest capital and social efforts on improvements assumed to be impossible.

Urban attitudes toward crime have fluctuated widely since the early twentieth century, ranging from Lombroso's extreme of believing in foreordained damnation to the other of believing that there is no such thing as a bad boy. In these swings society may simply be externalizing the inner conflict between the antisocial desires that occasionally flare in the best behaved and the need to repress them. As psychologizing has become more and more a part of the general culture, attitudes toward criminals, and prescriptions for dealing with them, have become more and more confused by the ambiguities implicit in the two polar beliefs about the essential nature of man.

Another source of ambiguity derives from the economic significance of crimes involving property. The Robin Hood legend may be historical balderdash, but romanticizing the process of economic redistribution, even by extralegal means, continues to strike a homely and familiar chord. Many urban people purchase stolen goods that they could not afford at normal prices.

Certainly they benefit economically from the existence of the second-level market in purloined goods. This benefit must have some moderating effect on the natural hatred of thieves and brigands; after all, the criminals supply the market. In fact, if one carries this train of thought a little further, the merchants who sell to the victims of crimes replacements for what they have lost by theft also benefit from the crime. Society even socializes the cost through the insurance process. Of course, the cost here described is limited to the obvious economic cost of replacing stolen goods; the social cost of rampant crimes far exceeds the dollar value of the physical losses. A further ambiguity in public attitudes toward economic crime is that some crimes are considered socially acceptable, if not laudable: smuggling, for example, and poaching. The ultimate moral confusion that surrounds crime is manifest by the fact that while some stolen goods—expensive jewelry, for example—are offered as though they were being sold legitimately, other goods, actually legitimate, may be represented as stolen because they then seem a better bargain to the purchaser.

New York's attitudes toward crime were very much affected in the immediate prewar years by the long history of Prohibition. The public, in general, was not afraid of violent crime in New York in the 1920s and 1930s. Criminals made little impact on the way people lived, except that they provided the general population with liquor that had previously been legal anyway. Its illegality seemed to many city dwellers a result of rural tyranny over them.

During Prohibition, great tolerance was felt for the bootlegger-gangsters, accompanied by a somewhat salacious interest in their way of life—or death. Everyone knew about their bronze caskets, extravagant floral tributes, and endless limousine corteges. The public curiosity was made up of equal parts of simple envy and horror, the kind indulged in movies about werewolves and vampires. The gangster of film and fancy was at once a figure of dread and a romantic hero, free or fighting to become free of the trammeling conventions of what people now call straight society: thus, Jay Gatsby, Little Caesar, James Cagney and his half-grapefruit in *Public Enemy*, Duke Mantee of *The Petrified Forest.* When Americans were not smiling at their obsequies, they were listening, fascinated, to the distant howling of the gangsters, secure in the knowledge that, like timber wolves, they would stay on their own side of the river.

The one area where some people feared that the gangsters might actually cross the river with something other than cases of suspicious Scotch whiskey (no one wanted to drink methyl alcohol at the price quoted) was kidnapping. That crime became popular in the Middle West in the 1930s, but it never caught on very much in New York City. In any case there was a certain snob appeal in appearing to be afraid that the children were about to be snatched. That dire fate was not available to the poor or the middle class, or even to the wealthy but unknown.

There was, in short, a rather ambivalent attitude toward gangsters in the 1920s, because one drank at nightclubs with which they had to be associated. How else could the speakeasies get their booze? Perhaps the pithiest expression of this attitude occurred in *Of Thee I Sing*, a Broadway musical by the Gershwins and Morrie Ryskind that lampooned presidential politics. A day in the Oval Office began with President Wintergreen at his desk. An equerry brought him a board attached to a long extension cord. On the board was a series of buttons, which the president had to push in turn to open some structure or start an event of major importance. One opened a dam. One activated a powerhouse. Finally, the equerry said, "And this button opens a speakeasy on 52nd Street." Said President Wintergreen, "I think I opened that yesterday." "You did," said the equerry, "but Treasury closed it last night."

As the depression became more serious, pressure grew for the abolition of Prohibition. The strongest arguments for repeal were that it would be good for business and that it would cut crime—organized, professional crime. The merits of the latter argument were not so solid as they had looked. Organized crime was too well organized to go out of business simply because a law was changed. Its executives were prepared with plans for expansion into other areas where legal bans on pleasures for which people would pay—prostitution and gambling among them—offered tempting rewards to those who were not afraid of a few legal complications. Those who now believe that legalizing drugs will stop present crime suffer from the same delusion.

The Prohibition era is often described as creating a disrespect for law that persisted for years afterward. It certainly did open up a new form of contact, quite unprecedented in New York, between society and business leaders on the one hand and the underworld on the other. The contact, however, was rather ephemeral: when Prohibition ended and the gangsters who had made Scotch available during the dry years turned to the satisfaction of other demands, no sympathy remained.

Far more important in opening the way for the eruption of the *disorganized* crime that has menaced New Yorkers in the postwar years has been the spread of ambiguity about guilt and morality. This ambiguity has eroded confidence in the moral standards that people of position had always taken for granted. During the depression, younger leaders of society—up-and-coming lawyers, bankers, and business people, all of whom would be leaders of the city in the postwar era—heard, and may well have echoed, depression-spawned criticisms of the capitalist system and its cruelties and of business leaders and their vacuous blindness. Some of this surely left its mark in a weakening of the insistence on obeying the rules of the existing order. The thirties were bad years for business people, and the ethics of the marketplace were satirized in numerous works. In Mark Blitzstein's *The Cradle Will Rock,* an informal opera, the main character, Mister Mister—a business tycoon—and his family were painted as hopelessly conventional clods. In *My Man Godfrey,* a movie with Carole Lombard and William Powell, Eugene Pallette, a tycoon, was represented humorously as he struggled to break free of the cramping conventionalities imposed on him by his wife's social ambitions. It can't be more than a step from feeling that all of society's conventions are stultifying and hypocritical to believing that all rules laid down by society must be judged by their inhibiting and stultifying impact on the individual people who are required to obey them, rather than by their effect on the social organization as a whole.

New York entered the postwar era believing that the era of major crime was behind it. In fact, its jail population was far lower than it had been in the prewar years. Some ascribed this fact to the fevered demand for workers during the war. Others said that the army had absorbed many young people who would otherwise have been in jail. Some drew from this the conclusion that if the army could handle these young people and make "men" out of them, so could the civilian world if only it tried harder. Others said that armies provide exactly the right opportunities for aggression that youthful criminals search for. Whatever the sequence of thought, most of those who cared about the size of the prison population concluded that if the postwar world were as busy, prosperous, and in need of labor as the wartime world, crime should remain at a low ebb. Few people thought that, despite general prosperity and high employment levels, crime itself would, within twenty-five years, be regarded as New York's most serious problem.

But as everyone now knows, the incidence of crime in the city took another turn and mounted upward.* At first, the crimes that attracted attention were those of youth gangs that struggled, violently and sometimes with lethal weapons, for control of the streets. Usually the gangs were recruited along racial or ethnic lines. Mayor O'Dwyer's response to the outbreak of juvenile gang warfare was the establishment in 1947 of a Youth Board, composed of representatives of the different ethnic com-

---

*Between 1947 and 1969, the average daily inmate count in the New York City detention facilities and its penitentiary for convicted offenders went from 4,454 to 13,170. Then, under the pressure of lack of jail space and humanitarian agitation, there was a change in bail practices and parole of defendants, and the population dropped to the 10,000 range. If similar standards had been applied to defendants in 1946, the 4,454 figure might well have been much lower. Between 1946 and 1983, the annual expenditures of the city's Department of Corrections rose from $3.6 million to more than $300 million.

munities. Some of the Board's employees did a masterful and courageous job of winning the confidence of the leaders on both sides of local gang fights. They were sometimes able to promote peace and to divert the energies of a least some of the young warriors into more constructive channels. But those youths who did respond were probably a specially capable fraction of the total membership. In any case, after a few years the meaningless violence of the so-called "rumbles" died out, to be replaced—temporarily, anyway—by gangs who fight for economic reasons, including the control of marijuana and other "controlled substances." Even the Youth Board and its courageous and dedicated employees were soon looking back nostalgically to the time when the young people were only fighting each other and, occasionally, killing each other on the spot. The slow, painful death after long years of addiction was worse.

Following the outbreak of gang warfare in the early postwar years, both crime, as measured by the number of serious felonies, and the rate of crime, as measured by the number of felonies per 100,000 people, increased steadily until 1983, when it began to taper off. No one knows whether the decline should be considered the beginning of a downward trend that will continue. Perhaps the declining birth rate, resulting in a decline in the number of males in the crime-prone years of late adolescence, portends a drop in random felonies. A single year's improvement in the statistics could be the beginning of a trend or a mere statistical accident. Subway felonies jumped ominously, by nearly 15 percent, in the first quarter of 1984, after several years of decline.

It is the nature of current crime in the city that is perhaps even more frightening than its high rate of incidence. As in the past, the newest arrivals in the city are those most responsible for antisocial behavior. That means, in general, the blacks and Hispanics. Together these groups are involved in about 80 percent of the crimes, perhaps an even higher percentage of the random street crimes. The difference in skin color, when it occurs, between the offenders and their victims doubtless gives the victims a special feeling of danger. These individualistic crimes differ from the offenses committed in the immediate postwar years in that they involve deliberate confrontations with people who are conspicuously not part of the gang world. Necklace snatchings, pocketbook grabbing, mugging at knife point, subway assaults—all are accompanied with oral threats, sudden spurts of violence, and senseless injuries, even killings. White victims of these attacks understandably find themselves thinking that they have been assaulted because of their race. They forget, for the moment, that blacks are even more frequently the victims of these random crimes. For the white victims, the crimes seem to promise the outbreak of a desperate race war; and older citizens perceive large parts of the city as a battleground, too dangerous for them at all hours.

Even the black victims of crimes committed by black youths find themselves believing that they too have become victims of a race war. Many blame white mistreatment of the black population for black broken homes, black undereducation, and black criminality. While this race scapegoating is not a universal phenomenon, it is sufficiently widespread to make very difficult the development of a biracial strategy to produce moral order among the black underclass—the children of those broken homes that lack parental authority, the children of transgenerational dependency on welfare, of illiteracy, truancy, and addiction.

Although the white victims of random crimes (and those who have not actually been victimized but fear that fate every time they venture from a safe haven) are not right in believing that they are the victims of a conscious racial war, the crimes could scarcely be more warlike if they were deliberately planned as a military strategy. The crimes limit the mobility of the enemy just as a shrewd commander hopes to do. Whites are afraid to travel by subway, to attend meetings at night, even—particularly in the case of older people—to leave their apartments to go to the market or drugstore after dark or to open their apartment doors. Since the very purpose of a city is to provide convenient access to the necessities and amenities of industrial civilization, it is no exaggeration to say that the crime that has emerged in New York City threatens the very existence of the city in its present form.

It may also be the case that the crime explosion among blacks and Hispanics has stimulated violence among whites and Asiatics. The Chinese, for example, having become more numerous in New York than ever before, have formed extortionist youth gangs, preying on proprietors of restaurants in Chinatown. Their purposes are economic, though the extraordinary violence they use cries out for a fuller explanation that no one can give. Hispanics are particularly active in the drug trades, especially in connection with the importation of cocaine from Columbia and its distribution throughout the metropolitan area. Nothing here should give the impression that white youths are not contributing to the crime wave and committing some horrendous, violent crimes of their own.

Before any discussion of the reasons for these crimes and what might be done to reduce their impact, it is important to understand that the violent crimes on the streets and in the homes are not crushing New York solely by the fear they engender. They are also keeping the police force, including the transit police, so busy with serious matters that the police have neither the time nor the energy to devote to lesser offenses that make the streets and subways seem outlaw lands. The ordinary rules of civility have been lost. Fare-beaters leap subway turnstiles. People smoke in the subways. The release of inmates from mental institutions has meant that some use the sidewalks and gutters as toilets. Always a slovenly city, New York has become even filthier.

It is all very well to adopt a self-righteously liberatarian attitude and pretend that such breaches of normal civility are of no importance. Few would disagree with the police, who feel that an armed robbery deserves more of their time. Yet such nuisance behavior conveys the unmistakable impression that the quality of life, despite all the conscious agitation to improve it, has been soiled and damaged in far more crucial ways that none can control. Ignoring the nuisance offense opens the city streets to further testing: If I can get away with this, what may I not do next? Yet if the police can stop the nuisances only by making an arrest for violating the sanitary code, they are disproportionately applying excessive force and irking those who wish they paid more attention to life-threatening offenders. The very presence of police, of strangers, of anyone, should inhibit the nuisance creator. If it does not, if there is no inhibition, what has gone wrong is so fundamental that the police cannot correct it any more than they can correct flagrant bad manners.

During the Lindsay administration, the police force expanded to record numbers, slightly over 30,000 members. In great part the expansion was intended to deal with the threat and the reality of rioting during the turbulent decade of America's involvement in Viet Nam. It is never clear just how effective the number of police is in the control of crime, because there is no generally acceptable way of counting the number of crimes that would have been committed were it not for the presence of additional officers on foot or motor patrol. Even a comparison of the percentage of reported felonies that are solved does not tell whether the additions to the force have resulted in more efficient clearing of offenses, largely because crime statistics tend to be highly subjective. Crimes described as felonies in the reports may ultimately be disposed of as less serious misdemeanors because of inadequate police work in handling evidence and gathering witnesses, in which case what shows up as a solved crime is, in fact, a botched investigation. Whether a police force increases its efficiency by increasing its numbers is no more certain than it would be in the case of any other type of organization. What is clear is that nothing is more reassuring than the sight of an officer, particularly one on foot patrol, when a member of the public happens to be in what he or she considers a dangerous part of the city. And yet the police are but the outer limits of criminal justice, often called a "system" but actually, in New York, a disorderly reflection of the doubts of honest people over the causes of crime and the methods that best control it.

One of New York's problems has been that its police officers have to spend far too much time in processing the arrests they make. The arresting officer must be present to give testimony unless the suspect waives arraignment. Court calendars are crowded. Other witnesses sometimes fail to show up. The Legal Aid Society, which provides lawyers for defendants who cannot afford them, is New York's substitute for the public defender system that prevails in many other jurisdictions. Its lawyers are very busy, because most of the people arrested for assaults and robberies are without means to pay for legal counsel. The Legal Aid overload makes arraignment proceedings drag on while police officers loiter in the courtroom, unable to function on patrol or on any other police duty, waiting for defendants' lawyers to get from one case to another.

Further delays and postponements are inevitable. Although the public hears about postponements as though they were generally granted at the request of the prosecutor, the fact is that most adjournments and postponements are at the request of defendants—some surely because their lawyers are too busy but many in the hope that prosecution witnesses will get tired of appearing or even die. The overwhelming majority of cases in New York City are disposed of by negotiation between the prosecution and the defense, a process that good citizens decry because it seems to allow people who admit their guilt to escape serious punishment by allowing the state to avoid the cost and delays of a trial.

That widespread impression is wrong. New York City simply cannot afford the costs and delays of trying more than a limited number of cases. Without plea bargaining, many more guilty defendants would go free. The city cannot afford to build courtrooms and detention space for holding prisoners who are waiting for their court appearances. Above all, it cannot afford the cost of jails to hold prisoners who are waiting for their cases to come up—a process that with the prisoners' own assistance is likely to take months. Finally, it cannot afford the space for confining people while they serve sentences of less than a year (sentences longer than a year are served in state prisons).

The verb *afford* as used above does not mean simply a lack of financial resources, although that surely plays a part in creating and maintaining the logjam in the courts and curtailing sentences to make room for the newer offenders. *Afford* also has a political connotation. It means that the central city government lacks the political means to compel the local communities and neighborhoods to accept the construction of detention facilities for accused or convicted offenders in their environs. On top of these impediments to the criminal justice system stands the federal judiciary, which not only limits the use of existing facilities on the grounds that further crowding would be inhumane and unconstitutional but additionally orders that other existing facilities be substantially and elaborately rebuilt before they will be constitutionally suitable.

These issues all bundled together indicate a great lack of clarity in the government's view of criminal justice, a lack of clarity that is shared by the people of New York City. The confusion has certainly not helped the city to deal with its increase in criminal activity since the Second World War.

In an earlier century, New York had a simple idea of the purpose of incarceration. It was intended to punish people who had been convicted of breaking the law. The city had, as noted, produced private agencies that dedicated themselves to seeing that the incarceration was not cruel or inhumane. These agencies recognized that most offenders are eventually released from prison, and the hope was that they would not have been made substantially worse as a result of their confinement with other offenders. Actually, the Quakers, in the early part of the nineteenth century, tried to guard against just that by imposing a rule of silence in prisons, so that the offenders would not contaminate each other. That quaintly rational but extremely cruel system was superseded by the efforts of reformers, but it was not until much later that anyone began to see the purpose of incarceration as not simply punishment, or even segregation of the offender from society, but as an opportunity for rehabilitation into a law-abiding citizen. Not until the 1920s did psychologists and criminologists assert (or did anyone in public life listen to their assertions) that causative factors in crime were not simply immanent vices but environmental accidents like unhappy childhoods, infantile traumas, and economic misfortunes. Once these ideas gained currency, a scientific—or at least a pseudo-scientific—basis was laid for the intrusion of simple humane ideas into the management of criminal incarceration.

That period saw the entrance of the psychological lingo into normal conversation. Everyone who claimed to be at least a fellow traveler of the intelligentsia started to sprinkle sentences with such weighty ideas as "inferiority complex" and "introvert." The trend carried over into penology. Segregation of youthful from older offenders had already become the rule. Now separate courts for the young were adopted; records of youthful offenders were sealed; their names were forbidden to be mentioned outside closed courtrooms. Probation, which kept convicted offenders from actually being incarcerated in an institution, and parole, which allowed for the early release of those offenders whom an independent board found represented no more than a reasonable risk to society—these became the rule. So did indeterminate sentences that left the length of the term of imprisonment to be fixed *after* the penal authorities saw what kind of "adjustment" to institutional life was made by the convicted offender.

None of these changes meant that a majority of New Yorkers actually believed that the old purpose of criminal justice—punishment of the guilty—had been abandoned. They still complained that prisoners were being coddled in country club jails, that justice had become a revolving door, and that only the return of capital punishment in the states where it had practically been abandoned would discourage criminals from committing more and more crimes.

The trouble with their position was not that it is wrong. No one knows whether it is wrong or right. Certainly as far as capital punishment is concerned, it is impossible to prove that it either increases or decreases the incidence of the crimes it is intended to stop. Life does not lend itself to being run in reverse so that we can count the murders that would have taken place either in the absence of or with the use of capital punishment and compare the result. What we do know is that those who have been electrocuted, gassed, or shot by the state have terminated their criminal careers. We don't know whether they would have continued them if they had been left alive, in or out of prison. Incarceration is more expensive than inflicting the death sentence; that's about the limit of our knowledge.

What's wrong with the punishment view of criminal justice is that the general American, and most particularly the New York, idea of government has changed to such an extent since the nineteenth century that it—government—now seems inconsistent with the punishment theory. Whereas government was then conceived of as a strong force whose major object was the enforcement of peace when possible, and the winning of wars when peace or order was impossible, it is now conceived of as a benign and loving instrument. It is meant to do good, to be humane, to solve people's problems, to heal the sick, or pay for healing them, to bind up the wounded and succor the orphan. Like it or not, this view of government is inconsistent with the successful pursuit of a policy of punishment, deterrence, and social revenge.

The view that government is now to be primarily a benign force continues, even though more and more experts in penology, to say nothing of the common folk in the street, have found that the "modern" penology that began to be heard from in the 1920s does not succeed in accomplishing what it set out to do. It does not rehabilitate offenders until they, themselves, have decided they are ready to be rehabilitated. In fact, it may encourage them to continue their old ways by giving them elaborate psychological explanations for their own behavior.

While parole and probation continue, they remain under heavy fire. The indeterminate sentence is criticized on all sides, and as juvenile crimes attract more attention, even the withholding of the names of young offenders and the sealing of their records are criticized.

The practical consequence of this conflict in attitudes toward criminal justice is that it undermines the governmental action that is necessary to stop—or at least that offers some hope of stopping—the seriousness of current crime. Since the public generally wants more stringent enforcement of the criminal laws, longer sentences, and more rigid incarceration in place of parole and probation, bigger prisons are essential to carry out its program. But the same public, uncomfortable with a government that is not humane and kindly and benign in its disposition toward citizens, refuses to allow the government to build prisons (even if they are called by some other name) near their neighborhoods. In New York City, this obvious conflict between what the public wants government to do to convicted offenders, and what it will allow the same government to inflict on the noncriminal public in doing it, means that government cannot build jails or prisons, cannot get citizens' consent to float bonds to finance penal institutions, and must continue to limp along with facilities that constrain its custody of alleged and convicted offenders. All the consequences of delays in the justice system, inadequate detention facilities, and shortened sentences follow. A society with a stern disposition to achieve justice should be able to impose a system that would depend on the deterrence of swift and certain punishment. Such a government would be encouraged to maintain a very large police force to compel those considering criminal acts to measure the certainty and the severity of punishment before taking action. But would such a society be able to win the cooperation of those very citizens who are loudest in their demands for a "tough" policy on criminals? They, the citizens, would find the police a palpable presence in their lives. Prisons would shadow their homes, perhaps reducing their value. Increased pressure for changes in criminal court procedure might even increase their own liability to prosecution for offenses they hardly consider criminal.

Obviously, not all of these changes would affect everyone. But the threat of building new penal institutions within the city has been enough to hamstring New York's own efforts to rationalize its present inadequate jail system by building new detention cells in every borough. Wherever one wants to put a jail, someone objects.

Only one effort to change the local criminal justice system has been more than halfhearted and has remained free from public interference, though not from public criticism. That has been the continuing effort by federal judges to make much milder—or, in the view of the judges, to make less unconstitutional—New York's treatment of prisoners held without bail for trial or, after trial, while waiting for assignment to another institution. The judges establish cell size and standards for visiting rooms and bathing, laundry, recreation, and library facilities, as well as total occupancy. They are not concerned with whether these changes are more or less likely to improve the conduct of offenders or increase the safety of law-abiding citizens on the streets of New York. Unlike the officials of the state and city over whom they assert control, they do not have to consider popular views or the political consequences of flouting them. Their power derives simply from the Constitution of the United States and their duty to uphold the Supreme Court's interpretation of its meaning.

Nor are the federal judges concerned with the cost of the changes they find necessary to make jails constitutional. If the city and state choose not to raise the taxes necessary to build these institutions, that will be their decision. They can do without them. There is no constitutional bar against failing to prosecute those accused of violating state laws. In 1981, Judge Morris Lasker forced the city to spend $20 million to fix up the old Tombs jail, alongside the criminal courthouse in downtown Manhattan. His rulings ultimately led the city to release several hundred prisoners whose terms had not expired or who had previously been unable to meet bail. Those who defended the judge from Mayor Koch's criticisms argued that it was not Judge Lasker who had released the prisoners, but the city's failure to cure the defects in the Tombs in time.

In any case, there is a startling contrast between the power of a nonelected judge to determine state policy and the power of elected mayors and governors to force their citizens to comply with his orders. New York's efforts to improve its jail situation have been hemmed in by state and local political problems. Forced to close the Tombs because it failed to meet constitutional standards, the city moved pretrial prisoners to Riker's Island, where they were housed in a prison originally built for men sentenced for misdemeanors rather than for people awaiting trial. The Riker's Island institution was found to be inadequate and poorly placed for a jail. The federal courts limited its occupancy. When the city tried to sell the island to the state government so that an institution for convicted felons could be built there, it had to find new jail space in the five boroughs, each of which must try, in its own courtrooms, those accused of crimes committed in the borough. The outcry against new jails made the proposal unworkable.

The state and city then tried to collaborate on a plan that would turn two former mental hospitals on the outskirts of the city into prisons. One, in Dutchess County, has been converted over the strong opposition of local residents. It is now a center for youthful offenders. The other, on Long Island, was closed in 1984 by Governor Cuomo, in fulfillment of a campaign promise. Faced by the inadequate jail space in its present institutions, the city tried to take over a former Navy brig in what had been the New York Naval Shipyard, better known as the Brooklyn Navy Yard. That, too, was greeted by violent opposition from nearby residents and their local legislators. Though the city was finally permitted to proceed with conversion plans, the federal judge who gave his permission imposed a ceiling on the number of inmates who would be housed there, reducing its value to the city and simultaneously increasing the conversion cost per bed. Then, in 1983, the people of New York City, complaining that crime was destroying the city, that bail practices were too lax, that sentences were too short, watched the voters of the state as a whole reject a bond issue that would have paid for the construction of 5,000 new prison cells in state prisons and helped finance local jails.

The lack of certainty about criminal justice afflicted not only the local people who, at this stage of the cycle of attitudes toward crime, want incarceration but still will not disturb their neighborhood in order to facilitate the program they support. It also caused state legislators to change their minds about the way to reshape the court system. Historic criminal courts, including New York County's General Sessions, for felonies only, have been closed. Arraignment procedures have been changed. Prisoners are being booked at a central office at police headquarters instead of at the local precinct houses. A Criminal Court has been established to handle arraignments instead of the Magistrate's Court where they were formerly conducted. Judges from upstate courts have been rotated into the city courtrooms, where their presence helps to speed the civil calendar, allowing more New York City judges to sit on criminal cases. None of the changes, dating in some cases back to the Wagner and Lindsay years, made a truly significant change in the administration of the courts. Or perhaps it's more appropriate to say that the increase in crime wiped out the effects of the changes. The changes may actually have kept the courts' delays from getting even longer than they are now. No one knows.

Yet the flood of random crime, supplemented by arrests on drug charges, fills the calendar and the jails. Anyone who does not present an immediate threat of non-appearance for trial is released on bail or, if bail is impossible, on his own recognizance. Many observers insist that defendants who plead guilty are given more lenient sentences than they should be, because the judges know there is not enough room to hold them longer and still leave room for future offenders to be incarcerated.

Judges deny this and complain that because the probation department charged with preparing a pre-sentence report on any convicted defendant is so understaffed and overworked, they do not have all the information they should have when considering a proper sentence for the prisoner before them.

It seems unlikely that, two hundred years after the prison system was invented to replace mutilation, whipping, transportation, and death as punishment for felonies, a new invention or organizational plan will come out of the blue to permit the courts to operate more swiftly, with greater dignity, and against a framework that everyone will acknowledge to be equitable and just. Nor does it seem likely that the New York public will be able to unify its conflicting views of the proper aim and technique for dealing with those convicted of crimes, minor as well as major. Nor will there come a sudden, clear answer to the possibilities of rehabilitation or the effectiveness of deterrence. What the city needs is what it seems unwilling to provide: correction officers as well as police officers, new jails as well as new patrol cars, an expansion of its probation department, and new courtrooms. It needs to spend millions more on the administration of criminal justice, because if there is one clear lesson to be learned from the current level of crime in the city, it is that it will not be self-corrective, as the previous crime waves following the arrival of new groups into the city were corrected.

The present arrivals in New York, those committing most of its current crimes—or, more precisely, those arrested for committing its most serious crimes—are not arrivals from overseas. Unlike their predecessors, they are themselves American, but they have been treated as no generation of Americans before them has been treated. That in itself would be a source of great difficulty in adaptation to the complexities of urban life. It is complicated further by the fact that their cultural background and civilization, their oral traditions for the organization of society, are different from those of the people who came here from Europe and Asia. The possibility of their being assimilated into the body of America, short of miscegenation on a massive scale, is repulsed not by language and custom, as was the case with the European arrivals, but by the indelible skin color. And their path is therefore more difficult. Jobs that were open to people of limited education and experience now lead nowhere, if they can be had at all. The authority figures that could once be relied on to point the way to the mainstream—the schoolteacher, the cleric, the cop, the precinct captain in the political party—have been chopped down. And in a world that has federalized much of its health care and what was its charity, human problems—even for the desperately situated—are no longer self-limiting: people, no matter how desperate, survive.

And a city which thought that massive lawbreaking and crime had been left behind finds itself facing new levels of danger in its streets while lacking the confidence in its own moral precepts to mount a consistent effort to reduce that danger.

Chapter VII

Counting on People

ONE OF THE ASSETS with which New York City expected to hold its position atop the postwar world was its remarkable population, its people. Of course, this was the Century of the Common Man, whose virtues were generally exalted. Advertisers learned to market products that had been made "with people in mind." The best ideas, they crooned, are ideas that help people. All enterprises, no matter how large they were and how impersonal their founders had been, hastened to assure one and all that they were motivated primarily to serve people. Long before Mario Cuomo would claim that the state he governed was nothing more than a big family, the United States Steel Company, then at the very summit of its power, announced that *it* was a family. And if Alexander Hamilton had complained in 1946 that "the people" is a great beast, he would have been demolished without the help of Aaron Burr.

In the case of New York City, however, the stirrings of pride in the quality of its population were on the whole justified. New York's population, drawn mainly from the descendants of

European immigrants, regarded itself as a major source of the
city's growth, its economic success, and its peculiarly diverse
and rich popular culture. Although it was a self-serving view,
the city's people were right in regarding themselves as the
source of the city's strength. What was not true was the belief
that the population would retain its remarkable qualities forty
years later. Nor was it true that the difference in population
over a period of forty years would be mainly a matter of skin
color.

Obviously, over the forty years of the postwar period the
number of nonwhite New Yorkers did increase dramatically.
Their representation in the city's population grew from less
than 10 percent to 30 or 40 (the exact count is in dispute). The
change in the appearance of the city's people was obvious and
would be even more striking if it were possible to juxtapose
1945 against 1985 without the intervening years. But the difference in the population was not only the increase in the number
of nonwhites; there were major changes also in the white population: it was much older in the 1980s than in the 1940s, for one
thing. In the nonwhite population, immense differences between age groups, classes, ethnicity, culture, and traditions—
differences that had been invisible to most white observers
when nonwhites were far less numerous—now became apparent to anyone who wanted to see them.

These changes in the population of the city reduced the size
and shape of its greatest asset, created problems to which no
solutions were apparent, and offered opportunities that were
inadequately exploited. The changes were made even more
complicated by changes in popular attitudes toward government and personal behavior. We can begin their exploration
by examining the facile assumption that the nonwhite immigrants to the city would follow the same path of adjustment
followed by European immigrants fifty, a hundred, or a hundred and fifty years earlier. They did not, and the path that had
been followed by the Europeans was not only different from
that opened to the blacks; it had in actuality been very different

from the way New Yorkers of the postwar period imagined it to have been.

In both popular and serious literature, Americans have tended to exaggerate the extent to which the previous identities of the immigrant arrivals disappeared in a melting pot. Happily, since the end of the Second World War a number of very popular books, including Oscar Handlin's work, Irving Howe's *World of Our Fathers,* and Nathan Glazer's and Daniel Patrick Moynihan's *Beyond the Melting Pot* have pointed out how cultural and linguistic differences shaped the adaptation of new arrivals to the American environment. But if the myth of the melting pot was not based on objective truth, neither was its opposite. Different national origins did not force the children of immigrants into rigidly stereotyped occupations.

Yet the stereotypes were applicable enough, at least in the first years of settlement, to give New York City a remarkably valuable diversity of occupations, a working force that could staff an equally diverse group of enterprises. It was not true, for example, that all Irish males became policemen, bartenders, or vaudeville performers; nor did all Irish women become waitresses, especially at a chain of restaurants and confectionary stores called Schrafft's. Yet enough of them did go into those employments (and into the construction trades) to open a path that eased the way for their successors. Not all Italians came to New York with barrel organs, barber's shears, or wheelbarrows, but enough did have a taste, talent, or predilection for these and other specific trades or professions or subprofessions to force an opening through which later arrivals with similar traits could pick their way.

Nothing in this process was as easy, or as successful, as modern Americans believe. The immigrant life in many cases required the separation of families for a number of years. The husband and father would often come first, establish himself sufficiently to pay for his family's passage. Sometimes he worked at a job for which he had been recruited before he even left home, other times at a job to which he had been led by a relative or acquaintance who had preceded him, or by a society dedicated to the mutual protection of immigrants with a common bond of local origin. If separation was painful, so was the reunion of a family in which one member had become partly familiar with the customs and standards of city life while the later arrivals, often estranged at first by their own initial clumsiness, eventually outstripped the first arrival as they, the children particularly, found it easier to adapt to the ways of a new society.

Literature and sociological studies are full of the tensions that arose in the immigrant family as it struggled to gain a foothold in New York. The strains were increased by the relationship between the new immigrant arrivals and the native New Yorkers, many of whom, coming from a northern and western European background, emphasized the differences between themselves and the newer arrivals from southern and eastern Europe. There were also rivalries, including some that were expressed in gang warfare, between groups from different nations or sections of Europe or even of their own homeland.

Yet, on the whole, the New York experience did work somewhat as the idealized picture of the melting pot would have us believe. Sections of the city tended to be settled by homogeneous groups who shared a religion, a native language, employment in similar jobs, and a route of public transportation that linked the place they lived with the places they worked. Nevertheless, there were opportunities for meeting and getting to know people who did not necessarily come from the same background.

The children of immigrant New Yorkers raised in the fifty years before the Second World War reminisce about the dangers they encountered walking to school through strange and foreign turf. Yet once in school, they often got to know other children of the very type who assaulted them on the street. As public education developed, athletics brought children from different schools and diverse ethnic backgrounds into more or less friendly competition. The second generation of New Yorkers rejected the rigid separatism, so often preached by their fathers, and the cautionary parental advice that no good could possibly come from close contact with "other" groups.

There were forces that worked to weaken the walls of separation at the same time new arrivals and their children recognized and even stressed their importance. Political organizations, once they came to understand that a new group was voting in numbers big enough to sway an election, moved to take in members of the new group. Political leaders who had always listened for a brogue or a German accent came to perceive that changing demographics made a "balanced ticket" more important than a familiar speech pattern. Newspapers helped breach the walls of separatism, particularly as the younger members of an immigrant group began to read the English language press, which featured news in which they were interested. Sports figures emerged from foreign-born or second-generation households, and professional entertainers left the early, limited foreign-language theaters to perform for a wider audience. From the press, and later from the radio, the children of diverse immigrant groups became familiar with the names, the styles, the antics, and the ideas of the elites whom they never personally saw or heard. Ethnic terms became part of New York slang.

Soon, immigrants who started businesses by selling traditional ethnic products to customers of the same immigrant stock, or by offering it familiar services, found that they could successfully sell them to members of other groups. In its simplest terms, Greeks who had restaurants found that non-Greeks would like moussaka and that they, the Greeks, could bake and sell challah, a Jewish bread, to Jews. The same broadening of repertoire and market crossed other ethnic barriers.

Another result was intermarriage. A far more sensitive area than cuisine, intermarriage was likely to start hesitantly between young members of two groups that shared a common religion despite their linguistic differences. Probably the earliest intermarriages in New York City in the mid–nineteenth century took place between Irish and German Catholics. Then came marriages between Irish and non-Catholic Germans who agreed to meet Church requirements about rearing their children. Then came marriages between Irish and Italians, still something of a rarity as recently as the 1920s or 1930s. Equally slow to come were the marriages between German and Russian Jews, marriages that later bridged the giant gap between Sephardic and Ashkenazi Jews, and, still later, marriages between observant and nonbelieving Jews.

What emerged from New York's multinational, multireligious ethnic stock by the beginning of the Second World War was a population that, without clipping off its national and ethnic traditions (in fact, members of the third immigrant generation are popularly believed to discover virtues of ethnicity to which their parents, the second generation, were blind), managed nevertheless to become a *New York* population. The common culture its members shared did not bridge the truly wide gaps— the feelings between the German-Americans and the New York Jews after Hitler's accession to power were as bitter as any that New York had ever seen. But the pool of people ready to work in different trades was no longer embittered by the enmities that once divided it. The police force, once almost entirely Irish and still that in most command ranks, now had societies for Italian, Jewish, and black officers. While members of each of these groups were not ashamed or hesitant to use group pressure to secure advancement or protection against unfavorable or unfair treatment, they generally acknowledged that the police force was now a force for all New Yorkers.

At the same time, it was accepted that, though weakened, the ethnic identification of certain groups with certain kinds of jobs would continue. Compounded by the fundamental structure of the city's economy—a harbor, a financial center, a printing industry, and a thousand lesser-known but equally important specialties like the manufacture of small bits of electrical equipment—the belief in continuing ethnic job ties gave New Yorkers in 1946 confidence in the future of their city and its continued preeminence.

The trouble with this picture as far as the 1946 work force was concerned—Irish women in the backs of banks and insurance companies, Italian women in the ship's brokerage offices, Jewish women in Jewish law firms and accountants' offices and in the department stores (except at Altman's and Best's), Jews and Italians in the garment factories, Irish and American Indians in structural ironwork, Jews as house painters—was that something drastic had happened to the ethnic communities more than twenty years before. The National Origins Immigration Act of 1921 had reduced the permissible number of immigrants from southern and eastern Europe to the same percentage level of total immigration that those countries had provided in 1900.

The advocates of the act had several purposes. In general they were motivated by a strong streak of nativism and a fear of the changes that were occurring in an America undergoing postwar revolutions in technology, employment, sexual relations, and social manners. It was difficult to pass effective legislation stemming any of these changes. Prohibition was one such effort, a futile attempt to delay the urban drift of an alcohol-seeking population from dry rural areas. Much easier was the passage of a law that would slow down the changing character of European immigration by forcing the immigrants who chose to come to the United States to be from countries that had produced most of the early nation's population.

On its face, the objective of stopping change was manifestly absurd. The changes that were occurring in American life—including the change that got the United States to involve itself in a war for the hegemony over Europe and the colonial world —had little or nothing to do with the number of former subjects of the Austro-Hungarian Empire now living in the United States. Though conflicting passions were aroused in New Yorkers before America formally took sides with Britain, they disappeared after April 1917.

The immigration battle in Congress, generated by the fear of further involvement in European complexities, finally settled down to a siege around the issue of whether the laboring class in the United States was large enough to keep the economy booming. Those who supported quota restrictions unfavorable to the so-called newer immigrants recognized very well that no law could increase the number of British, French, Scandinavian, and German immigrants coming to the United States. That number had not been determined by American law but by conditions of life in England, France, Scandinavia, and Germany, and, as important, in the British dominions in Africa and elsewhere that competed with the United States for British emigrants.

The net effect nationally of the National Origins Immigration Act was the political achievement of making white nordic supremacy legitimate. Of greater importance to New York was its cutting off the city's ethnic populations from further replenishment from Europe. The point was that the ethnic communities of New York no longer could supply cheap, hungry labor, fleeing from Europe's teeming shores and delighted for the opportunity to work in an American factory. Instead, as the younger people in the ethnic communities moved to meet their destinies as skilled workers, business people, and professionals, the traditional industries of New York would be unable, sooner or later, to find the labor whose low price and high productivity had been the foundation of their success.

Stopping the influx of immigrants in large numbers from southern and eastern Europe also undermined some of the vitality of the ethnic communities. The foreign-language theater was the first to go; then went the foreign-language press and radio stations. Ethnicity became more a matter of cuisine, decoration, and folk singing at annual festivals than a cohesive political force. Localism, the support of neighborhood or communal positions on public improvements and zoning matters, took the place of a neighborhood's common ethnic heritage as the cohesive force. On the whole, the disappearance of the European ethnicities of the past was bad for the centralization of government. Ethnicity had served to link widely separated parts of the city, because there were communities of German-speaking people, for example, in such widely separated parts of New York as Yorkville, in Manhattan, and Glendale, in Queens. Until immigration policy changed again, a decade after the war, the New Yorkers who spoke German as their first language declined in number. Despite the fact that many people in both sections were of German ancestry, Yorkville and Glendale seemed to have nothing in common; when it came to a fight over zoning, Yorkville and Glendale were utterly indifferent to each other's fate.

A major change that was to some extent encouraged in New York by the passage of the National Origins Immigration Act was the massive movement of southern Negroes (now blacks) to the North, including New York City. That movement began in the 1920s and 1930s and quickened after the Second World War. It was accompanied by the arrival of Hispanic people. The first waves came from Puerto Rico, a United States territory, and were broadened later in the postwar years as the Puerto Ricans were joined by Dominican aliens, many with falsified Puerto Rican birth certificates.

The major difference in the postwar years between the population that most people predicted that New York would have and the population it did have was the great increase in black and Hispanic people. The *New York Post,* in an article published in May 1976 by Anita Alvarez, stated that the black and Puerto Rican population of the city just before the outbreak of the Second World War was 520,000. By 1980, the population of these groups was four times greater, or about 2.4 million people, according to census figures that, according to the city government and leaders of the minority communities, still represent an undercount of black and Puerto Rican residents.

At the end of the Second World War, although there was no legally imposed racial segregation in the schools of New York City, the social separation of the races was pervasive and quite rigid. In the prewar years, whenever Joe Louis, heavyweight boxing champion of the world, came to New York, he stayed only at the Hotel Theresa in Harlem (it no longer exists because it is unnecessary). He might not have been refused lodging at one of the city's downtown hotels, but he would have felt unique, uncomfortable, and embarrassed. The Housing Authority built public housing projects on the assumption that those in Harlem would be lived in by blacks, while those in white sections of the city would be lived in by whites. When the Metropolitan Life Insurance Company built Stuyvesant Town on First Avenue in Manhattan for nearly 9,000 middle-income families, it not only refused to accept blacks as tenants, but also tried to avoid renewing leases of white families that had invited blacks to stay in their apartments. To show that it did not dislike blacks as such but believed only that mingling races in desegregated housing would not "work," Metropolitan built another project, Riverton Houses, in Harlem, to be occupied by black families only.

The pattern of housing segregation was merely one aspect of the separation of the races. Restaurants in New York would not serve people of color, unless, perhaps, they wore turbans. When the National Association for the Advancement of Colored People, in those days presided over by whites, with numerous members of both races on its board, sought a place to hold a dinner that all board members could comfortably attend, it had to pick a restaurant in Chinatown; midtown restaurants did not welcome blacks. The managers of Broadway theater box offices were instructed not to sell orchestra seats to blacks; blacks frequently found themselves waiting in department stores until all other customers, including those who had arrived after them, had been served. No black entertainers were welcome on the radio before the Second World War. Except for a few outstanding celebrities like Duke Ellington and Louis Armstrong, jazz records by black musicians were euphemistically labeled "race records" and sold separately from other jazz. Not a single black played in organized baseball before 1947, when Branch Rickey flouted his colleagues and brought Jackie Robinson up to play for the Brooklyn Dodgers. Robinson's treatment by other players, including some of his own teammates, reads like the cruel hazing that was a feature of serial stories about English boarding schools in the illustrated boys' magazines of years ago.

One could walk from one end of the offices of every major corporation in New York to the other and not see a black face except for that of an occasional porter. If a firm for whatever reason sought to hire a black secretary, it encountered great difficulty in attracting a candidate. As late as 1950 in midtown Manhattan, fear of not being able to find a place to eat lunch combined with fear of social ostracism kept candidates away, even if they were specially requested from a Harlem employment agency. No other agencies listed blacks.

Yet there were signs at the end of the war that things were beginning to change. A black elite middle class had long existed in the shadow of American life and literature. Its members were artists and intellectuals, a few business people who catered largely to a black clientele, politicians, and government civil servants. But although the nation was engaged in a war for its very survival, the armed forces of the United States remained strictly segregated by race until the very end of hostilities in Europe, when some black replacements were posted to units that had previously been all white. As late as 1943, officers of the United States Army were known to tell their white soldiers officially, not in a whisper, that though they were expected to salute any black officers they happened to pass, it was not too hard to arrange not to see them.

The progress being made by the end of the war tended to obscure, even from sympathetic whites, the seriousness of the difficulties that faced blacks in the United States. The blacks whom such whites met were either servants in their homes or else members of the black aristocracy—that is, the intellectual, artistic, and political elites. It was inevitable that the whites who were moved by the outrageous treatment of nonwhites assumed that all the blacks in the United States were more or less like the exceptionally gifted and educated people whom they met in politics, the arts, or the organizations dedicated to removing legal obstructions to desegregation. In fact, most sympathetic whites were themselves products of an upper-class private education and had rarely met whites who lacked educational experiences similar to their own. For them, it was not merely that working-class blacks were totally strange; working-class whites were, too.

By the early 1950s, a number of blacks were serving as judges in all but the highest court of the State of New York. J. Raymond Jones, a black from the Virgin Islands, had been elected head of Tammany Hall, the regular Democratic organization in Manhattan. Hulan Jack, a black, was elected borough president of Manhattan. He was followed by another black, Edward Dudley, before and afterward a New York State judge, and then by Constance Baker Motley, now a federal district judge, also black. Finally, Percy Sutton, once a state senator and more recently a businessman, was borough president of Manhattan for two terms. He is the last black to have occupied the post that was opened to white recapture when he chose to run for mayor in 1977.

The election of black politicians to high office in districts in which many whites vote is a heartening sign of progress in race relations. So has been the great increase in black employment at all but the very top levels of the corporations making their headquarters in New York City and the employment of blacks throughout the civil service of city government, many at the commissionership or deputy commissionership level. So, too, has been the almost complete eradication of discriminatory customs in places of public accommodation. Even in housing, one of the strongest bastions of segregation, there has been progress, not only in the expansion of the black population into white areas but in the maintenance of integrated patterns in some attractive areas of the city after blacks have moved in.

These signs of progress, together with the much-increased attention that previously neutral governments have paid to overcoming the effects of discrimination and the repeal of those laws that actually fortified discrimination, sent up a wrong signal to sympathetic whites. They expected that black progress in New York (and in other northern cities) would mirror the progress made earlier by other newly arrived groups, the European immigrants particularly.

Because so many blacks have failed to share in the progress and instead turn up as arrested and convicted offenders, welfare recipients, drug addicts, and social deviants in numbers that far exceed their proportion of the population, the primary reaction of successful blacks and sympathetic whites has been a nagging disappointment. Why, both groups ask themselves, haven't blacks as a whole done better? They do not come up with the same explanations, a fact that deepens the sense of disappointment, particularly among those whites who long ago envisioned a multiracial society.

One aspect of this disappointment—the comparison of the black lag with the recollection of European immigrant progress —badly calls for factual correction. The immigrant experience was not only more difficult than Americans choose to remember; it was also less universally successful. While contemporary Americans of foreign stock like to brag about the progress they and, more particularly, their forebears made, they do not brag about the failures. For the most part, the failures have no descendants to talk about them. Many—perhaps as many as 30 percent of the European immigrants—returned to their native lands. The much simpler, crueler, and technically less proficient society they had found in New York in the nineteenth and early twentieth centuries killed off many, probably those who were doing less well than their luckier contemporaries. They died of undernourishment, diseases since eradicated, and industrial accidents. Others moved on to other parts of the country. Expunging the failures from social memory does not mean that they did not exist; nor does anyone seriously suggest that current failures be left to starve or die of causes that the society can control. But until mastery of social problems achieves the same level of success as mastery of organic and technical problems, the failures will remain visible among urban dwellers.

Nevertheless, the differences between immigrant life and the lives of underprepared black migrants are significant also in setting fair standards for black achievement. The comparison with an idealized immigrant experience has helped to obscure from sympathetic whites the wide gap that exists between the social culture of the blacks who are entering the city's economic life and those who are not. Naturally some whites (and some blacks, too) ascribe the failures to genetic inferiority or genetic difference. That is a hazardous and needlessly complicated theory, although it may well be true that a combination of cultural adaptation and cultural selection prompts certain ethnic or racial groups to produce individual members who consistently excel in specific types of activities. In any case, even if this selection and adaptation process takes place, it does not seem rigid enough to explain the even wider span of differences between members of the same group. Not every Jew can play the violin; not every black can tap-dance. What sympathetic whites, who have known primarily distinguished blacks, probably underestimate is the depth and persistence of cultural differences between an African and a European past, especially when those differences have, as in the United States, been reinforced by a peculiarly degrading form of slavery and post-Emancipation customs and laws.

The cultural gap is not so great that it cannot be bridged, but bridging it will take longer than sympathetic whites expected. In keeping in mind the immigration pattern of the past, they have failed to emphasize to themselves the cultural differences between European life, even rural European life, and the situation of the black slaves. Though the Europeans spoke English poorly, if at all, while it was a native language for most recent migrating blacks from the South or the Caribbean, the Europeans were familiar with a money economy. They had not been immured in a system of near-total dependency, in which all important decisions were made for them by others. Even if Europeans were individually illiterate, they were familiar with the printed word; they had not, like blacks in slavery, been held under a system that made teaching them to read a felony. Their family life was not subject to interruption at the bidding of a third party; and even for those who worked in the fields, entrepreneurship was not an unknown idea, nor was the mastery of a trade unfamiliar.

All these differences between the European and the black experience (and to a lesser extent between the mainland black and the West Indian) added to the unfairness of the expectations that their adaptation to urban life in a new setting would be similar. Of indeterminate importance was the whole question of skin-color difference, which arouses subliminal fears and hatreds not fully comprehended by those to whom they are not a part of daily existence. Those who argue that the European immigrant was also distinguishable from earlier arrivals by appearance, accent, clothing, and religion (in many cases) do not fully understand the difference between a distinction that will gradually disappear in subsequent generations and one that travels with the genes and is immutable—particularly when the characteristic is historically associated with legally enforceable lower status.

It is not enough, however, to *explain* why the black and immigrant experiences in New York diverge; both blacks and whites struggle with the question of what to *do* about it. Neither side has a valid prescription, although there has been a proliferation of inadequate ideas, which are pushed forward with more and more vigor, the less successful they are in practice.

While whites, even sympathetic whites, express their disappointment in black progress in jokes about black inferiority that they would have scorned to repeat only a few years ago, blacks, even middle-class blacks, tend to claim that they are the victims of white prejudice and conspiracy. They make these assertions despite the achievement of public and private goals that would have seemed visionary only a generation ago. If whites misunderstand the problems and conditions that are an intrinsic part of black life in the United States, so do successful middle-class blacks misunderstand the nature of white life. Frustrated by events like the failure of black policemen in New York City to pass, in the same proportion as whites, a specially designed, racially unbiased promotion examination for sergeants, they complain that while the examination is not culturally biased, the results were. What this means, logically, is unclear. Politically, it means that the blacks who are impatient with the progress of their least successful fellows are determined to blame their problems entirely—the crucial word—on white conspiracy. It has become all too common to hear blacks who know better complain that whites have too easy a time of it in the United States and that, essentially, none of them really work but merely pass the benefits of a corrupt society back and forth among them.

These charges amount to the assertion that the United States is so corrupt a society that only by bending the laws backward can blacks hope to achieve their fair share of America's benefits. This supposition underlies the black demand for affirmative action, a demand in which some whites join them. Affirmative action no longer means what some originally took it to mean, that blacks had been so handicapped by their inferior status in American society that the state would have to take steps to improve their education, remedy their inferior status, and enable them to compete on equal terms with whites. Affirmative action now means the elimination of competition as the determinant of who gets what. Instead, jobs and promotions are to be assigned to minority-group members, mainly blacks, in accordance with a mathematical formula that represents someone's idea of what a fair share of the benefits should be, all else being equal. It is, obviously, a policy of despair. It seems to cry out that blacks cannot compete on equal terms with whites and that therefore invidious discrimination, favoring one person over another by reason of skin color, must be a permanent feature of American life. Sometimes its supporters are heard to claim that affirmative action will not be permanent but will be abandoned as soon as blacks attain a fair share of American rewards. There have been no clear signals that suggest how anyone will know when a fair share is achieved, or what will happen, after affirmative action withers away, if blacks fail to retain the fair share for which the program was instituted.

The whites who favor such a program do not merely acknowledge that blacks have been subjected to invidious discrimination in the past. They seem to feel that their own decision-making would be made easier if a numerical standard were established to substitute for the exercise of individual judgment. If a white personnel manager tries to pick an indeterminate number of blacks (or of other minorities) for a specific job level in a company, he or she must decide each case on its merits. Given a numerical assignment, or "goal," as it is politely called, for black employees, the manager simply picks that number of blacks and leaves behind all questions of balancing the contributions that might be made by an originally unqualified black against the contribution of a white competitor who starts with better qualifications. That such a system was abhorrent led to the civil rights revolution in the first place; one of the arguments made in favor of the movement was that eliminating color bias would improve efficiency in the society. It is ironic that current thinking should seek to reverse the process.

Some of its proponents argue that the numerical goal set by affirmative action provides a measure, otherwise nonexistent, of fairness in hiring blacks. The trouble is that there is no numerical standard for fairness. Establishing one is either a purely symbolic gesture or a fraud. If one tries to set a standard for all job categories—say, the same percentage of people holding each job as the percentage of blacks in the general population—one has simply ignored the universal experience that each population group, blacks included, excels at some jobs or professions and eschews others. A numerical goal that would demand the hiring of as high a percentage of black mechanical engineers as black center fielders would be absurd with respect to both occupations in 1984; the center fielders would be kept at a ridiculously low number, while the engineers' quota could not be

filled. Who would decide when a goal should be raised or lowered? and to what fairer number?

The sad feature of the argument, which is embittering relationships between blacks and Jews particularly, the latter having had so much trouble with anti-Semitic quota systems in the
past, is that its advocates demand the goal system for the apparent reason that they no longer know what else to ask for. While
a very large part of the black population moves upward, its rate
of progress generally following the state of the economy (and
perhaps—inversely—the employment of women in the work
force), the number of blacks at the bottom, in dependency on
government handouts, increases or stays about the same. Surely
it has not declined. The record of black achievement indicates
that when blacks are given a fair chance, they do better than
whites in some occupations, less well in others. As more qualify, in more and more fields, the better the general record will
be.

The problem to which no one has an answer is what happens
in the meantime, until more do qualify, and until the dependent
population diminishes. It is because there is no ready answer to
the immediate, though interim, problem that the affirmative
action proposal arouses so much passion. The passion they
express is probably much stronger than their conviction that
affirmative action is indeed a solution to the most urgent problem affecting American blacks, the reduction of dependency.

It does seem clear that a program like affirmative action is
perversely designed to increase dependency rather than to reduce it. It announces to blacks that they must be dependent on
government intervention and support to take jobs that they
cannot win on the basis of merit.

The fundamental difficulty, the reason why the present population of New York City is not the asset that it once appeared
to be, is that the increase of dependency has spread through the
society. This is not to suggest that it is good for a society that
some should be hungry and others homeless, but rather that a
society that fails to draw a clear line between the ethic of

dependency and the ethic of self-support is doomed to an increase—a continuing increase—of dependency. A society that rewards young women for producing illegitimate children is a society that has failed to draw a line clearly at a vital juncture. Such a line cannot be drawn by government, nor should it. But a society whose elites, black and white, fail to understand that a line should be drawn between moral and immoral conduct is failing in its duty to the dependent and to their offspring, generation after generation.

Unfortunately, that prescription—the intervention of the elites—leaves the immediate problems of the dependent untouched. Whatever is to be done to keep these people alive, and to lessen their destructive influence on the society around them, must be done by the black and white elites in concert. If both the long- and short-term solutions to the problem of black dependency cannot be found, New York's City's fall cannot be broken.

Chapter VIII

The Costs of Accomplishments

IT IS RELATIVELY EASY for an economically successful society to repair the damage inflicted on its members and their posterity by carelessness, lack of foresight, and bland assumptions about progress that turn out to be mistaken. One of the major social impulses of the postwar period has been to try to redeem the damage done to the physical environment by foolish and misguided industrial processes and careless and hasty improvisation. Filthy rivers have been cleaned; damage to bird life by dangerous insecticides has been reversed; some of the incidence of foul air resulting from careless burning of fuels or release of noxious chemical vapors has been reduced significantly.

Indeed, it can well be argued that the feelings of guilt that have motivated much of this restoration work in the environment are altogether too powerful. There seems to be a kind of wallowing in the *culpa maxima* of trying to satisfy human needs and hungers, as well as human desires. Some beneficial processes, such as nuclear power generation and solid waste disposal, are being held from production and use by fears that are irrational and overheated, although they are stimulated, no doubt, by earlier fears of environmental damage that turned out to be solidly and reasonably based.

When it comes, however, to dealing with the consequences, sometimes extremely unfortunate, of programs and inventions and discoveries that were motivated by humane considerations and dedication to the values of life itself, society has been much slower to take remedial action. Its leaders feel no sense of guilt over what has been done. They feel properly proud of their dedication to the good of humanity and are able, with no effort at all, to avoid looking at the unintended side effects, some of which are menacing to society as a whole.

Long before the outbreak of the Second World War, New York City had prided itself on its generally progressive and humane concern with the well-being of its citizens. It pioneered in constructing municipal hospitals, passed social welfare legislation of its own, and took advantage of powers given it by the state legislature to enact health codes, build advanced water supply systems, and provide help and refuge for indigents and for children needing supervision. It offered protection from factory accidents and unsanitary working conditions before these bits of social legislation were generally adopted by the other states and cities. Its support of health facilities and hospitals and its standard of assistance to the destitute put it in the front rank of cities in the nation in its concern for the poor and helpless, the exposed, the weak.

It certainly was not clear in 1946 that the city's welfare and health programs had some unintended consequences that made more difficult the development and maintenance of civil order in a city populated largely by new arrivals. The new arrivals in the postwar period, as we have noted, were in great part peculiarly handicapped by the racial feelings of native New Yorkers and by the mismatch that existed between their cultural background and the demands made on them by an unfamiliar and frightening society.

The National Origins Immigration Act had so drastically cut down the heavy flow of immigrants to New York in the twenty years before the Second World War that most New Yorkers had forgotten the city's earlier fears that it would never be able to establish civic order in so large a city populated by so polyglot an agglomeration of people. In Paul Boyer's study *Urban Masses and Moral Order in America, 1820–1920,* cited in chapter 6, Boyer begins with a quotation from Tocqueville: "I look upon the size of certain American cities, and especially on the nature of their population, as a real danger."

In retrospect, it may be easy to believe that this possibility of danger was a chimera exclusive to Tocqueville. On the contrary, it was a real fear, shared by the French observer, who was so fascinated by the real prospects of democratic life, with many Americans. The danger was that the theory of representative self-government, put forward by a small group of philosophers and landowners in a pre-industrial society, would be unable to impose the necessary controls on the behavior of crowded, rootless urban residents. How could democracy be prevented from becoming simply mob rule? What would provide the unifying system of beliefs if self-direction and self-discipline could not be counted on? Although Tocqueville could not foresee the future media of communications that would put urban ideas and modes of behavior before the whole country, he surely understood that if the cities were unsafe for their residents, they could not provide safe seats of government. In that event, a society that was both democratic and libertarian would not survive.

Boyer's book stresses the institutional efforts to instill responsibility in the wayward and frightening youths of the cities. It is clear, however, that the most important institutions in turning European peasants into American industrial workers were the familiar ones of family, church, working environment and unions, political parties, and other voluntary associations that either continued old world relationships or created new ones. The part of the population that was most at risk were those young people who had no solid family life, who were inadequately prepared for regular work, either by temperament or training, and who were out of touch with religious or other institutions. It was on these young people that the reformers of the nineteenth century lavished their dedication, humanity, religious fervor, and simple generosity—as well as, some would argue, their drive for power. They established settlement houses, trade schools, work programs, boarding homes, reading rooms, and youth associations, to mention only a few from the top of a long list. All were to some extent successful in nursing the desire for order that hides somewhere in every human breast. Yet they were on the whole unsuccessful in pinning angels' wings on the shoulder blades of street urchins. The city's crowded and mobile population produced more than could be cured by uplifting influences, however sincere and ingenious.

Some were saved for the work force by the presence of a host of informal educators, of whom the most important in the late nineteenth century was probably the policeman with his billy club. Unrestrained by review boards and civil service regulations, the police were not trying to create angels or win the affection of their youthful enemies, but simply to enforce order. In some cases, a sharp rap on the shins with the nightstick must have been more effective than twenty sessions with a Youth Board therapist would be seventy-five or a hundred years later.

The main influences in keeping the potential urban mob under general control, however, were three forces not often discussed: the lure of the frontier, the need to be self-supporting, and the high death rate.

First in importance during the period Boyer writes about was the thin settlement of the West, which made the frontier a tempting possible alternative to city life. To suggest nowadays that the poor, particularly the disorganized poor who have not found work in the city, can move elsewhere is considered unrealistic and offensive—unrealistic because nice people understand that poor people cannot afford to move, and offensive because it implies that the poor are not wanted in the city. Nice people in this case can be wrong: the poor have frequently moved to the city in search of work and can move elsewhere if better opportunities can be found elsewhere. And it is quite obvious to the poor themselves that they are not wanted, because they are not working and must support themselves by begging or worse—or, at least, that's what they had to do in the period of which Boyer writes.

The frontier, according to Frederick Turner, remained open until 1890, and even after it closed the West continued to beckon and often to be hospitable to displaced New Yorkers. Sometimes the results were unfortunate: Billy the Kid, a New York boy, obviously made no better an adjustment in the West than he had in Hell's Kitchen. But thousands of men who were incapable of anything other than casual labor found a place to work on the railroads, in the mines, and on the cattle ranches. Their sisters found work as wives, or entertainers and bar girls, or hired girls, or even as waitresses in the Harvey restaurants or their equivalent. The move westward continued during the depression, when the Okies moved to California, finding opportunities there more often than Steinbeck's *Grapes of Wrath* suggested they would.

A second major influence contributing to the achievement of order in the nineteenth-century city was the lack of a system of public assistance. Under the present system, the federal government provides half the cash required to give a family with dependent children the minimal income that a state establishes as necessary for survival. The adoption of this law was a giant step forward in compassionate government. It has saved countless lives, enabled countless families to survive intact through periods of unemployment and disability during which all their assets were exhausted, and no doubt played an important role in saving young people from being institutionalized or sent to foster homes. No one in his right mind would want the nation to abolish a system of government support for those families who have become unable to support themselves.

Yet that is not a balanced appreciation of the public assistance law. As Gertrude Himmelfarb points out in *The Idea of Poverty*, England has been wrestling for centuries to find a way in which the poor can be sheltered and kept from starvation by government programs without at the same time being turned permanently into paupers. Certainly the Aid to Families with Dependent Children program has saved the countless families described above from degradation. Among its costs, however, is the pauperization of countless other families for whom public assistance has become no mere temporary protection against involuntary unemployment, but a way of life freely chosen—as much as any human decision can be so described.

Welfare is a deplorable way of life, as anyone knows who has had to visit the barren New York apartment of a family supported by AFDC. Although it is not impossible for a child in the fourth generation of dependence on AFDC to turn into a second Beethoven, such an outcome is highly unlikely. Raised in a world without objects to treasure, without the obligation to work, without reason to respect one's parents or parent, raised in a world in which those who work are assumed to be foolish and feckless and those who do not work, smart and street-wise, a long-term beneficiary of welfare has a minimal chance of turning into a member of the working population. The AFDC system, in short, inadvertently accomplished precisely what the British had sought to avoid in their dealing with the problem of dependency: it created a permanent class of people outside the working population. Obviously, that did not happen to those who had to accept welfare to survive a temporary emergency for which they had no responsibility. It did mean, however, that those for whom it became a way of life were now anchored by it in the place where they were receiving it.

There had been no such system in the less compassionate world that died in the Great Depression. When the welfare system was inaugurated, its legislation was more or less deliberately framed to keep the level of public support from competing with employment in the states that had the lowest wage levels.

Those states with the lowest wage levels obviously established the lowest permissible standards for welfare assistance, because they did not wish to do anything that would exert an upward pressure on wages; high levels of welfare might compete with the wages that men and women could earn in the economy. New York, where wage and, consequently, welfare levels were high, could not expect its welfare population to move. However, in the nineteenth century, only the relatively flimsy tie of private charity could have kept the indigent in big cities like New York. Civic order was therefore less menaced by a large, permanent group of people who lived on public assistance and raised their children to do the same.

This unintended consequence of the welfare system is not easily avoided. Nor is it easy to avoid unfavorable comparison between the net earnings of families working at the minimum legal wage and the net benefits of welfare, including such incidental fringes as food stamps and Medicaid health insurance. It may not be possible to design a system that will sustain the poor without creating a subclass of paupers, in which case common humanity suggests that welfare must be continued despite its inadvertent risks. But if the American nation continues on that course, it must redouble its efforts to prevent the welfare status from becoming a permanent part of life. That has not been done, not in New York and not in the nation as a whole.

Some of the remedies that seem most obvious are clearly impossible. It would be unthinkable to terminate welfare benefits after a specific length of time unless the recipients agreed to move to another part of the country where unemployment is lower. The prospective "receiving" states would surely block such a proposal in Congress, even if the forced relocation it hints at did not seem wholly inconsistent with American views of the powers of government. Forced relocation from one state to another recalls the treatment of Japanese-Americans during the Second World War, of which Americans are now ashamed.

That leaves the cities with the hopes of the evangelical reformers described by Boyer and very little else. In a nation whose advertisers can sell cigarettes effectively while the Surgeon General prints on their package a warning that they can kill you, it should be possible to make even something as dubious as work attractive to the idle. The welfare benefit is not so generous that it frees recipients from the desire for more money. The selling job is only to make work (assuming that work is available) more attractive than mugging. That idea may not be as preposterous as it sounds, for the problem is real.

The directly financial costs of welfare in New York City are not the only costs, but these are important. No program for putting people to work would ever save all the expenditures on welfare. Large sums will always be required to support those who are only temporarily in need or cannot work for irrefutable reasons. But the postwar years have seen an almost steady climb not only in expenditures on welfare, but, more ominously, in the number of people who are its beneficiaries.

The annual reports of the New York City comptroller and mayor reveal that in fiscal 1946, the city spent $70 million on its share of welfare (making up one-half of the state's total share). Within four years, the cost had increased by 140 percent. Within nine years, welfare costs were 300 percent over the 1946 level. School and library costs rose by only 80 percent in the same period. In 1945, 300,000 people received welfare aid in New York City. By 1969 the number had exceeded one million. For a while during the Koch administration it dipped below that figure, but it has started to climb again. The important thing to remember is that this growth in welfare cases has occurred against a background of growth in business activity and in employment generally. What it portends is a permanent growth in the number of people living in New York City who cannot take the jobs that the city economy offers.

How many people can live permanently on welfare, not working, not attending school regularly, committing far more than their proportionate share of the street crimes that make the city's streets unsafe for its residents? How many can the city permit to destroy what's left of its cheap housing or allow to terrorize the weaker children of families living in public housing? How long can the business climate of the city stand the taxes needed to protect citizens against the permanent welfare population? How long can wasted and futile lives, filled with inactivity, pile up in the city without rendering everything else meaningless?

As a matter of cold fact, the situation gets worse, not better. Below the welfare permanents, a new subclass is beginning to grow that is not even entitled to welfare because its members have no addresses to which their checks can be sent. These are the homeless. Some became homeless when the owners of the single-room occupancy buildings cleared them out in favor of a less taxing group of occupants, able to afford full-service apartments. Others were released from the state's institutions for the mentally ill, in the expectation that with the help of new drugs that controlled the effects of mental disturbance, they would be able to sustain themselves in the outside world.

New York's treatment of the mentally ill was described by Jacob Riis in his books on the darker side of the nineteenth-century city. On cold winter nights, Riis wrote, the police would allow mentally disturbed men and women to sleep on the floors of police stations, which if nothing else were warm and dry. The police managed at least a touch of humanity in their dealing with these helpless people.

In subsequent years, the state built a massive system of large institutions for the mentally ill. Their treatment was at best rudimentary, and it seemed a blessing when a series of new drugs, starting with lithium, offered hope that the symptoms of mental disease could be kept under control. Once the drugs had been tested in the institutions, it seemed possible to allow the inmates out and to establish community-based care centers where they could get the drugs and such assistance as they might need to sustain themselves. The Civil Liberties Union quickly involved itself in a de-institutionalization campaign, successfully persuading the courts that it was unconstitutional to keep people confined unless they were dangerous to themselves or others.

Thousands of inmates were released, but no significant progress was made in establishing community centers. The former patients do not take their drugs regularly, probably for the same obscure reasons that make them behave in a bizarre fashion to begin with. They sleep in doorways and at municipal shelters, disturb and frighten fellow citizens, and constitute a living reproach to those ideologues who think that freedom gives its beneficiaries the right to live in destitution on the streets.

It might be possible for charitable institutions that are privately owned but helped with public funds to develop a housing pattern in which some of the least antisocial homeless people would be able to live more comfortably than they did in the old S.R.O. buildings or in the mental institutions. Such a program, however, would be more than expensive; it would be precarious, because it would depend on the continuing willingness of private philanthropies to run the new institutions. What they would have to devise is not housing in the ordinary sense, nor health care institutions in the ordinary sense, but some new form of sheltering and nurturing establishment in which the homeless who are not quite ill enough to be in mental institutions, yet not quite well enough to go it alone, can survive. But how many former mental patients would stay in these places voluntarily, and how many, driven by the impulses that the physicians can neither fully understand nor treat, would resume their feckless and dangerous camping on the city streets? Moreover, institutions that might be developed under such a plan would not only be difficult to run but nearly impossible to situate. The city has had difficulty in pushing its plans for temporary shelters through the city's governing body, because local people do not want them in their neighborhood, not in any neighborhood. The acceptability of community shelters for the mentally ill will depend on their being able to weed out the cases that frighten neighbors and need the more intensive care of a fully staffed mental institution. We can imagine the same guardians of liberty who ejected these cases from the mental institutions in the first place rallying to keep them from being sent back. The advocates of de-institutionalization seem impervious to the fear that the presence of disturbing people on the streets imperils the whole program of treatment in a community setting. It also undermines the ability of the city to win approval for establishing or funding these new shelters by heightening resistance of their future neighbors.

The homeless former mental patients who have been deemed to be safe while they take their prescribed medications constitute a rather small example of the way in which another monumental human achievement—the improvement of medical care —has had unexpectedly bad side effects on urban life. Looking at the urban masses and their disorderliness, we come to the third factor that enabled the cities to establish order in the nineteenth century: their lack of modern medicine.

Life expectancy was much shorter in the cities of the nineteenth century. The major killers were the bacterial diseases that flourished in conditions of poverty and degradation. Without public health measures to assure cleanliness in foods, adequate and clean water supplies, and effective sewage systems, those most at risk in the nineteenth-century cities were, as usual, the poorest of the poor, those living in the most savage circumstances. In the past fifty years there has been a virtual explosion in medical therapies. Death rates for the poor, and particularly the addicted poor, are still higher than for people of greater means, and the life expectancy of nonwhites is shorter than that of whites, probably because their incomes are lower and their living conditions worse. Nevertheless, life expectancy for the entire population is much greater than it was in the nineteenth century. With caution, one must wonder whether the higher death rate, winnowing with singular cruelty the ranks of the disorderly and poor urban masses, was not a very significant factor in making possible the achievement of a measure of civil peace in the older cities—and whether anybody or any institution has begun to glimpse the size of the challenge needed to meet a problem whose limits have been stretched by the achievements of a humane civilization.

Such a hypothesis, even if it is correct, surely does not mean that the medical achievements that have lengthened life should be discarded. It is hard to imagine an ethical system that would not attach supreme value to extending human life and freeing it from the threat of disease and disability. The hypothesis does mean, however, that in exchange for the gift of longer life, residents in the new cities have to assume a much heavier social burden—either that of living with a constantly growing group of people who cannot impose order on themselves or that of finding new ways to strengthen the impulse to create order.

The figures alone are quite persuasive that something fundamental distinguishes the demographic pattern of the late twentieth-century city from the same city in the earlier years of this century and in the nineteenth. There are many ways of looking at health statistics. The data can be sorted by age cohorts or the several diseases can be separated and the death rate for each calculated separately. Death rates can also be tabulated by race. New York City's health statistics are remarkably thorough, although changes in tabulation that reflect changed medical opinion and knowledge sometimes make comparisons difficult. Nevertheless, no matter how the statistics are looked at, they tell the same general story.

Over the past century, New York's death rates per year per 100,000 population have plummeted. Life expectancy at every age level has risen significantly. Furthermore, the diseases that kill people in the early years of their lives have been reduced dramatically, as have the death rates caused by diseases known to be communicated by bacteria under crowded or unsanitary conditions and to bodies weakened by defective diets. The diseases that now kill people in their later years are those that are related to rich diets and to environmental factors that are themselves associated with improved material standards of living. The death rates from those diseases have increased significantly, along with death rates from homicides. The increases are found both in gross numbers and as percentages of the population.

John Duffy's *History of Public Health in New York City*, published by the Russell Sage Foundation in 1974, sets forth the data in its appendices. The crude death rate in New York City in the decade of the 1860s was 31.86 per 1,000 of population. Ninety years later, in the decade of the 1950s, the rate had been reduced by two-thirds, to 10.4 deaths per year per 1,000 of population.

These figures, though startling, do not sufficiently differentiate the parts of the population that were primary victims of the diseases that caused the higher rates in the 1860s. The most striking information is that relating to the deaths of children below five years of age. Duffy points out that as late as 1900, deaths of children under five accounted for 40 percent of the deaths annually in New York City. Generally, these children were killed either by infant diarrhea, particularly serious in the summer months and generally the consequence of eating spoiled food, most commonly in households that could least afford ice, or from highly contagious diseases, such a diphtheria, which spread under the most crowded conditions, where the poorest children were most likely to live.

The correlation between poverty and the infant death rate is made particularly clear by records that connect the infant death rate to temperature and humidity. Dr. Elisha Harris, then the city's registrar of vital statistics, pointed out that in the summer of 1874, no less than 63.5 percent of all deaths in the month of July were deaths of children under five, while in August they were practically as high, 61 percent. For the whole year following, infant deaths were 47.5 percent of all deaths, indicating that in the winter months, when food spoilage was less likely even without ice, fewer children died.

To illustrate the impact of overcrowding on the population, Duffy quotes Dr. Abraham Jacobi, reporting on behalf of the Committee on Hygiene of the New York County Medical Society. In 1891, Dr. Jacobi reported that between 1860 and 1890,

43,000 people, mostly children, died of diphtheria and croup. Another 18,000 died from scarlet fever, a streptococcal infection, in the eighteen years between 1871 and 1900. In 1882, Dr. Jacobi told his medical colleagues, the city's hospital facilities for communicable diseases on Ward's Island "were so crowded with smallpox, typhus, and typhoid fever cases that there had been no room for patients with diphtheria and scarlet fever."

The death rate for children in New York, staggering to the modern reader, remained high well into the twentieth century. In 1909, when the city population was four million, 16,000 infants died in their first year. In 1981, when the population was 7 million, the number of infants who died in their first year was one-tenth of what it had been in 1909, 1,678 against 16,000.

Records published by the city's health authorities in recent years are far more complete than those published in earlier years, and it is now possible to study the death rates within various areas of the city. Because these areas can be generally characterized according to income and ethnic character, the figures make clear the relationship between generally accepted indices of social disorganization and a high child mortality rate. In 1981, although for the city as a whole the death rate of infants under the age of one was 15.5 per 1,000 live births, the rate in central Harlem, an area dogged by poverty, overcrowding, and illegitimacy, was more than a third higher, 21.2 per 1,000 live births. The citywide percentage of illegitimate births was 35.5 percent of all births. In central Harlem, illegitimate births were 79 percent of all births. Throughout the city, the costs of 32.4 percent of all births were paid by Medicaid; in practical terms, that means that 32.4 percent of all women giving birth were receiving public assistance or welfare. In Harlem, that figure was 69.9 percent.

Harlem today is much better served with medical assistance than it was in 1909. The high correlation between the indices of social disorganization and infant mortality rates means that even with better facilities, poverty imposes a tremendous burden. In poorer households, mothers are less well fed, both because they lack the money to do better and because they lack the knowledge of how to make the very best of the meager resources they command. It is more difficult for poor, young, unmarried mothers to get proper prenatal care. For one thing, they may have a harder time finding someone to take care of other children while they seek aid. The poor had an even heavier burden when the disease rates were much higher. It is hard to resist the belief that those families among the poor population who had the hardest time taking care of their children, and were thus most likely to lose them, were, by and large, the families who provided the least promising home in every sense. Their children would be the most likely to follow antisocial, disorderly patterns of life if they survived infancy.

Turning from infant diseases to those of older children and adults, we find the difference in demographics between the older city and the new one equally striking. Of children up to the age of fifteen, scarlet fever took 67.6 lives per 100,000 population in 1901. In 1950, it killed no one. Diphtheria killed 159.3 of every 100,000 people in 1900. In 1950, the rate was one-tenth of a person for every 100,000 in population. The statistics for tuberculosis are similarly dramatic. In 1901 it killed 248 people of every 100,000 per year. In 1981, the rate had dropped to 2.2 people per 100,000. Pneumonia, which is associated with malnutrition as well as with hypothermia and preceding infections, killed 263 per 100,000 in 1901 per year; in 1981, the toll dropped to 36 per 100,000.

Disease was not the only threat to life and health that oppressed the poor in older New York. They were, one must suppose, the primary victims of the appallingly high rate of accidents. Many contemporary Americans believe that the automobile has greatly added to the accident rate since its invention. Though the automobile, which caused no deaths at all in New York in 1901, caused 542 in 1981, it has declined steadily as a cause of death since 1930. In that year in New York City, it reached its peak efficiency as a killer, disposing of more than twice as many victims as it would fifty-two years later. The annual rate of automobile fatalities in 1930 was 17.5 per 100,000 population. By 1982, it had dropped to 7.7 per 100,000.

It is even more pertinent to the population control of the city in earlier days to note that the rate of accidents other than motor vehicle accidents has tumbled. In 1978, the Health Department recorded 950 fatalities due to accidents other than automobile accidents, a rate of 12.5 per 100,000. In 1901, 3,591 New Yorkers lost their lives in such accidents, a rate of 93.5 per 100,000 population. It seems likely that in the days when factory regulation was rudimentary, if it existed at all, and crude outdoor work was done with inadequately powered machinery, the work place was dangerous indeed. It also seems likely that the most probable victim was the poorest unskilled worker, who had to take the most dangerous job under the worst working conditions.

In short, if it remains true, as the record suggests, that the sections of the city in which the poorest people lived were also the sections with the highest death rates from disease and accident, the effort to achieve moral order in the city was somewhat easier because the impact of these premature deaths fell heaviest on the class that was producing the greatest number of disorderly people in a turbulent time. The same sections of the city, incidentally, were characterized by the highest suicide rate. It was three times as high per 100,000 population in 1901 as in 1981. The homicide rate, however, has risen sharply, going from 3.8 deaths per 100,000 population in 1901 to 20.8 deaths per 100,000 in 1978. The relative drop in the cost of firearms has doubtless had something to do with this doleful figure.

Public sanitation, clean water, and government inspection of eating and health facilities have all played a part in the immense and heartening reversal in health statistics. At the same time, they have not been without cost.

Part of the cost is simply economic. A just society must surely accept the idea that all members of the population should have the right treatment for disease when there is a reasonable chance for a cure. Unfortunately from the point of view of economics, that statement creates a rising demand for health services as the number of treatable diseases rises. Coupled with a finite supply of doctors and facilities, of laboratories and technicians, the increased demand means that the cost of medical care has gone up faster than costs for most other goods and services. So far, the demand for health services has stimulated the invention of new diagnostic and therapeutic devices, also tending to push immediate costs up (though long-run costs may be reduced). The cities, New York in particular, have been struggling to bear the health care costs of the very large part of the population that gets its only deliverance from medical indigence through Medicaid.

The second cost of health care is more ticklish to discuss because it deals with the intangible costs that result from increased life expectancy. In a highly congested city, if health care has the effect of increasing the number—or changing the demographic pattern that formerly decreased the number—of dangerously uncivil people in the population, the cost of trying to impose moral order on them must rise significantly.

No serious person can claim that in past years tuberculosis, with miraculous aim, wiped out all the potential New York criminals and spared the poet and the philanthropist. No one would suggest that cures for diseases should be taken out at night and buried, as Tom Sawyer buried his cat, to avoid warts. Yet it would be equally nonsensical to overlook the fact that unconscious blind forces, by helping reduce the size of the potentially disruptive population, made easier the job that the city must now do consciously: imposing moral order. The hard part is to determine how moral order can be encouraged; clearly, it cannot be imposed by any regime, no matter how tyrannical. Like the environmental consequences of technology, the demographic consequences of medicine have to be offset so that physical health does not triumph at the expense of social health.

Yet that is not what New York City is doing, nor is any other city doing it on a scale that approaches a solution to the problem. The city—perhaps not the political city, but the private city, the religious city, the institutional city—should be expending a significantly greater effort in the search for moral order than did the reformers discussed by Boyer. In fact the opposite is the case. Moral order is still condemned, as it was in the 1960s, as a code word for race prejudice and class pride. Those who would argue that people are not born civilized, that they do not take to civilization easily, are told that they are trying to impose middle-class attitudes on the poor. They are denounced as kitchen imperialists.

Far from attempting to impose moral order on the poor, society has adopted a neutral attitude on moral matters, in some ways a neutrality that amounts to opposition. Consider the case of a hospital in New York City that dedicates a ward to the treatment of patients with subacute bacterial endocarditis, an infection of the heart muscles and valves. In this ward are placed those patients who contracted their diseases by injecting their veins with narcotics, using an infected needle.

The process of curing these people from their once always-fatal disease is long and expensive. It requires bed care, sophisticated antibiotic drugs, and a course of treatment lasting six weeks or more. In addition to their debilitating illness, the patients suffer from the unpleasant withdrawal symptoms that follow the denial of narcotics to an addict and from all the personality problems that contributed to their addiction in the first place. They are graceless, even insulting, impatient, destructive, dirty, doomed people, snatched from addiction unwillingly and usually prepared to return to it upon their release from the hospital. With the renewed addiction will return all the nasty and dangerous ways of getting the money to pay for the narcotics: stealing, mugging, perhaps even murder.

In a few months' time, many will be back in the hospital, suffering from another infection of the same germs from another dirty needle. Yet these patients are remarkably free from the death rate that accompanies the same disease when the infection is brought on by another form of exposure. Curing the endocarditis that follows injection into a vein produces a scab on the right side of the heart; in other patients, the scab is more likely to form on the left side. In the noninjected patient, the scab often breaks off and is carried by the arterial system to the brain, where it causes instant death. In the addict, the scab is carried to the lung, where it will probably form an abscess that can be treated surgically with relative ease.

The treatment of the patients in this ward is paid for by government or given free by the hospital, in keeping with medical ethics and the principles of the society. The patients are, in effect, treated no differently than they might be if they had incurred an infection while trying to save someone else's life rather than in the process of trying, in a long and tortuous passage, to end their own. It is altogether proper that they should be saved. No one can conscientiously advocate saving money by letting them die, as they inevitably would were their disease left untreated. Yet, somehow, to say that they should be saved is not quite enough.

What seems missing is the passing of judgment on the matter. No one with any experience with addicts would entertain the hope that psychiatric counseling or any of the other forms of treatment that might be imposed in the hospital would make a significant difference in the long-term prognosis for these people. The physical disease is curable; the mental predisposition to addiction is not. Yet it remains impossible for a society in which the notion of individual responsibility has been undermined and that of societal implication in individual failings has grown weighty, to say what has to be said: that these addicts are immoral and that society has not only an excuse for contrasting them with people who are innocently ill, but a duty to do so. Not shrilly, not hysterically, but plain out, society has the obligation to distinguish between physical illness that involves no act of will and physical illness that does.

Of course, it can be argued, probably correctly, that passing moral judgments on the people you are treating for endocarditis will not accelerate the cure nor terminate the addiction. It is not intended to do that. It is, rather, intended to counteract another of the unintended side effects of the great medical advances that have brought the city hope and despair simultaneously. The ability of medicine to solve human problems, and its reaching out to include what were once called moral problems and bring them into its ambit as though they too are primarily medical, has tended to make good people quail at the prospect of passing judgment on others. In the jargon of the social workers who have colored much of the way in which government and private institutions treat troubled people, the helpers should avoid being "judgmental." The advice may be good tactically in winning the confidence of somebody to whom one is talking, but it is absurd strategically. Unless one is willing to form an unspoken judgment in one's head, at least, one has nowhere to stand in trying to alter behavior.

The basic fact is that the refusal to be judgmental has been based on a highly optimistic—better called naive—view of life. It assumes that people are born good, and civilized as well. Even those who advocate not being judgmental do not really mean what they are recommending. If they did, they would not also urge that society rely on "education" to solve human problems. That, too, has been one of the misunderstood disappointments of the postwar period in New York.

Chapter IX

A Little Learning

ONE OF the great hopes for a better world that emerged after the Second World War was based on widespread public education. The G.I. Bill of Rights included, as one of its most novel and important provisions, a free college education for every veteran. For those veterans who chose not to attend a college, the Bill also provided for vocational or professional education. It is not necessary to drag out statistics to indicate how education grew to meet the demands of a growing population, of which a continually increasing portion went on to study at colleges and universities. New schools went up all over the country. The teaching force multiplied. A previously unheard-of institution, the community college, took root all over the nation, offering specialized training to prospective health care assistants, computer operators, and workers in a number of other subprofessional occupations, many of which did not exist before the war. Students could also transfer from community colleges to senior colleges. The networks of state- or city-owned colleges and universities grew and proliferated. Even the Air Force opened its own institution of higher learning, a mighty campus at Colorado Springs, with traditions that came with the blueprints. New York State's Board of Regents, whose state university never had a campus, found themselves in charge of a full-fledged university system that continues to grow, at least in its community college sector, even though the number of students in its regular senior colleges has stabilized.

New York City's university system had started to grow long before the war broke out in 1939. After the war, its growth accelerated, stimulated in part by the development of community colleges. The elementary and high school plant also grew tremendously, not only because the number of students increased but because they lived in different parts of the city from their predecessors. Some school buildings became obsolete not because they were old, but because they were located in areas no longer attractive to families with children—in some cases, in areas that were no longer attractive to anyone as residential districts.

There was hardly a subject of conflict, puzzlement, or moral ambiguity that people in the early postwar years did not expect education to simplify or even to correct. Education was trumpeted as the solution for race prejudice, even though the enrollments of the nation's most prestigious private universities would have disclosed to any investigator that race and religious prejudice played important roles in the selection of students and faculty. Even in the late prewar years, the leading private universities had practically no black students, and the situation did not improve much for nearly twenty years after the war was over. When black students were in great demand, in the late 1960s, preference was given to those with the shakiest background, the least likely to succeed. No one will ever know certainly whether the selection was accidentally misguided or deliberately tendentious.

Education was expected to eliminate international conflict, if only by teaching American children foreign languages and giving them some idea that children in other nations did not differ from them very much. Education was expected to alert children to the wonders of sex and family life, reducing divorce and illegitimacy. It is not easy to determine the results of sex education because no one can establish how much, if any, higher the rates of both would be if there had been no sex education in recent years. Education was expected to eliminate superstitions, prepare children for scientific work, even out the level of intellectual achievement between the races, raise the level of public discourse, and eliminate corruption and malfeasance from American politics.

In some surprise, one can look back over nearly forty years of postwar expansion of formal education and find that it has become one of the most controversial subjects in the nation's life. First of all, bitter arguments have arisen over who is to have control over the educational process. To what extent should the federal government be empowered to establish rules by which the money it has made available to colleges and schools should be spent? The Supreme Court disappointed many people who style themselves liberal by deciding that the federal government's power to insist, for example, that equal sums be spent on female and male sports programs does not extend to an institution that accepts no money directly from the federal government, even though some students have federal loans. The Court acknowledged, however, that Congress could extend federal power over such an institution simply by rewriting the law to assert it.

That dispute, however, was much more sophisticated and rarified than most of the disputes that have arisen over education. Parents want to know why their children cannot read; some write books about it, bulging with remedies. Others want to know why their children cannot write or solve mathematical problems or speak foreign languages or be familiar with simple facts of their country's history. They argue whether teachers have a right to join unions and go on strike; whether homosexuals should be permitted to be classroom teachers; whether pregnant teachers who are unmarried should be permitted to teach after their pregnancy becomes noticeable. They argue over prayer in schools, whether brief prayers should be conducted on school property and whether observing a moment of silence is in effect a religious observance that violates the principle of separation between church and state. They argue over the extent to which, if at all, the state or city should be permitted to extend help to Roman Catholic and other religious schools that also teach the regular school curriculum. They argue with peculiar fervor over the question of the origin of the human race and whether children whose parents want them to be taught that men and women were created by the Deity on a certain day should be required to hear about dinosaurs and evolution. And, in New York especially, they argue over teaching Hispanic students in Spanish. Will it help or hinder their lives in the future? And, though surely it is bizarre when considered in recollection of the hope that education would dampen racial prejudice, they argue violently over whether or not black children should be bused to white schools, white children to predominantly black schools, or city children to suburban schools in order that school classrooms can be desegregated.

Of course, in local school areas the arguments can also be narrowed down to financial questions that have no wider application than decisions by the educational authorities about priorities in spending limited funds. Should we first redo the inadequate cafeteria in which the children in the Hill Street School eat their breakfast and lunch, or should we build a chemistry lab at the Valley Street School, the only junior high school under our jurisdiction that does not already have such a facility?

The ferocity of these arguments can only be understood by recognizing that, for the parents involved, the arguments are not merely about cafeterias or riding in buses; rather, they are about the future of their children. Children's lives stretch out from the cafeteria: will my children be able to live fuller, better lives than we have had? Or will their careers, whatever they may be, be no better than ours because they aren't getting the proper education? Perhaps feelings on this subject were equally intense a hundred years ago, but that seems doubtful. Something has happened to the class structure of American life, or at least to its class consciousness. The leadership position of elite groups in the social order seems to the people below them less firmly set. Avenues of advancement that were not in evidence have now been opened, but that does not mean they have been opened wide. In fact, they have been opened only to those whose knowledge is up to the mark, who will be equipped to deal with the new, more technological society that lies ahead. Similarly, white parents worry that their children will be unable to stay ahead of the new crowd—maybe black, maybe Hispanic or Chicano, or maybe Oriental or Russian refugees— that is catching up from behind.

Obviously, this expectation of the advancement of the children of the lower middle classes has its effect on people at still lower levels. The fight over control of the schools then becomes even more divisive. Not only are parents involved, but community leaders, foundations, racial and ethnic protective organizations, and practical politicians get involved in the question of control of the modern school.

In New York City, the unsettled problem of school control has beyond question stimulated the division of the city into neighborhood enclaves. It has weakened the centralizing power of the mayor, the comptroller, and the president of the City Council, who between them control six of the eleven votes on the Board of Estimate, the city's governing body.

The issue of who would control local schools came to a head in a very complicated way, in the battle for control of an experimental school district in Ocean Hill–Brownsville, a black section of Brooklyn. A leading role in establishing the district was played by the Ford Foundation, then headed by McGeorge Bundy, formerly a Harvard dean and a high White House official during the Kennedy and Johnson years. Bundy strongly held the view that the schools were the natural institution for making possible a frontal advance by black Americans into the American mainstream. But he also seems to have believed that blacks would not fully perceive the benefits of schooling for their children until most of the teachers and administrators in predominantly black neighborhoods were themselves black. The board running the local school also had to be controlled by local blacks, including some black school parents.

Coming in 1967, when the cities were already resounding to cries for community control and for "power to the people," the Bundy view, backed up by the Foundation's offer to fund the costs of establishing such a model school district, was accepted by the Board of Education. A local school board was elected by a small percentage of the people actually residing within its boundaries. A black professional educator named Rhody A. McCoy was chosen by the board as the administrator of the district.

Unquestionably there was friction in the district long before the local school board was set up. The teachers, members of the American Federation of Teachers, were predominantly Jewish. Although some were respected, others had encountered difficulty with parents who blamed them when their children had disciplinary problems. It was not unusual to hear blacks accuse Jewish teachers of intellectual "genocide." A talented administrator, determined to make measured progress in developing black confidence in the school, might have succeeded in increasing the number of black teachers and winning voluntary transfers of others who were unacceptable to him or to the local board. McCoy, however, had no intention of working things out quietly and patiently. There is even evidence—of threats and violence by blacks who can only be described as *provocateurs* —to show that the extremist leaders would not have tolerated a gradualist approach if McCoy had tried that. He did nothing of the kind. He suspended teachers without hearings, posted observers in classrooms in violation of the AFT's contract, hired faculty members who had not been formally qualified, and finally achieved the result that he seems to have wanted from the beginning: a strike against the school district by the teachers' union.

The strike enabled McCoy to bring in more new teachers, mainly young and idealistic people who lacked formal teacher training. They kept the students busy with such matters as consciousness-raising and black history and songs, but they did not teach very much arithmetic and spelling. McCoy had the support of a significant number of parents and of a large fraction of the school board. Far more important to him and the media were the militants in their dashikis who came from all over the city to express their solidarity with what the McCoy administration had done. It was the first significant confrontation between Jews and blacks in New York since the end of the Second World War.

In the early days of the strike, prominent New Yorkers (including some rich, well-placed, and liberal Jews) tended to side with the local school board and McCoy. In part this was the product of the maddening condescension sometimes shown by upper-class whites to the black people whom they regard as primitives, and in part it was due to a sincere feeling that local government was more likely to promise decent school conditions than the bureaucracy of the immense Board of Education. Beneath these two responses must also have been a deep suspicion of the teachers' union and particularly of its president, Albert Shanker. Shanker was far too articulate and intellectual (and tough-minded) to inspire condescension in the breasts of wealthy observers and civil libertarians, who took sides against union members who were merely defending their rights against an obvious breach of contract.

Shanker did, however, inspire respect in the breasts of the Board of Education and its chancellor, and ultimately they decided that they could not risk labor problems throughout the entire system in order to support a questionable decision by an administrator whose own motives were, at best, mixed. The Ocean Hill–Brownsville experiment came to an end; McCoy left for Boston, and the model was abandoned in favor of the establishment of local boards throughout the system whose powers were carefully delineated; and the Board of Education was also restructured in an effort to remove it from the control of the mayor and the central government of the city. Each

borough president became entitled to appoint a member of the
Board, a change which has had the effect of making each member
a full-time board member. That was not the intent of the
legislation, but as the members represent the borough presidents
who appointed them, they feel a responsibility to keep an
eye on school activities in their individual boroughs. Their appearance
on the job is also more or less guaranteed by the fact
that they are paid on a per-diem basis. The more often they do
the Board's business, the more they collect.

Today local boards are regularly elected, and each local board
picks its own district superintendent. It may be difficult for an
outsider to get a clear picture of the extent of local control in
the school system, or its effect. In times of intense racial feeling,
some militant local superintendents take actions that start a
new, small-scale version of the Ocean Hill–Brownsville episode.
But a conscientious district superintendent who tries to
improve educational standards and performance can accomplish
worthwhile improvements through the narrower focus of
concentrated attention.

The New York school system is so large an enterprise that it
can be evaluated only with the greatest difficulty. The performance
of students falls generally below national averages, though
it probably ranks on a par with other large cities having as
heavy a concentration of children who have only recently arrived
in the city. The schools with the best performance records
are those specialized schools able to choose their pupils by
examination and academic standing. In such schools the student
is motivated to excel in music, art, computer technology, science,
the performing arts, or in all subjects. Their success probably
reflects the simple fact that the special schools attract the
best pupils and the best teachers. Yet some schools with no
specific specialty may, under the leadership of an outstanding
teacher-administrator, achieve a record performance greatly at
variance with the average level of schools throughout the city.
Formal education is one of many areas in which the personal
characteristics of the people in direct contact with the students

matter more than the pedagogical theories of those responsible for running the entire system from a great distance.

It is difficult to make parents believe that. When fears for the future are as serious among parents as at the present time, many parents overemphasize the value of expenditures on education. Some even insist that children with minor handicaps be placed in the special education classes intended to help the severely disabled overcome their physical and emotional problems. The parents who demand special education for minimally handicapped children are apparently acting in the belief that because more money per pupil is spent in these classes, the education must be better. Other parents assert the same belief differently, by arguing for newer schools, better physical plant and athletic facilities, and more teaching aids.

While good facilities and better paid teachers are of help in improving the quality of education, an important fact to be remembered about the city schools is that no matter how much hope is placed in them for improving the quality of public life in the city, they do not operate in a walled garden. A school education is but one of the formative influences that mold the characters of children. Much of what children learn has been implanted before they set foot inside the schoolroom. Its tone is set by the parent or parents and reinforced or amplified by the informal educators who fill the city: the policeman, the cleric, the storekeeper, the landlord. Just as teachers' ability to communicate and enlighten their students depends on their own motivation and morale, so are the city's informal educators influenced by their own perception of what the city is and what is expected of them. If one expects to understand the role of urban education, one must look both at formal teachers and at these informal educators and compare their performance with that of their predecessors a hundred years ago.

The first indication of change begins with the position of the teacher. It seems strange that in a period in which parents take seriously the role of education in enabling children to progress beyond the achievements of their parents, teachers should have less rather than more prestige, standing, and respect. Yet that appears to be the case. No longer, if contemporary accounts are to be believed, does a child fear to bring home an unfavorable report from the teacher; the teacher, not the child, is automatically held to be at fault. Surely the record of physical assaults on teachers, bringing with it a cry for police protection inside the schools, is unprecedented. In part the new attitude follows a loss of belief in the importance of authority figures generally. In this sense, the century has indeed become the Century of the Common Man, who is believed to know better than the trained scientist or the specialist. Community activists are presumed to know more about the real dangers of nuclear power than the atomic physicists and nuclear engineers do, and parents know more about schools than teachers do.

Thanks to this view of authority, it seems that parents of the striving generation hope that education will unlock their children's future at a time when, according to public opinion polls, Americans have a much dimmer view of the future than they once held. *Unlock* is a word to be taken literally. Parents today do not believe that education trains the mind and prepares children to meet the future challenges of life. They think, rather, that there are some secrets that constitute the subject matter of education and that they are revealed or withheld according to the whim of the teacher. Why, therefore, should one respect the custodian whose good faith has not been established?

Unfortunately, this mistrust of the motives of the crucial teacher figure hurts more than the relationship between the teacher and the pupil in school. Traditionally in New York, especially during heavy flows of immigration, the teacher served as part of the Americanization and urbanization process for the parent as well as the pupil. Pupils carried home some of the information that their parents, who had been living in small rural villages or on plantations, needed to adapt to city life. What kinds of help might be available to them from private organizations, how to store food without spoiling in a tenement apartment, how to create a nutritious diet out of foods that were unfamiliar to new arrivals, how to obtain citizenship—these were the kinds of questions to which the answers were brought home before the questions themselves were formulated. The pattern of such education by children is described in numerous books about immigrant life in New York.

One of the complicating difficulties for black arrivals in New York is that they are treated like immigrants when in fact they are Americans of long standing, probably longer standing than many of those who talk about them as though they were immigrants. Naturally this labeling causes fierce resentment, as does the patent condescension that accompanies it. That the native-born black has perhaps eight or ten generations of American ancestors does not make the informal education into urban ways unnecessary, but his or her treatment as a greenhorn by New Yorkers with one generation of native-born ancestors does make more difficult the acceptance of the teacher as an instructor of the adult as well as of the child.

Families coming from southern villages in which they were members of an inferior caste—in which, often, they lived in a non-cash economy, having been staked to their necessities by the landowner whom they repaid with part of the season's crops—need to be educated in the rationing of cash so they will have what's necessary for major expenses that come due on a long cycle while their own receipts come in on a much shorter one. People who regulate their activities by the calendar or by the movement of the sun, as people do who live on farms, must become accustomed to the more arbitrary weekly differentiation of tasks and the tyranny of the clock. Ralph Ellison, in *Invisible Man*, catches this last feeling when he describes his protagonist, soon after arriving in New York from rural Alabama, feeling that the faces of the clocks were staring at him with disapproval because he was not moving fast enough.

If it were true that people adapted to the urban environment, or any other, without being carefully if unconsciously taught, it would not matter so much that the schoolteacher no longer has unquestioned authority. But it is not true that the teaching is not needed, nor is it true that the teacher still has the authority he or she once had.

The teacher's role as an informal educator is supplemented by that of the policeman. But to the American black migrant, he recalls the sheriffs of the South, who were enforcing a whole code of interracial conduct, the main purpose of which was to remind blacks of their inferior status, a lesson to be dinned in at every occasion, from the greeting to the departure. It is scarcely a surprise, then, that whether the minion of the law comes in a blue city uniform or the gray or khaki of a rural deputy sheriff, the black person recently arrived in the city expects the worst. All too often he has received it. Even in the New York City Police Department, which has made a conscientious effort to instill among all ranks an understanding of the necessity for equitable treatment of all people regardless of race, there are officers who vent their personal hostilities. Some officers, conscious of the higher crime rates among black males, believe themselves to be endangered at times when cooler reflection would rule out the use of deadly force. At least two major postwar riots by blacks broke out because of shootings by white policemen of black juveniles, one of whom was later shown not to have carried a weapon at all.

The basic estrangement between the white police and black males, particularly younger black males, has made impossible the spontaneous use of the nightstick as an immediate, well-understood measure for the control of petty offenses. A white policeman cannot tap a young black male with his stick without raising a host of memories that make the reaction serious rather than salutary, lasting rather than momentary. The charge of police brutality still raises black suspicions of the police and their motives, and there are still enough instances of clearly indefensible use of force, sometimes with fatal results, to give body to the complaints of blacks that the police are eternally out to "get" them.

At the same time, it has to be remembered that there is no

question that blacks commit the overwhelming majority of violent crimes in the city today and that police look for black offenders not necessarily because they are prejudiced but because the odds favor the assumption that certain types of offenses are committed by blacks. The difficulties and ambiguities of the situation were clarified starkly when a world-famous black photographer complained that he had been stopped and questioned about his identity by a white policeman. He charged, probably correctly, that the policeman would not have treated a white man in the same way. The incident, it turned out, took place at two o'clock in the morning on a side street off Park Avenue in the midtown area. The photographer was hurrying down the street, carrying several very expensive cameras and a large bag containing extra lenses and other equipment. Obviously the police officer did not recognize the photographer; he may never even have heard of him. He must have wondered whether a black man hurrying down a lonely street in the middle of the night with expensive camera equipment was not a sneak thief. One can also wonder how the famous photographer would feel if someone stole his equipment and if the thief, carrying it through the streets late at night, passed a police officer who did not bother to stop and ask him where he was going with all that expensive stuff.

These ambiguities are only somewhat dispelled when black officers, including black women, are added to the force, as the city has been making a serious effort to do since the Lindsay years. Koch, as mayor, has in fact appointed the city's first black police commissioner, Benjamin Ward, who was formerly in charge of the city's jail and penitentiary system. Black officers have never been charged with brutality toward a black suspect or prisoner resulting in death, but they are frequently accused, in general, of being hostile to blacks who behave in an obstreperous manner. Their accusers say that the black officers act aggressively toward blacks in order to solidify their relations with white fellow officers. It might also be true that, as police officers and blacks, they would like to teach appropriate standards of civility to others with whom they identify themselves and other people identify them. Which of these explanations is right in what case, and whether or not the fundamental charge against the black officers has any merit or not, there is little question that the educative function of the police officer on the streets of the city is not as effective as it was many years ago. It is sad that this should be true when the quality of police officers is generally higher than it was, the merit system for appointing them to the force is firmly in place, and the commanders are dedicated to racial fair play.

One process in which the New York City Police Department has not been so forthcoming as it might be is in the hearing of civilian complaints against the police. This issue came to life in 1966, when Mayor Lindsay sought to establish a review board on complaints that would be controlled by a civilian majority. There had been, and is now, a so-called Civilian Complaint Review Board. But the board has no members outside the police department. All complaints are investigated by police officers, and there is no actual hearing, no chance for the complainant and the officer to confront each other and hear the other's side of the story unless the investigating officer decides the complaint has merit. In the great majority of cases, investigating officers decide the opposite, and the charge is, in effect, dismissed without any explanation to the civilian who made it.

Mayor Lindsay attempted to replace this system with a civilian board, but that attempt was torpedoed by a clever move on the part of the Patrolmen's Benevolent Association, the police union. The Association got together enough signatures to place a City Charter amendment on the ballot. The amendment was worded in a somewhat confusing way, so that a "No" vote would permit the establishment of a review board controlled by civilians, while a "Yes" vote would forbid it. The strategy of the union seems to have rested on the theory that those opposed to civilians would study the matter carefully and vote "Yes," while those who wanted civilians would be less careful and also vote "Yes." Whether that theory accurately analyzed voter behavior, the fact remains that the civilian review board was handily defeated.

Although the Police Department is now forbidden by the charter to put civilians on the board, it is not forbidden to adopt procedures that might give greater satisfaction to complainants: letting them feel that they have had a fair hearing, letting them hear the police officer's defense, and giving them the reasons why their complaints are ultimately dismissed, if indeed they are. Probably the reason why the department has been reluctant to take this step is the opposition of the union. The union fears confrontation will expose its members to reprisals. In 1984 the first black police commissioner, Benjamin Ward, instituted new, better procedures.

Another set of informal instructors in urban ways in former times were the religious leaders. The churches over which they presided served as rallying points for those who shared the same religion and came from the same ethnic background. Their focus was, of course, religious and moral. While individual clerics interpreted morality in a strongly political and economic sense, standing up for causes that were not generally popular, most confined their preaching, like that of Calvin Coolidge's preacher, to being against sin. Among the exceptions (according to the biography *Rebel, Priest, and Prophet* by Stephen Bell) was Father Edward McGlynn, a Roman Catholic priest who was removed from his pulpit and later excommunicated because he dared to tell parishioners that they should support Henry George for mayor. George, author of *Progress and Poverty*, was a land tax reformer who championed the radical doctrine that if cities taxed the locational value of land instead of the value of the improvements put on it, they could raise enough money, without discouraging productive development of vacant land, to pay all the costs of government. Naturally, this doctrine was offensive to large landowners, who appealed to the church to muffle the priest. Years later, Father McGlynn was reinstated.

Most clerics tried to defend individual parishioners from mistreatment at the hands of the law or of more powerful citizens, but they generally subscribed to the theory that the best way for a newly arrived constituency to strengthen itself individually and collectively was by hard work, sobriety, good habits, and clean living. Generally speaking, they offered spiritual support for the values to which American society claimed to adhere, while most of them understood that no society ever completely fulfills its own moral expectations. In that sense, they were important parts of the informal educational network that made New York civilized.

The situation of the clergy today is very different. Its members tend to have a different view of the endless ethical conflict between group and individual rights and responsibilities. While the older clergy talked about individual responsibility, large sections of today's clergy think primarily about social responsibility. They seem to acquit individual people of doing wrong except when that involves not thinking properly about social problems in distant countries. It is not necessary to condone apartheid in South Africa to feel that how a white New Yorker treats black New Yorkers is a better measure of his or her moral stature than sending money to an organization dedicated to promoting American disinvestment in Pretoria. But the clergy, much of it, seems to take the opposite view. To judge by the remarks of the Reverend William Sloane Coffin of the Riverside Church (once known as the Rockefeller Church), it is far more important to think badly of South Africa than to comport oneself honorably toward one's neighbor. Indeed, it seems clear that if a neighbor thinks well of apartheid and sympathizes with the fear of white South Africans that the economy they put together will collapse under the pressure of migrants from other parts of Africa, one owes that neighbor no decency whatever. He is beyond the pale.

In the religious history of the city, like that of the entire Western world, there has been a tradition of support for those who defend themselves against threats to their life and safety. Exactly where one's right of self-defense begins and ends are the crucial questions for a truly religious appreciation of the problems of normal human conduct. Certainly, for the ordinary new arrival in a metropolitan city like New York, unfamiliar with the complexities of urban life and surrounded by people who wield far greater power and influence, the supreme moral questions involve how far one can go in using tactics that bear the onus of immorality. To say the least, the modern clergy offers very little help on this subject. If one listens only to their disquisitions on the maltreatment of minority racial groups, homosexuals, women, and the poor, it would seem that there are few unpardonable deeds in the advancement of the interests of such groups. The point is not that people fighting for a toehold in the urban conglomerate should be expected to live by the code of the educated, the wealthy, and the accepted. But neither should they be given to understand that nothing they do has moral significance because their position in life is so humble that no human responsibility attaches to them. That, it seems, is the true lesson preached by the modern clergy; it's the same lesson preached by the modern social worker, for the very good reason that both derive their ideas from the same Zeitgeist.

In the spring of 1984, the largest religious delegation ever to visit the Soviet Union was put together by the National Council of Churches. It went to investigate the condition of religion under the Soviet government and came back with the cheery message that religion was in fact thriving under the chilly auspices of a government that came to power with the pledge to exterminate religion. The evidence for the good health of religious sects was that there was a busy Jewish congregation in southern Russia, using textbooks and hymnals printed seventy-five or more years ago; that people did go to church and were excited by their Christian fellowship; and that church buildings were being preserved as evidence of the importance of the Russian past. The American church group made no apparent effort to learn how prisoners in the political work camps are given access to religious teachings, nor what the Russian government does with those men and women who refuse service in the armed forces because of religious scruples against taking human life. What, one must wonder, would have been their reaction to an American government that made so little provision for the safety of those who do not agree with the moral and religious principles of the white majority? How much help are people who follow the teachings of this body to those who want to find their way out of poverty—an effort that does require some individual and personal will, in which fortification by religious teaching has in the past been a source of strength?

Chapter X

What's Government for, Anyway?

ON A SUMMER EVENING, just as the sun is setting, the high buildings of lower Manhattan burst into the sky like the final extravaganza of a fireworks display as though rows and rows of rockets have exploded and miraculously become stone. A visitor from the West, seeing them, would be inclined to think of them as the work of individual entrepreneurs, scrambling for the best sites and the biggest buildings, risking credit and capital in the hope of more profit. The observation would be true only in part. The two tallest buildings that came to dominate the vista in the 1970s were not the work of private entrepreneurs, many of whom grumbled at the competition. They were erected by the Port Authority, to provide a haven for activities connected with world trade. When the buildings were opened, there were too few world traders looking for space to fill them, and they became instead a haven for the State of New York, which installed many of its offices in the buildings at bargain rates. They are a symbol of the encroachment of government activities into areas formerly not merely dominated but monopolized by private interests. In 1984, Mayor Koch, echoing previous statements by former Governor Carey, demanded that the World Trade Center be sold to private interests so that it would be fully taxable.

Yet a more careful view of even the privately built and operated office buildings of the city, the buildings that make Manhattan as shining (though partial) a representation of their age as reconstructed Carcassonne is of its, would reveal that the skyscrapers are not quite so exclusively the product of private enterprise as they appear. Up to the Second World War, the main purpose of municipal government was to contribute to the city's growth by encouraging the use of land for private development. Its primary mission was to be accomplished positively as well as negatively. On the positive side, it assumed the obligation of installing public facilities, such as streets, piers, water, sewage, and transport facilities that gave the land value. On the negative side, it stayed out of the way of developers, once having established minimal regulations guarding public health and safety.

Government also helped to create a climate of public opinion that encouraged risk-taking. Those who survived could expect not only to benefit financially from their success but to revel in the admiration of their fellow citizens. They could expect to move into the more exalted ranks of society and to open to their children opportunities that would be closed to those who did not risk and win. Perhaps one of the intellectual bequests of Marxism has been a general tendency to underrate the importance of nonmonetary benefits in motivating entrepreneurs to risk their money and their energies in productive schemes. A New York developer, one of a family noted for the apartment houses it has built and the skill and care with which they are managed, privately said in the mid-seventies that most of the family's business activity would henceforth be carried on in Boston and Atlanta. He explained that the market for their kind of construction in those cities was very good. Furthermore, he added, "When we come there to discuss our plans with city government, the mayor meets us at the airport, or if he can't make it, sends his car." In New York, he said, "the general impression is that my family and I are public enemies." The family had reached a point of financial success at which gold was worth less than a greeting.

New York city government, helped by bursts of energy from the state, which first helped the city grow (over its initial opposition) by sponsoring the Erie Canal, had been active since the early nineteenth century in what is now ponderously called economic development. DeWitt Clinton, as mayor, had the street pattern of Manhattan Island mapped, not to stimulate beauty nor to emphasize the majesty of government, as Major l'Enfant did in Washington, but simply to divide the city's land up so that it could more easily be sold to people who would then put structures on it. The lots that resulted, twenty-five feet wide and one hundred feet deep, in a rigid rectilinear pattern except for Broadway, which angles east and west on its general north and south course, have defied city planners since the end of the nineteenth century. They imposed a deep, narrow shape on buildings, so that providing adequate light and air was impossible. The obvious remedy came into governmental hands when the state constitution of 1938 offered cities the right to use the power of eminent domain to acquire land on which to build housing for people of low income. From that power came the superblock.

The superblock assembled sites for city housing and, later, slum clearance projects, without regard to the city blocks or the lot lines adopted in 1811. Free-standing apartment houses that were oriented to the sun instead of to the street lines became the basic site plan of public housing projects. It took only a few years after the invention of superblocks, however, for a new generation of city planners to discover virtue in the old 1811 mapping. The street, with its line of houses and shops, was found by younger planners to impose a needed symmetry and order on the urban vista. They argued that the physical frame of the street was necessary to give a sense of order to human experience. The free-standing, unaligned building breaks the street line and contributes to community disorganization. Once these criticisms had been aired, it became a little easier to understand that the plan of 1811, although it tried to flatten and make banal all the natural contours of the city's topography, was very successful in its basic intention of stimulating the growth of economic activity and development of the land. This message has not yet sunk in with those groups in New York (and elsewhere in the nation) who understand that economic growth is necessary to alleviate poverty and stimulate the emergence of the underclass of dependent people into the economic world, but who do not understand that economic growth inevitably requires the sacrifice of other values.

New York City's government throughout the period up to the Second World War was prepared to make that sacrifice. It built the streets without which all economic activity would have stopped. As buildings went higher into the air and the number of people working in them multiplied, city government took on the burden of making the streets strong enough to bear the increasingly heavy vehicles required to carry the larger work force and the goods they needed. The city built the docks and bulkheaded the river edges. It built sewage systems to drain the streets and take away household and industrial wastes. In doing so, it sacrificed the cleanliness of the harbor waters to discourage the spread of disease among the people—a perfectly rational decision that later generations found themselves in a position to modify. The municipality also created a water-supply system. It was allowed by the state to establish a Board of Water Supply directed by three appointees with lifetime tenure, a move that gave them freedom from political pressures. The result of their work was a municipal system that has become the envy of the world.

New York's city government recognized that civil peace was essential to economic activity. Even before the city had consolidated to form the five boroughs of today, it built up a metropolitan police force that took over its functions from pri-

vate agencies under the aegis of the state. It did the same with
the fire-fighting forces. It developed courts and jails. It built
almshouses and hospitals for the poor. (The almshouses were
criticized as inhumane institutions and were abandoned, but
the current cries for housing for the homeless suggest that a
revival of the almshouse may be around the corner.)

Under the state constitution, the city exempted religious and
educational institutions from taxation, because it felt that they
made a significant contribution to public order and public
preparation for productive work. For the same reasons, it early
established public education, including higher education. By
the end of the Second World War, its system of colleges was
most impressive and the record of their alumni spectacular. Its
park system, its highways, the airports that it started and later
conveyed to the Port Authority, all mark New York's government as active and progressive. Yet its eyes were firmly fixed
on economic growth as the necessity prerequisite to a generous
interest in the health and welfare of its needier residents.

New York City's government at the end of the war had
another advantage over that of most of the cities of the United
States. New York was genuinely a metropolitan city, combining
suburban districts with the central business district that they
surrounded. The implication of the union was that the families
whose income increased and who could be expected to move to
the suburbs would, instead, move to those parts of the city that
seemed suburban. They would continue to pay taxes to the
metropolitan city, and as their incomes and taxes increased,
they would make decreased demands for service. As more affluent citizens, they would be more able than the poor to exert
pressure for legislative aid for the city. They would give the city
a more diverse population of lower, upper, and middle-class
people than most cities have, with good effects on the public-
school population and on the political process.

No one believed, of course, that New York City's government
was perfect. To begin with, it was a one-party city. Customarily
it voted Democratic. True, Fiorello LaGuardia, a Republican

with Labor and City Fusion party support, had been elected to three terms as mayor, but the overwhelming majority of City Council members and of the other important elected officials were Democrats. At the war's end, Council members were elected by borough-wide proportional representation. In the 1930s, the reformers who pushed that procedure on their fellow citizens had considered differences in political party of supreme importance, far more decisive than differences in race or geographic districts. The system provided for two at-large Council members from each borough. They could not be members of the same party, but they could be members of the same race, and they were: white.

Without exploring the complicated consequences of the amended Voting Rights Act, which has given the Justice Department the right to overrule local government election districting, it seems apparent that the metropolitan nature of New York's government has been somehow out of step with the times. Just as in the early days of the United States there were population differences between the states, so were there wide differences in population totals among the five boroughs when the city was unified. Those differences had made unification difficult. Four years after the charter of 1898 was adopted, it was changed to provide that while the Board of Aldermen would generally reflect the differences in population between the boroughs, the city's Board of Estimate would not. The Constitution did not design Congress to reflect the population differences among the states. The Senate has two senators per state, even though the total population of Nevada may be smaller than a single congressional district in California. In the House, no matter what the disparity in the number of constituents involved, each state must have at least one representative. In deciding how the states may apportion themselves, however, the Supreme Court has ruled that the national Congress should set no precedent. One person, one vote is the rule. That decision has already removed New York's at-large Council members; it now threatens the present composition of its unusual corporate executive body, the Board of Estimate.

These changes are much more in tune with the current temper of the times. They emphasize the growing wish for decentralized government, a movement that, like environmentalism, sees the good but rarely calculates its cost. Obviously, also, they reflect the current illusion, fostered by amendments to the Voting Rights Act, that the federal government knows better than the voters how many members of minority groups should win office. The federal government is now authorized by law to try to assure its view of an election's preordained outcome by annulling the local legislature's work in apportionment under certain circumstances.

Most of the changes in New York government since 1946 reflect a trend away from metropolitan government in favor of local district independence—loosely called "community participation." Acts by such reform organizations as Citizens Union also helped undermine the metropolitan character of the city government. Originally, borough presidents had executive responsibilities in their boroughs. They were in charge of maintaining all thoroughfares but the crucial arterial highways. They had their own asphalt plants and employed sizable groups of laborers. Highway maintenance and other administrative chores not only kept them busy but gave them a patronage base with which they could hold on to a voting bloc. Party loyalty and mutual service were two much stronger elements of government than they are today, when "sunshine" laws exposing all government papers to public scrutiny and other institutions such as investigatory commissions make negotiation between political figures much more difficult. The borough presidents now have no trinkets to throw to their constituents, and they therefore cannot afford to support the mayor very often on matters that are unpopular with the people of their individual boroughs. The mayor also has fewer favors to grant. There is no independent political boss of the party—meaning the Democratic party—

who is able to command the loyalty of the borough president to the mayor. The nearest approximation of such a boss was Meade Esposito, the Brooklyn leader, who retired in 1983 after years in which he described himself as a legend in his own time and controlled enough votes by Brooklyn council members to force passage of unpopular but needed mayoral legislation enacted by the City Council. He was replaced as county leader by the borough president of Brooklyn, Howard Golden. Obviously, the borough president of Brooklyn will not often persuade himself to do things that are against his political interest in order that the mayor may look better to posterity. In Queens as well, the positions of borough president and county leader are held by one person, Donald Manes, with the same result. These are the two most populous boroughs in the city.

All of the above may simply be an extended way of saying that the central government of the city has lost its power to execute policy, because the voters now are more under the control of their television screens than of a block captain. The block captains are still there, reporting to the district leaders while they keep their own political ambitions glowing. The district leaders are connected, like dry bones, to the county leader. But the whole apparatus is more valuable in promoting the election of candidates for offices so minor that television ignores them. And there really is more to the matter. It turns out that the basic principles of metropolitan government have been undermined by a growing lack of certainty over just what it is that local government is intended to accomplish.

The faith in metropolitan government that burned in a pure white flame among students of public administration after the war was based on the theory that the flight to the suburbs was destroying the economy of the central city. Certainly the flight did not help, but it is clear now that the problems of the new, largely black population were much more important. Moreover, those problems related to race were far more intractable than anyone but incurable pessimists had assumed them to be. The widening difference, not between the white and black worlds as set down in the Kerner commission report but between those in the black world who have become part of the American economy (though not yet of its polity) and those who seem to be forever mired in dependency, addiction, and family disorganization, has demanded the urgent attention of the municipal government.

Acknowledging that economic development is essential to replace dying industries and lost jobs, municipal government wants desperately to stimulate job growth. And the moment it does so by offering relief from the burden of real property taxes, primarily on the improvements like factory buildings that the city wants new industries to build, it comes under the fire of those who argue that the city is giving away tax revenues to provide jobs for people who live in the suburbs and don't really need them anyway. This dispute simply emphasizes that those who are trained and psychologically ready for office jobs get them; blacks on the wrong side of the widening gap do not. Then the city finds itself involved, as seems after all only fair, in preparing blacks who have never worked consistently to take their place in the work force. That's roughly what the city did quite informally for some of the underprepared white immigrants from abroad who preceded the present arrivals from the South by seventy-five or a hundred years.

One trouble turns out to be that the problems faced by the two groups are not the same, as we have noted. Dealing with the present problems is much more difficult and expensive, even after allowance is made for the changing values of the currency in which expenses are stated. And while the simple education and informal training given to European arrivals were not trumpeted as steps toward erasing monumental injustice, that is precisely how the situation is portrayed with respect to black Americans. The expectation that justice is to be done leads to a cruel hoax and frightening stupidities. Mayor Lindsay's Manpower Commissioner, a bright young black man, told a radio audience that he would not send a black applicant for a job in a concrete block factory or as a taxicab driver because these, he said, are "dead-end" jobs. That characterization would probably not apply to the cab drivers who have told over the years of their children becoming orthopedic surgeons. And if it is true that these are dead-end jobs, so also is the mayoralty of New York, except in the case of DeWitt Clinton, who, as we saw, went on to become governor. Would the commissioner not back a black man for mayor for this reason?

Furthermore, it turns out that the problems of the inner city are not necessarily simplified by the effort of keeping the middle class from fleeing to suburbia. Two factors that have encouraged the middle class to remain in the city are rent regulation whose impact on the housing problem we have already examined, and the hidden but very genuine real estate tax concessions on small houses. Every study of the taxable value of one- and two-family homes in the city outside Manhattan indicates that they are appraised at far below their market value. The practice of assessing apartment houses, especially elevator apartment houses, is altogether different. Small houses are valued at about 30 percent or less of market value; apartment houses with elevators at 80 percent or perhaps more. The discrepancy is complicated by the difficulty of estimating what the value of an apartment house really is when its rents are controlled by law. Should the building be valued after considering what it might rent for if the owner were free to ask whatever rents the market might bear? Or should it simply be valued on the basis of its actual rental income?

The result of the under-valuation usually means that the owner of a one-family house in Queens, located a hundred yards from the Nassau County line, pays about 30 percent of the taxes that a home owner pays for a similar house a hundred yards away, over the border in Nassau County. Homeowners are thus being bribed to stay in New York City. The bribery consists not only of tax breaks but of newer schools and the banning of changes that might have an adverse effect on their homes. That certainly does not mean that the city government meets all the wishes of residents in the semisuburban areas of the city. On the contrary, Queens residents can complain with justice about their crowded subways, their lack of sewers, the slowness of the city to clear their streets after a heavy snowfall, and a number of other issues. All together, these issues raise the question of the appropriate standard by which the city should be made to measure its services to those who live in the outlying sections. Should they be served at the level generally offered in the suburbs outside the city? Or are they entitled to all the services provided in the crowded central district, where taxes are higher and so are the dangers of contagion and fire that flourish under higher densities? Because no one wants to answer these questions, no one asks them.

The shift in the government's attention—from programs that naturally support economic growth to programs that help the unskilled prepare themselves to take the jobs that successful economic growth might produce—has been gradual. It coincides with the decline of the political organizations in New York City and the rise of reform Democrats. The reformers started out as young lawyers in the late 1940s or early 1950s; many of them are now senior judges on the more illustrious courts of New York City and New York State. A younger flight of reformers watched their younger children enter college in the fall of 1984. The first batch consisted of people who not unnaturally, considering their law background, wanted to get into politics. They were stimulated by two events. The first of these was the Kefauver television hearings of 1948. The second was the Stevenson candidacy for president in 1952.

The two events were very different in their nature and their effects both on the reform movement and on public opinion generally. The same differences make up part of the continuing contradictions in reform Democratic policy. The Kefauver hearings were intended to expose the ties between big city politics and organized crime. They were an exercise in expressing the ideology of good government for its own sake and reached one peak in public excitement when Senator Charles Tobey asked why the cities could not hang a leper's bell around people taken to be racketeers and follow them through the streets crying, "Unclean, unclean!" Presumably the senator was referring to the racketeers and not the streets themselves. The second highlight was the picture of faceless Frank Costello's fingers, tapping on the arm of his chair as he testified; his face was kept off camera at his request, a decision that merely enforced his image as a mysterious figure with ties to organized crime and Tammany Hall. In fact, there was little or no evidence to suggest that New York City government did in fact have major ties to organized crime.

There were—and always have been—ties between specific people in the police department and crimes that the public prefers to be hypocritical about, usually with good reason. These include gambling and prostitution. Stamping out such crimes is not only impossible but also not particularly desirable because of the massive invasion of privacy that would entail. What one wants is to avoid staining the public scene with them, giving the young and impressionable (two different classes since the Second World War) the impression that the body politic is indifferent to them. Society can live with these weaknesses—it has done so for centuries—but if they were officially allowed to exist, government would have to tax them and allow those who profit from them to demand major concessions in regulation and enforcement by the legislature. That has been the result of legalizing vice in other states.

New York has suffered from an unknown amount of bribery; the challenge it poses is to develop a government efficient enough to make "honest" bribery unnecessary. Municipal government can eliminate graft only by finding a moral equivalent for it. Graft is an important safety valve against the possibility of ineffective government. If a government is weak enough, the official who takes graft and accomplishes something in return can be a hero. Of course, one would prefer that the official act from nobler motives and refuse to accept money in return, but in desperate situations, one does not look for motives but for whatever escape one can find.

In a government as good as New York's has been, much graft is of a minor, rather benign sort. It is the price the body politic pays for its inability to achieve what the payer of graft achieves instantly. The payer draws attention from the general rule to his or her individual case. That is what an ombudsman is expected to do but is far too busy to accomplish. Graft becomes possible when the general rule applies unwisely to a specific case, or the time involved in taking a formal appeal is unjustified. New Yorkers have traditionally paid graft to building inspectors. The inspector takes a certain risk in acceding to a violation of the standard rules and is paid for taking that risk. But it's a rare inspector who would overlook a truly dangerous condition and approve it. Of course, there's the danger that the inspector may judge wrongly and approve something that is not in fact harmless.

There's also the damnably corrupting effect of money; the person who takes it becomes a little less ready the next time to resist an offer that he or she knows should be resisted.

That, of course, is the same old slippery slope of public morality that even people who do not accept money for favors have been observed to slide on. The legislator who wins favor for sponsoring a bit of popular but wasteful legislation—perhaps imposing a condition on the electric light company or the landlord that neither can readily meet and that is expensive to comply with—finds it a little easier to sponsor still more wasteful legislation after hearing his praises sung for his first indiscretion.

Good Government, with capital G's, is not necessarily good government in the sense that it does well and quickly those things which it can and should do well and quickly. Government that attends too much to the proprieties accomplishes too little, a statement that does nothing whatever to clarify what too much propriety really is.

In any case, when the reform Democrats wandered into established Democratic clubhouses in 1952 and offered their service to help get Adlai Stevenson elected, they found themselves confronting older men and women who looked at them suspiciously. "Are you one of them Volunteers for Stevenson?" they were asked, and the implication was quite clear. The clubhouse types did not want to get involved in national politics unless the top of the ticket were certain to help the state assembly candidate whose name appeared at the bottom. Most of them were probably going to vote for Eisenhower anyway. The volunteers and future reform Democrats really did not know what Stevenson stood for—in retrospect, what did he stand for, other than good diction and a meritorious education?—but Stevenson pushed them toward a more substantive view of politics and local government. It was not until much later that the reformers discovered that what they really wanted was to make their way into public office, an impossibility so long as the suspicious old clubhouse types were still in power. When the reformers themselves finally achieved power, they were just as tough on their adversaries as their adversaries had been on them.

What it took even longer for the reformers to recognize was that when it came to actual programs, there was very little difference between their program and that of the Democratic regulars. Both groups favored rent control. Both were opposed to new highways cutting through their terrain. Both tended to oppose public housing, unless it was in another section of the city or catered to old people. Both wanted frozen fares on public transportation, less-crowded subways, better schools, and cleaner streets. Neither group cared much about taxes, because their constituents were for the most part renters, who thought of federal income taxes and not real property taxes when the word came up. There might have been some difference between the two groups on the question of race. The reformers were much more outspoken, long before the decade of the 1960s, in their advocacy of rights for black people, but it was the City Council's majority leader, a bibulous regular named Joseph Sharkey, who with two colleagues got the Council to pass a bill forbidding housing discrimination on the basis of race and religion. It was Tammany Hall, the very bastion of Democratic regularity, that first elected a black leader for New York County, J. Raymond Jones, and it was the regulars who voted in the first black borough president of Manhattan, Hulan Jack. As a mayoral assistant said, the only real difference between the reformers and the regulars is this: When the regulars vote against something unpopular that the city needs, they feel guilty and they know they owe you one. Usually they pay. When the reformers vote against something the city needs, they think they've stood up for the people against corrupt government, and you owe them one. You always pay.

One subject on which the two groups agreed was Robert Moses, who left a bigger, more constructive, and, naturally, more maligned mark on New York City than anyone else in its history. Moses was the last successful practitioner of what had been the city's fundamental strategy of economic growth. He was totally without ideology, except for a basic belief that the whole was bigger and more important than the sum of its parts. He had been associated with Governor Alfred E. Smith in Albany in the 1920s and was called on by Mayor LaGuardia to restore the city's park system in the depression of the 1930s. He combined federal, city, state, and who knows what other money, who knows how, and cleaned up the park system with the largest work force the parks had ever seen. He built the suburban parks, including such treasures as Jones Beach, and the less-well-known Riis Park within the city limits on the Rockaway peninsula, which juts out into the Atlantic. His highways gave New York a matchless road system, although even it jams up on summer holidays. He built the Long Island Expressway, which helped make Nassau and Suffolk counties the busy and prosperous places they became. He was in charge of the New York State Power Authority when the St. Lawrence Seaway was built. He insisted on building up the hydropower resources of the St. Lawrence River at a time when no one believed there was a need for the surplus supply. It is now the cheapest power available to the people of New York.

Moses was never elected to any office. The one time he did

run, as a Republican against Herbert Lehman in the 1930s, he destroyed his own campaign with his first speech. He attacked Lehman, regarded by the Jews of New York as the nearest thing to a saint that their religion would tolerate. Since Moses himself was at least partly Jewish in ancestry and never identified himself in any way with the Jewish community, the breach of ethnic ethics was fatal. He was denounced on that and many other occasions as arrogant, dictatorial, imperious—in short, unbearable. He was all of those things. He was also courteous to a fault with the aged and charming with children. He removed his hat in elevators when any female person entered, regardless of age, race, or previous condition of servitude.

Moses held and wielded power to carry out the plans he thought essential to the city's future. Since he was, in effect, unelectable, he held a long list of offices by making himself essential to the governors, mayors and others who appointed him. His language was scathing, and his appetite for acquiescence by others was limitless. He had no patience with fools, a category that included everyone who disagreed with him, not without a certain justice. Those who yelled back at him and had something to say were treated with grudging respect in which a certain genuine affection was concealed. To lunch with him and his staff on Randall's Island, the headquarters of the Triborough Bridge and Tunnel Authority, which he ran for years, was a treat for those who respected him. The meals were incredible in quantity and variety. He liked his guests to drink with him before lunch, and his stories of the socialites of Long Island were inexhaustible; he seemed to regard the very rich estate owners whom he talked into giving him rights of way and magnificent trees as his wards, children whom he alone could keep from accidental self-destruction, the inevitable result of their soft upbringing.

The mayors and governors called on him to solve problems that no one else could; they both loved and detested him, because they could not get along without him. A great regret among those who knew both Moses and Edward I. Koch is that they never had a chance to interact. It would have been quite a spectacle.

Koch was originally a reform Democrat from Greenwich Village, one of the group for whom Robert Moses sat in the number one seat on the sinners' bench, next to Carmine DeSapio, the Tammany Hall leader with the sinister dark glasses (he suffered from conjunctivitis). Automobile ownership is low in New York City, a statement that must be tempered with the knowledge that since the city is very large, the low rate of ownership nevertheless permits an extraordinarily large number of cars. Reform Democrats in those days—we are now in the early 1960s —lived in Manhattan. Few owned cars; Koch bragged that he did not even drive and that the whole road network was to him as foreign as kielbasa. He accused Moses of bulldozing communities, not really an unfair accusation if both parties could agree on what, exactly, constitutes a community. In later days, Congressman Koch was strongly opposed to Westway, the elaborate offshore highway designed to complete the interstate highway system in New York City without impinging on Greenwich Village and Chelsea, two sections of Manhattan along the Hudson River shore. Koch may not have known that Robert Moses was also opposed to Westway. Their reasons, however, were somewhat different. Until he changed his mind to help Governor Carey hold down the subway fare, Koch argued that Westway would cause havoc in Greenwich Village and stimulate real estate developers to change the type of housing there. Moses objected to Westway because, he felt, it was grossly extravagant in its efforts to spare the Village by the use of an offshore tunnel that would make it the most expensive highway, mile for mile, ever built in the United States.

What finally clipped Moses's power was the same burgeoning "nicety" of the elites, the spreading feeling that the body politic as a whole had forfeited the right to interfere drastically in the lives of individual people and families. More crudely, television brought Moses down. It had been his slogan that you can't make omelets without breaking eggs. In his halcyon days, both omelets and eggs were abstract and unreal. When television arrived, it could not show its viewers the omelet—the finished highway, the glorious beach, the spectacular park. It lay off in the distant future, slowly solidifying. But it could show the broken eggs—the crying mothers watching bulldozers crush their homes, the torn-up trees, the non-English-speaking family with their meager belongings, wailing through an interpreter that their apartment had just been flattened and they had nowhere to go: those broken eggs were all over every living room carpet in the city. Moses first lost the newspaper editorialists, and then he lost his political leverage. His sharp tongue was blunted when it was inadequately reported. The Sunday magazine sections began to print Moses's fancy but pallid literary criticism—Sean O'Casey was one of his favorites—instead of his thumping denunciations of city planners and critics who never drove a car.

His fall was hastened by his involvement in housing as chairman of the Mayor's Committee on Slum Clearance. The committee's name was unfortunate. Its role was to use federal money to bulldoze dilapidated sections of the city that yet had residual value and to offer the land to builders who would pay bargain prices and replace the worn-out buildings with new and better ones. The first mistake was to call a place in which people were living a "slum." They did not like it and objected strenuously. Then Moses had the idea that he would not clear land or even have the city acquire it until he had his personally selected builder all ready to buy it and start work. This horrified the good-government people who had previously been his strongest supporters. They wanted him to obey state law and hold an auction, selling the land to the highest bidder. Moses protested that he did hold auctions, but that if a second bidder ever showed up, he would call the auction off. History has proved Moses absolutely right in this matter; his method avoided the sad, empty spaces common to other cities that acquired land and razed buildings, only to find that no one wanted to build on what they had cleared.

Years later, Moses in all seriousness unveiled for friends and associates his housing master plan. He wanted the city to acquire a square mile of vacant land, put up housing on it, and then relocate from the heart of Brooklyn's slums everyone living on a specific square mile, moving them into the new buildings. Then the city would bulldoze the area in which they had been living, put up a square mile of housing, relocate everyone from another square mile, and so on. A return to reading oxen entrails in Times Square would have been equally incongruous in the 1970s, but hardly more so. Moses wanted to help people —he seemed quite without prejudice in race or color—but he did not see people quite as clearly when they were out from behind their windshields.

Moses's lifelong doggedness in pursuit of goals that he knew the people wanted made his last years reverberate with angry criticism from people who had no knowledge of the times of which they were writing, little understanding of the techniques of road and bridge construction or of municipal finance, and a phobia on the subject of political and governmental power. Robert Caro is the outstanding example of this kind of criticism. The first few hundred pages of his book on Moses, *The Power Broker* (if there was anything that Moses was not it was a broker for someone else's interests), demonstrate a magnificent understanding of Moses's interest in nature, recreation, and conservation. But Caro simply uses these glorious pages to set off the later, power-mad Moses, whom he grossly maligns and misunderstands. It would be too bad if the Caro portrait were the last word on Moses. For a long time to come, Moses will be the last embodiment of the ability to accomplish difficult projects on the municipal scene. Following in Caro's footsteps, people denounce him as an arrogant dictator for trying to satisfy the public demand for freedom to move with the magic of the modern automobile. Yet they do not think of themselves as dictators for trying to impose their contrary will on the people's desires.

Chapter XI

A Wealth of Ideas

IN CULTURAL MATTERS, the popular prewar view was that Boston was straitlaced, Philadelphia senescent, and New York not serious. Boston was known for its symphony and for clubs with strange names like Athenæum—if, indeed, it was a club in Boston. Philadelphia reached its cultural high with Benjamin Franklin and the framing of the Constitution. It had a brief resurgence when Thomas Eakins painted someone rowing on one of its rivers, and then, in New York eyes, it went back to sleep forever. New York had Broadway, the Algonquin, and *Partisan Review,* the Smart Set of the Left.

The best feature of the live theater in the United States was the difficulty it had in trying to take itself seriously. Many of its playwrights cried over the emphasis on commercialization that, they claimed, prevented them from bringing forth their most important work. They cried, as the old saying goes, all the way to the bank.

New York in the prewar years had other cultural institutions besides the Broadway stage, but out-of-towners knew little about them. It had at least one great university, two world famous cultural institutions, the Metropolitan Museum of Art and the Metropolitan Opera Company, no connection between them, and some art galleries. As a city it was engaged in a constant tussle with its past, made more combative than the similar tussles of other cities that had been fed by a smaller stream of immigration. In the ninety years between 1850 and 1940, New York's population was always made up in large part of foreign-born adults who had no recollection of that past and who naturally preferred to concentrate on the future. As the stream of new immigrants from abroad diminished, the population of the city increasingly was composed of people with a New York past. Recognizing that the changes in the city's racial composition and structural texture was not always welcome, many very ordinary people followed the lead of the elites in supporting a movement to preserve the physical remains of the past. Landmark preservation became an important activity, for which the city established a special agency. It soon discovered that much of its supporting constituency was more interested in slowing the pace of change than in preserving past beauties for their own sake. For the elites, however, deference to the past became intertwined with other aspects of the movement to make New York the cultural capital of the world, a goal to which commercial and industrial development was expected to defer, and in many cases had to.

The upsurge in cultural interests in New York in the postwar years was expected by many in leadership positions to be an omen of the city's future growth in importance. It led to such phenomena as the construction of the Lincoln Center for the Performing Arts, when other cities were building domed football and baseball stadiums. It produced a startling proliferation of art galleries and auction houses, attended by a steadily growing and steadily more affluent crowd. Music busted out all over the city, filling concert and recital halls; two major and many minor auditoriums housed opera and operetta companies. Even the sidewalks were used for impromptu concerts. Art museums grew in size and in the number of people who attended them, although attendance was not necessarily a reliable indicator of a deepening interest in art itself. Beginning in the Viet Nam years, many of the young who thronged the Whitney Museum of American Art, in its new headquarters, were clearly there to make love, not Warhol.

The first cause of this cultural spring was the European turmoil that began with the Russian Revolution and continued with the rise of fascism and Nazism, followed by the war itself. Performing artists like Toscanini, Bruno Walter, George Balanchine, and Rudolf Serkin; painters like Hans Hoffman, the "founder" of abstract expressionism; composers like Bela Bartok; poets like W.H. Auden, and thousands of lesser lights in all fields except the stage—Equity and other theater unions were too powerful—flourished in and around New York in the prewar and the war years, and stayed on afterward. Unlike previous artistic travelers, they had not come simply for the money or the fun of inspecting their cultural inferiors.

The presence of European artists in New York gave young Americans an alternative to the Paris years of a previous generation. Ultimately, the old habit of temporary self-imposed exile to the Boul' Mich' revived (it had never been lost to black writers, musicians, and dancers). But the revival of interest in Europe did not come until after New York had started to think of itself as the Paris of the New World, and artists started to move into loft buildings whose manufacturing tenants had left.

Another influence in raising New York's seriousness about its own culture was the arrival of the United Nations. That New York had been selected for the honor of becoming the capital of the new, almost–world government imposed obligations on the city to make itself worthy of its singular distinction. Not all New Yorkers welcomed the United Nations. Some felt that its major effect would be that a bunch of foreigners, with money cheerfully supplied by Uncle Sam, would compete for the notoriously scarce apartments for which New Yorkers themselves were already fighting. Some resented the amount of land that would become tax exempt. But, especially after the United Nations helped establish Israel, there would have been no way to keep the U.N. out, not even if more New Yorkers had visualized that in addition to the problem just mentioned, the U.N. people would disregard parking violations, enjoy diplomatic immunity for offenses for which New Yorkers of impeccable character paid a high price (breaking contracts, for example), and cost the city a fortune in overtime for police officers protecting dignitaries from assassination. The opposition of some New Yorkers to the location of the U.N. in their city stimulated other New Yorkers who supported its presence to form voluntary organizations, as well as an official municipal body, devoted to making the permanent civil servants and the foreign delegations feel at home. There's no way of judging exactly how much the U.N.'s presence—and the sound of foreign languages on Manhattan's East Side—contributed to the city's inflamed desire to become cultured, and quickly. But the effect must have been considerable, not only on culture but on cooking. In culinary terms, the city's postwar pastry course stretched from pizza to quiche to croissant.

Naturally, official and elite New York felt good about the growth of culture. Some of this was high-minded, in the sense that some genuinely felt that exposure to high art was first an essential and then an ennobling experience, without which life would be less rich for some, barren for others. Some, of course, loved art but loved just as much the opportunity to exercise their fund-raising and administrative skills in organizations that produced, supported, or displayed culture. Others frankly saw an opportunity to ennoble themselves through culture in ways different from the heightened perception and understanding that art critics promise. They saw art as an opportunity to launder money, or perhaps to de-launder it. Taking the monetary gains piled up through years of making or selling washing machines or crying towels, they built up collections—often magnificent ones—with the help of very good (and very expensive) advice, ultimately giving the collections to museums for display in rooms that would forever bear their own names. The same, of course, could be done with the lively arts, and it was. And there were also those who saw that the growing depth of

New York's cultural position would also help it commercially, just as the Tintorettos may have made Renaissance Venice seem a more trustworthy place to invest in trade because the local merchants who owned the fleets (and who sometimes, as Shakespeare would have it, lost their ships on "merchant-marring rocks") had good taste.

Finally, of course, there were those who felt that an increased appreciation of culture in New York would have a most salutary effect on the young attending the city's schools. Their civic pride would ignite their interest in their studies, enriching family life and lightening, one would hope, parental duties in disciplining children who might otherwise tend to neglect their studies.

Most New Yorkers, one may suppose, paid no attention to any of this. They were busy trying to earn a living in the new postwar world, some going back for professional educations in an effort to catch up with contemporaries who had not been in the army and navy. But art, not social problems, increasingly interested the leadership of the city, the families who set the pace, who presided over the banks, who owned the newspapers and broadcasting companies, and who sat on the boards of trustees of the leading universities, which, in turn, tended to be copied by other institutions of higher learning. These people— the overlapping elites of the city—contributed to the major cultural institutions and made the decisions, with the city government itself, that set New York City on its course. Increasingly that course was plotted to enhance, solidify, and expand its cultural institutions for the edification of its citizens, and for all the other reasons we have touched on, that course found support among other families of wealth.

In 1949, the federal government established a slum clearance program designed to assist the economies of older cities. Washington offered to subsidize the acquisition of deteriorated central city areas, so that their fading tax payments to the city could be expanded by the much greater taxes that would be levied on the new residential and commercial structures which

would replace what was there. Though New York had lived
with its characteristically shocking "Dead End" contrasts, one
of which had placed the Metropolitan Opera house from 1883
to 1966 in the midst of Seventh Avenue's dress factories, the
city took some of its federal slum clearance subsidies and used
them to create Lincoln Center, a wholly tax-exempt cultural
center into which moved the Metropolitan Opera House, along
with the New York Philharmonic orchestra, the Juilliard School
of Music, and a new noncommercial theater. Out went thousands of poor families. In a city with New York's long history
of concern for housing problems, Lincoln Center was a dramatic
example of the new importance attached to cultural matters by
the elite and, consequently, by municipal government itself.
Incidentally, when the Metropolitan Museum of Art wanted to
expand in the nineteenth century, it was given a site within
Central Park. When, in the late 1960s, the museum sought to
use more of the site than it had actually occupied in the past,
many New Yorkers objected to the displacement of trees the
expansion entailed. Trees, they pointed out, were God's cultural
artifacts, raising a point that had not been made about people
in the Lincoln Center site.

The only difficulty with the attention paid to cultural activity
on the postwar municipal agenda is that culture is not necessarily a socially constructive activity; or, perhaps more modestly,
it can be said better that culture, like most human activities, can
be overdone. The human relationships that move an audience
watching a play, or a reader with a novel in hand are, at best,
somewhat confusing in their relationship to life itself as well as
enlightening. They are necessarily distorted by the creative
mind that produced them. As Plato insisted, poetry is for similar
reasons seductively dangerous for the young. Music, like dance,
is or can be an intoxicating delight, but like other intoxicants,
it can produce a loss of equilibrium when overdone. It is important for society that creative artists "overdo" their involvement
with the arts, so that they become all the more productive. But
when people who are not truly artistic themselves "overdo"

their interest in art, allowing it to become a substitute reality, the result is not constructive at all; this theme has become an object of ridicule and scorn in literature through the ages. Two examples that come immediately to mind are Moliere's "les précieuses ridicules" and Gilbert's Bunthorne and his admiring maidens. When civic leadership begins to regard art and culture not as the source of enriched understanding of reality but as a substitute for it, ridicule serves a social purpose: one cannot afford to underestimate the extent to which nature imitates art.

We have referred to live theater as New York City's major and characteristic cultural endeavor. To glimpse some of the difficulties engendered for social policy by an oversensitive appetite for what the theater has to say about it, one might take a look at how the Broadway theater has dealt with the American race problem. In the hands of a great playwright, social problems become the igniting force for an examination of basic, recurring patterns of human existence. The incidents become generalized without losing their specificity. In the Broadway productions that we will examine, what happened was quite different. The problems of race never lost their specificity; they remained always and particularly the problems of white and black against a background of prejudice and invidious discrimination. Meanwhile, the characters involved in the situations never themselves achieved enough specificity to produce worthwhile generalizations. They remained stock characters in plays, never taking on the dimensions and shadings of life.

In any case, the Broadway theater did deal with the racial problem in the United States long before the general population was prepared to think about it as a moral dilemma. Its first efforts were to mimic black habits and language, perhaps condescendingly, perhaps sentimentally, but certainly with more respect than the minstrel shows and comic routines of an earlier day. *Green Pastures,* a big hit of the 1920s, was in effect a kindly, even a respectful version of such condescension. It elicited sympathetic interest in the blacks by describing their religious feelings in a way that made them resemble those of a child: sincere, but naive.

In 1927, *Show Boat,* one of the great successes of the New York musical stage, made its first appearance, to return many times thereafter. Set on a Mississippi floating theater, *Show Boat* inevitably caught the juxtaposition of the white and black castes in the South and the border states. It contained two pioneering episodes in the theater in its treatment of the black and white relationship, both depicting blacks in a serious and dignified manner. The first was the song "Ol' Man River," later associated with Paul Robeson. As sung in the show, "Ol' Man River" is a concise, manly statement of the difficulty of roustabout and longshoreman life, in this case almost exclusively the province of the black male. The pioneering aspect of the song was the intense masculinity and the great dignity that the song lent to the black singer.

The other unusual episode in the show (adapted from a novel by Edna Ferber) was the subsidiary love story between Julie, a partly black singer, so light-skinned that she passes for white, and a white actor in the show boat company. The story was a melodramatic but extraordinarily sympathetic view of miscegenation and an implicit attack on the inhumanity of laws outlawing marriage between the races. To say that this idea was ahead of its time would be a crude understatement: it was years before similar incidents were played again on Broadway. In *Show Boat,* the sheriff comes aboard, having heard that a black female and white male are cohabiting as man and wife. To protect them against the charge of illegal miscegenation, the white actor cuts Julie and, sucking her blood, claims that he has thereby become as black as she. To audiences of the 1920s especially, it was a stunning moment in the theater.

Another prewar play that was more of a throwback to the *Green Pastures* tradition was *Porgy,* by DuBose Heyward, the story of some poor blacks living in Charleston. The hero, a legless beggar on a cart pulled by a goat, is in love with a black woman who deserts him for a flashy wastrel. The play was an attempt to humanize blacks for a northern audience. A mark of the extent to which it succeeded is the fact that George and Ira Gershwin turned it into a folk opera, a genre they invented themselves. The blacks had not been humanized so much as super-humanized, like Carmen and Don Jose. Witty though the lyrics were, and charming, even moving, as were some of the sequences, it served not to turn the blacks of Charleston into recognizably human creatures of the same species as New Yorkers, but into exotics, no more real than the Athenian artisans of *A Midsummer Night's Dream.*

Nothing could more starkly contrast with *Porgy and Bess,* the Gershwin version of *Porgy,* than a virtually contemporary play, *They Shall Not Die.* Written by John Howard Lawson, whose Communist affiliations were widely discussed, the play was a dramatization, with liberties, of the Scottsboro case of the 1930s. The case involved a notorious and flagrant abuse of the rights of seven young blacks, riding a freight train in Alabama, who were ultimately conceded to have been framed by a southern sheriff for allegedly raping two white prostitutes who were riding the same train. The sheriff based his charges on perjury he suborned from both prostitutes. In Lawson's version, the seven young men are urged, by black clergymen who represent liberal interracial defense organizations, to confess to the crime they have not committed. Their lives, in the play, are ultimately saved by the sardonic brilliance of a white New York lawyer who is clearly a Communist. Since the basic facts of the false accusation of rape were true, the play cannot be described as a fantasy; yet its conclusion was at variance with the facts of a terrible episode in the racial history of the country. The play was not so much an effort to depict the plight of blacks in the southern United States at a time when they could not get justice, but rather to demonstrate that to alleviate their distress and provide justice for them, the liberal method was useless; the only hope for blacks in America lay in a radical restructuring of society, as personified by the Communist lawyer. Since the audience had to take it on faith that a Communist society would automatically extend justice to blacks, it cannot be argued that the play did in fact offer the solution that it claimed to be offering. That does not mean, however, that it was not extraordinarily suspenseful theater, very effective in arousing anger.

Another prewar play about the desperateness of the black situation was set in Chicago. *Native Son,* by Richard Wright, described the destruction of a lower-class black criminal who could find no place for himself in a society torn by racial animosity and hatred. Its moral ambiguity made it compelling in a very different way from Lawson's play. What it aroused in the audience was compassion for a character who in real life would have aroused little but fear and revulsion. As a "consciousness-raiser"—to use a phrase totally anachronistic to the time referred to—*Native Son* was singularly affecting when precisely such an effect was badly needed. A present-day revival would be almost out of the question; it would seem irrelevant to a problem for which compassion, however sincere, no longer offers a solution, or even a relevant response.

Similarly, postwar treatment of blacks in the Broadway theater consistently sought to inspire compassion for their situation in American life. It was no longer necessary to assure a New York audience that blacks were indeed human. The playwrights of the postwar period wanted the audience to appreciate fully how grievously the society afflicted blacks, and how that evil corrupted those who participated in mistreating them.

As in the case of *Show Boat,* one of the most effective bits of packaging for that message was provided, almost casually, in a musical comedy. *Call Me Mister* was a revue whose unifying theme was the readjustment of veterans of the Second World War to civilian life. In the midst of songs like "He was a bum before he went into the army," whose point was that he was still a bum after his discharge, and skits about the last G.I. left on a Pacific island after the end of the war, there came a number about the army's Red Ball Express. A black former G.I. recalls in song the Red Ball Express, the long line of trucks that sped across France to carry supplies, including gasoline, to the tanks and motorized units of General Patton's Third Army, which was racing for the German border. Blacks were excluded by army fiat from most combat formations of the American army and relegated to such support functions as truck driving. In effect, they *were* the Red Ball Express. As the singer, on a darkened stage, finishes his song, the lights come up enough to reveal that he is standing before a small wooden booth bearing a sign that reads "Hiring Office." A wicket is cut into the side of the booth facing the audience. There's a white man behind it. He has just nodded and shaken hands with the white man standing on line immediately ahead of the black singer. The white man, just hired, moves offstage. The hiring boss turns to the black singer and looks at him. Without a word, he shakes his head and pulls down a wooden shutter, closing the wicket. The black man turns to face the audience. Blackout.

More sensational, but equally determined (and probably somewhat successful in evoking compassion) was a play of the same period by d'Usseau and Gow, *Deep Are the Roots.* It dealt with a situation that strained credulity. The heroine, scion of a southern family, comes home, having been away during the war. She has fallen in love with a black man. Her father is a ranting southern racist who worries about the future of a world in which old racial barriers have broken down and the races are no longer socially segregated. He little dreams (the plot seems to make such rhetoric inevitable) that his own daughter is not only in love with but actually thinking of marrying a black man. Further ramifications of the plot are not germane. The crucial moment in the play is when the white girl passionately kisses her black man in full view of the audience. The audience invariably gasped as though it were on a roller coaster. It was one thing to show a white man kissing a black woman, but even in relatively liberated New York City in 1946 it was quite another to see a white woman kiss a black man. That simple act unloosed all the repressed sexual attitudes toward dark-skinned people. It would be stretching a point to call this drama; it was, in effect, a mass psychological apperception test. The audience was invited to face its own lingering racism. Whether audiences actually did so, and felt guilt, or whether they simply blamed the playwrights for having taken advantage of them remains an unanswerable question. In any case, it would be impossible to prove that the play made interracial marriages more generally acceptable or that audiences were made more compassionate by actually seeing her embrace the black man. It seems more likely that the audience would have felt greater compassion for her misfortune in the selection of a father than for her progressivism in the selection of a possible husband. For those who insist on knowing how the story ends, let it be recorded that the two recognize that society is not yet ready for them and do not marry. The final scene of *Tristan and Iseult* is somewhat more moving.

Finally, as the theater's gift to racial consciousness-raising, there is the curious case of Arthur Laurents' *The Home of the Brave.* The main action of the play unfolds in a military hospital somewhere in the South Pacific near the end of the Second World War. A soldier cannot walk; his affliction is diagnosed as psychological. The sympathetic military psychiatrist discovers that the soldier is Jewish, and by hypnosis or the use of a narcotic drug (one cannot help but run out of details) he manages to elicit from the soldier that he became paralyzed after his Christian buddy was shot, when his first thought was, "Thank God it's him and not me." He then feels guilty about this reaction, because he ascribes it to the fact that he is Jewish, the other man gentile. The doctor explains that that is no reason for guilt. The reaction of gratitude that it is your friend who was killed, not you, is a perfectly normal, natural human reaction, exacerbated in his case by the displays of prejudice and dislike of his Jewishness by other soldiers.

What has this to do with the theater and its interest in black-white relationships? Nothing, really, except that when *The Home of the Brave* was made into a movie, the Jew was made into a black.

The facility of that transfiguration is a vulgar but effective key to the limitations of culture or art as a medium for examining the problems of race and politics. Carl Foreman, the writer who performed the transracial surgery, may have thought that the substitution of a black for a Jew deepened the significance of the social comment of the play. At the same time, however, it testified mutely to his belief that there is no significant difference between the black and the Jewish experience in America. One might as well say that there is no significant difference between Hamlet and Macbeth except that one lived in Denmark and the other in Scotland. In short, in its effect on the public view of social problems as large as the American race problem, the theater is of help only in arousing sympathy. It not only does not matter very much whether the sympathy is aroused by the treatment of the Jew or the black, or whether some other minority—homosexuals, American Indians, poor whites, or even a mistreated majority, women—is the subject of the play. All these plays can do is make the audience leave the theater with the feeling that the treatment of minorities is bad, and that it's important to feel that it is bad.

Since New York's cultural world is largely an elitist audience much of which is involved in politics and civic work, making the city a center of theatrical entertainment may strengthen a misleadingly simpleminded view that a serious and venerable American social problem is to be solved by good feelings without any knowledge of the specific facts of the specific issues. A bright child might see an operetta about a fabulous kingdom in a part of the world that once was the Austro-Hungarian Empire and might leave the theater wondering why in the real world the problems of Austria-Hungary could not have been solved by the same music heard in the operetta. But many adults have become so habituated to the theater that they continue to believe, without bothering to think about it, that the marvelous surge of righteous self-admiration with which they set themselves above the portrayed villains of the bigoted South is actually the way to ridding the world of the effects of invidious discrimination.

What the theater has done for New York City is not only to encourage an out-of-town couple to stay an extra night to take in the hit show that everyone in Chagrin Falls is talking about. It also made New York an important radio and then television center, though in the long run the city lost out to the West Coast. It also made it an advertising center, a publishing center, a place where words seemed of the same order of reality as granite and potatoes.

New Yorkers who are employed in the lively arts have no illusion that the magic of the theater is the triumph of truth; they know it is the triumph of illusion. Unfortunately, they begin to believe that the real world is also illusory, so that what works on stage should also work in real life, and ideas in the theater—such as the victory of good over evil and the essential fine nature of man—might apply as well to real life. In the theater, good can often be distinguished from evil as easily as the pugilist wearing black trunks can be distinguished from the one wearing white. The essential nature of man seems as easy to discover and describe in commercial theater as a peach pit.

In postwar New York City, the cultural heights of serious drama were infrequently climbed. That was a blessing. As the years passed, serious dramatists turned their attention from social problems, like the racial situations in the early postwar plays, and focused instead on abstract but weighty examinations of the order of reality, rendered in symbols whose true points of reference were deliberately obscure. One thinks of the ambiguities of *The Iceman Cometh* or *Waiting for Godot* or *Venus Observed* or *Rosencrantz and Guildenstern*. Whatever their authors were saying, if there was a whatever, its meaning could never be settled. The pith for most of the audience was that there is no such thing as meaning, a conclusion that can have deadly impact on the moral bearings of the community. If nothing has meaning, then nothing is wrong but interference with what others choose to do. Thus, among much of the older aristocracy of New York, a city in which it was not always necessary to

have inherited money or position in order to become an aristo-
crat, a moral framework for social behavior was coming apart
like lattice secured by rusted nails. That description did not
apply to all the old money and the old leadership, but to part
of it; and to much of the aging leadership, and to some of the
new leadership, it did apply very broadly.

All of this questioning of the reality of meaning reached its
apogee in the postwar period in New York City in the disci-
plines of painting and, perhaps less important in New York,
sculpture. Although the rest of the nation associated New York
with the theater, because no other American city had anything
like the Broadway phenomenon, the characteristic art of the
postwar period, reflecting and shaping the leadership mentality
of the city, was abstract expressionism. Galleries and auctions
attracted tremendous crowds. Special exhibits at the Metropolitan were overwhelmed to the point where tickets were sold out
months ahead of time and the crush was like that in the subway
at rush hour.

Art had also become a well-accepted form of investment,
indeed a very lucrative one. The ability to select a painter whose
work would ride the crest of the next wave of collector interest
was worth, literally, millions. Since art was so valuable to both
the collector and the painter, new waves of style rose with the
regularity of giant combers on the coast of Hilo. Abstract Expressionism made its millionaires, followed by Jackson Pollock's action painting, Pop Art, Op Art, Minimalism, art that
burst from the frame—the list is practically endless. It was
apparent that many contemporary artists no longer sought what
older artists had thought of as beauty; the very word now
sounded as vulgar as crackerjacks. Inevitably, the paintings
looked as though they must have a meaning, a curious, modern
form of iconography made up of vocabularies as numerous as
the painters themselves. But the meanings defied explication.
The more the critics or the artists themselves tried to explain
what their meaning was, the more elusive it became. Detached
from natural objects except when natural objects, such as rub-

ber tires and minimalist planks, were themselves part of the palette, this art could not be taken seriously by its collectors unless they were willing to forswear any precise definition of the meaning that the unusual character of each new painting seemed bulging to express.

It would surely be overreaching to suggest that the spirit of nonobjective art forced New York into its financial difficulties of 1975, or that it continues to hold before the city the specter of other severe difficulties that it may face in the future. But it is not overreaching to suggest that when the institutional leaders of the city make modern painting and sculpture their most prized art form, and when they devote as much time, intelligence, and, not least, money to its pursuit as the New York leaders of the postwar world have done, they demonstrate a set of values that endangers those needed to keep an urban polity on a firm, reasonable, and safe course.

To manage public affairs it is necessary to believe in their importance. It is impossible to believe that decisions about public courses of action are important unless one believes also in the ethical significance of what appear to be the minor distinctions between one course of public conduct and another. Ethical significance in the public sphere is also dependent on the understanding of the relationship between facts and values, enabling government officials to decide how major principles must be shaded so that their enactment becomes possible. Accepting as a form of high and serious art an arrangement of colors and shapes that has no relationship at all to objects of the world outside the canvas inferentially denies the value and importance of understanding the relationships between those objects and the observer. It offers the viewer instead spatial relationships that relate the paints (and sometimes, the objects used as paints) to each other within the canvas and nowhere else. It is, of course, true that sympathetic critics of nonobjective art ascribe meaning in portentous statements that the intracanvas artifacts allegedly express. Unfortunately, real life cannot survive on portentous statements; it requires the knowledge that iron is hard, and exactly how hard, and how much harder it is than flesh. It is the value of precisely such discrimination that the canons of nonobjective art proscribe.

The image of New York as the world's cultural center built up gradually over the mayoralities of the six men who governed it during the postwar years. A dedication to seeing that no sick person was allowed to lie untreated became, by the mid-1970s, a "commitment" to closing one's eyes to the real differences between individual people. A new spirit of egalitarianism swept through the city. The process cutting commitments to fit the available resources was eliminated as elitist and inhumane. It did not matter much whether the subject was serious or trivial. The *New York Times* revised its traditional style book, advising its writers that henceforth all males mentioned in news stories were to be referred to with the honorific *Mr.*, even if they were convicted criminals, except for a few who had been found guilty of extraordinarily heinous (undefined) offenses. At the other end of the spectrum, universities of high academic reputation tumbled all over each other to admit a certain number of students with aptitude scores far below the minimum that had been found over the years to identify students able to study successfully at the college level. There was only one other requirement: the student had to be black and from a lower-class family background. Most of the students admitted under such perverse criteria suffered through a year or two of academic life and many became involved in protests against racism that were all too easy to explain as the natural reflex to their own unhappiness and sense of worthlessness. Many dropped out and, one imagines, have been paying the price of wounded self-esteem for the university's rather slavish adherence to what seemed the spirit of the Chinese Cultural Revolution in American terms.

It would be a tragic mistake to believe that the only victims of a culture-oriented civilization were those of racial distinctions. Just as the police sergeants' examination, specially tai-

lored under court supervision to eliminate cultural bias, turned
out to pass a far higher percentage of white than of black
applicants for police promotion, so, as we have seen, the fire
department entrance examination was altered, on orders from
a judge, because women could not pass the physical strength
tests. If one cannot lower the water, one must raise the bridge.

The costs of this attempt to overlook, ignore, or override real
differences were high. It was not so much a question of the
direct costs, which were sometimes difficult to establish.
Rather, the heavier cost was in the indirect costs—the loss of
efficiency and the loss of morale. It's only a short step from the
realization that merit can be overruled by social policy to the
recognition that performance can be obliterated by egalitarianism. Once the courts had decided that minority promotions that
fell short of proportional representation of minority groups in
the general population were evidence of invidious discrimination, they had to rule that older standards of fair dealing and
contract equity must be replaced by new standards. Never mind
what the contract says, the courts began ruling in the 1970s, the
question is whether it affects blacks and women more adversely
than it affects whites and men. If such a trend were to continue
over the years, the list of hampered groups would inevitably
grow longer and longer. Certainly efficiency and productivity
would become less and less crucial to jobholding, and ultimately the cost of everything in the economy would go up.

For a city—New York, for example—a tremendous cost of
the egalitarian spirit of the times was the cost of bribes to the
nonbenefited minorities. Without them, civil peace would have
been difficult to maintain, or as New Yorkers are still saying,
"Our city will become a refuge only for the very rich and the
very poor." We have already seen some of the programs that
were developed for good social reasons and then distorted to
confirm the middle-class view that government should treat
them as well as it treats the low-income population. At the
same time, the benefits had to be concealed behind a language
screen of universality, or they would have undermined the

usefulness of the egalitarian programs intended to satisfy the elitist urge to give help, constructive or not, to the victims.

The New York programs that balanced help to the poor included the impressive middle-income housing program already discussed, the institution of rent control as expanded to include newer apartment houses, the large school construction program, the generous pension and other benefits given on a large scale to municipal employees, and a host of building and improvement programs intended to improve the amenities of middle-class neighborhoods. There were others, too numerous to list separately.

Meanwhile, the leadership elite of Manhattan got a much smaller slice, but it was studded with raisins. The elites got, of course, the conscience-relieving programs of aid and comfort to the poor, coupled with the refreshing understanding that distinctions were no longer to be made in the cold, inhuman way they had been made in the past. They got a landmark preservation program, and they got a budget of financial aid for the cultural institutions to which so many members of this group dedicated a large part of their time and hearts.

No one noticed that this was expensive; no one noticed that the ability of the city to produce wealth had dwindled and that a serious gap had developed between what the city had to do and what it had to do that with. In 1975, out of the blue, the richest city in the world suddenly became one of the poorest.

Chapter XII

Down for the Count

IN NEW YORK CITY, the music stopped in February 1975.

Actually, the momentum carried the dancers on for a few extra pirouettes, because they were so intent on finishing the steps they had been choreographing over a long period of years that they simply did not notice the silence around them. Sponsors of middle-income housing continued to seek loans from the city government, although the bank account was nonexistent. Unions were continuing to talk of major raises. People at dinner parties continued to complain about the minimal decencies of civilized life that were still lacking, but their voices fell, the urgency was gone, and finally, after a few moments of silence, people started to ask friendly officials whether their city bonds would ever be paid off.

Clever officials, fearful of the consequences of misleading people about investments in which they were expected to have insider knowledge, told the truth. They said they did not know. It had been a great dance while it lasted, even without a Cinderella.

The episode that brought on New York's fiscal crisis has been discussed in detail, and very well, both by James Ring Adams in his articles in the *Wall Street Journal* and by Charles R. Morris in *The Cost of Good Intentions*. Those interested in further details can find what they want, and probably a great deal more, in official reports from the Treasury and other government sources. Steven Weisman's reporting from City Hall in the *New York Times* threw great light on the state's role in helping to end the crisis satisfactorily. We will examine here not the details of the fiscal problems that become inflamed simultaneously, but the major issues that brought the city to its fiscal knees.

The trouble began when the Urban Development Corporation, a state agency, found itself unable to sell a new series of one-year notes. If it could not sell them, it would be unable to pay off an equivalent series of maturing one-year notes. That meant that an agency of the State of New York, the Empire State, whose motto was Excelsior, was broke. If an agency of the State of New York was broke, the natural presumption in the financial world would be that the state itself could not be very healthy. And if the state was not, neither was the City of New York, always somewhat more populistically inclined, likely to be robust.

The Urban Development Corporation had been established under the Rockefeller administration to act as a public developer of moderate-cost housing. Its powers to override local wishes in planning, zoning, and building-code matters were tremendous. The money it borrowed went into mortgage loans on housing developments it conceived and constructed. The developments were owned by private business people or by cooperative corporations owned and run by those who lived in the projects. Since the purpose of these buildings was to provide moderate-cost housing for people of moderate income (moderate-cost housing can be defined only as the housing built by corporations empowered to build moderate-cost housing), it did not matter very much to anyone that the residents did not pay enough rent to cover operating costs and the carrying charges on the mortgages. Their rents were insufficient to cover costs even when they were supplemented by all but the most generous federal subsidies. As with the city's own moderate-cost housing programs, the object of the game was not to ring the bell for sound fiscal management, but to provide better housing than unaided private industry could, particularly after the rent control laws had worked their perverse magic.

Governor Hugh Carey quickly understood that the state's own credit would be impaired by the U.D.C.'s default, even though it had no direct legal responsibility in the matter. New York State had bragged about its moral responsibility. If it did not stand behind the gratuitous acknowledgment of moral responsibility for the U.D.C., the credit standing of all the other "moral obligations" that New York State had undertaken would plummet even faster than the state's own credit. Thanks to ingenious ideas that, among other things, involved assignment of the federal housing subsidies to a newly established Project Finance Agency that was able to sell bonds to refinance the U.D.C.'s maturing debt, and to some direct appropriations by the legislature, the U.D.C. was saved from liquidation, and the state from even worse embarrassment.

The U.D.C. problems made it impossible for investment bankers to overlook New York City's own credit-worthiness, a subject to which they had always preferred to let sleep, having made lots of money by ignoring it. The look, when they finally took it, was upsetting. The city's own short-term debt stood at $3.4 billion on 30 June 1974, having tripled in the previous four years. Much of it was debt incurred, like the U.D.C.'s, to finance housing mortgages. The rest was secured by real estate taxes yet to be received and payments from Albany and Washington that the city claimed to have coming to it. Records were skimpy. There was no way to ascertain if all the taxes would be collected, or indeed if some might not already have been collected. The exact amount due in intergovernmental payments was apparently in dispute. The most questionable part of the short-term debt was the housing part. The only way those notes would ever be retired was through the sale of long-term bonds. But if short-term notes were a risky proposition, what investors smart enough to have money would also be stupid enough to lend it to the same New York City for terms as long as thirty years? Answer: none.

Other accounts of the fiscal crisis have spelled out in detail how New York City escaped from a formal default on its obligations. Few have noted the crucial element in the crisis: the city's—and the state's—willingness to use public credit to finance housing without realizing that if users of the housing do not fully pay for the public credit they benefit from, the taxpayers will have to do their paying for them. Since rent controls established the facts that apartment house dwellers are unwilling to pay adequate rents and that legislators are unwilling to force them to do so, the taxpayers' ultimate burden in moderate-cost housing should have been foreseeable far in advance. That it was not foreseen was probably the result of three important rules in human behavior, at least in New York in the postwar years. First, the tenants who benefit from public subsidies feel no gratitude to their fellow taxpayers who provide the subsidies. They consider themselves entitled to the subsidies as a matter of right, the proof of which is that the public subsidized them in the first place. Second, when the party system has become too weak to assure incumbents their reelection, legislators generally will place their own political survival ahead of the soundness of the state's economy.

Third, rent controls, in New York at any rate, make life economically difficult not only for private owners but for taxpayers whose collective assets are invested in apartment houses with rents that must be competitive with those in the old regulated buildings. Furthermore, when the government seeks to raise rents in subsidized middle-income housing at a faster rate than rents in controlled housing, tenants will refuse to pay them, and will get their assemblymen and senators to intervene.

If miscalculations based on ignorance of these axioms—so easy to discern now, so hard before the fiscal crisis—were responsible for the overextension of New York's credit and its fiscal disaster in 1975, why did it happen? It happened for one reason above all: it happened because the lower-than-moder-

ate-income families were living in such bad housing that a
federally subsidized public housing program was developed to
provide them, at significant public expense, with housing that
met enlightened standards, not much more. To moderate-
income families, to the legislators who represented them, and,
remarkably, to the elite leadership of the city, it was offensive
to develop programs for the poor without doing something for
moderate-income families. And although moderate-income
families in the prewar period scrimped and sacrificed to keep
up the mortgage payments on cooperatively owned, bank-
financed apartment houses, in the postwar period they quite
naturally believed that you should take everything you can
get from government, because it does not really need your
money. After all, was this not exactly the philosophy of the
elites, who insist that government soothe their consciences
and succor the poor, helpless, and downtrodden, doing their
charity for them while they are out looking for tax shelters?
This was not true of all the elites, of course, but all the elites
as perceived by moderate-income families, the only perception that politics requires.

Imprudent borrowing to finance moderate rental housing in
New York City produced the fiscal crisis, only coincidentally
with the U.D.C.'s problems in 1975. It would ultimately have
produced a crisis all by itself. Losses piled up in financing the
developments. They are still piling up in the case of the least
successful projects; the more nearly successful projects were
taken off the city's hands by the federal government. In 1976
Washington decided that it would issue mortgage insurance on
municipal housing mortgages, an act of charity that enabled
New York to sell its mortgages. The federal government, however, not twice-bitten but bitten a hundred times over, would
insure only what it agreed was the true worth of a mortgage,
after a valuation based on the rental income of the building
whose development costs it had paid for. That was usually
quite a bit less than half the face value. In other words, if New
York, at a reasonable guess, invested $3 billion in housing mort-

gages, it got back significantly less than $1.5 billion. Its taxpayers are still paying off the balance, even if not one in a thousand knows it.

If, indeed, there had been no fiscal crisis, the worthless housing debt would be greater, probably much greater. The only thing that kept the moderate-income housing program from continuing forever was the crisis itself. Residents liked it (until their rents rose, though not nearly enough in most cases to cover costs). Builders liked it, because they made money on land and construction. The building trade unions liked it, because it kept them busy. The financial world liked it, because they could buy city obligations which were, effectively, guaranteed by taxpayers as well as by residents. Even legislators liked it, despite their discomfort over rent increases. Ultimately, every threat of a rent increase gave them an opportunity to appear heroic while arguing against city approval of the rise. The heroism was hardly worth a congressional medal. None of the officials in charge of supervising the program liked to raise rents; after all, they were usually in or close to the political world, and some of them had started out as idealists.

One of the remarkable features of the fiscal crisis was the evidence it gave of the persistence of another important truth: money matters. Once convinced that there really was no more money, even the most intransigent tribunes of the poor, the most persistent advocates of middle-class amenities, and the ladies from the upper East Side who had been crying for greater generosity to their favorite museums lapsed into an acquiescent silence. Reality is the best possible cure for dreams. It is, however, a short-lived antidote. Now that the city's budget is balanced and money that is labeled "a cash surplus" piles up in the city's bank accounts, the familiar cries for generosity are rising. The faces change. In a few years, unless New York should have another fiscal crisis, no one will be left who remembers the battle of '75 and the glorious victory.

Solving the crisis involved major acts by three different centers of power. Governor Hugh Carey, who arrived innocently enough in Albany in January 1975, had one month of relative calm before it all started. It was his prodding, pushing, and leadership at great personal risk that managed, very successfully, his end of the crisis. He set up the agencies that managed to refinance New York City's debt even while supplying it with much of the additional money it needed to cover its continuing budget deficits. In this he was helped by shrewd advice from Felix Rohatyn, an investment banker, and Richard Ravitch, a builder who had taken over the chairmanship of the U.D.C. in its darkest days. The precise details of how a pitiful debtor was made to look like a muscular tax farmer will be of interest mainly to students of magic and public relations and to those who live in cities that face similar problems. There are, of course, critics who say that New York should have been allowed to go into bankruptcy, so that the bankers would be punished suitably for their role in stimulating, aiding, abetting or acquiescing in public imprudence.

People who actually lived through the crisis are somewhat slow to agree that the pleasure of discomfiting the bankers would have made up for the anxiety of trying to run hospitals, schools, prisons, police forces, and sanitation workers—for starters—without cash for payrolls. Those few members of the public who sat in on Mayor Beame's top secret bankruptcy task force also took a dim view of the luxury of liquidation. They were worrying about how a federal district court would be able to approve the use of cash to pay for milk deliveries and oxygen, and how it could establish a receivership or a legal equivalent that would satisfy creditors, secured and unsecured, that assets to which they looked with some hope were not being squandered on political nonessentials.

Mayor Beame's role in the crisis was as important as the governor's, but he received far less credit. Unfortunately from the point of view of fairness, he had run for office in 1973 on the slogan that he "knows the buck." When the city ran into the financial wall, his critics were quick to allege that he did not know the buck at all, for the city was in deep trouble. Actually, the depth of the trouble reflected his understanding of municipal finance, perhaps to the exclusion of a bit of municipal reality. The system of borrowing to the limit of the city's legal borrowing limit was well established; the comptroller, the office Beame had been elected to before his mayoralty, was interested in the concrete realities of constitutional borrowing limits and the marketability of city obligations. The comptroller also had an interest in what it was that people wanted. The abstract question of long-term fiscal prudence was secondary, or tertiary, or immaterial altogether.

Once the markets closed down, Mayor Beame realized that he had to carry out the toughest part of the rescue. His assignment was to reduce the city's operating budget. He had to cut the payroll, eliminate promised services, refuse to give pay raises, defer improvements, and conduct a great many other equally unwelcome duties. Anyone who did not know how persistent Beame could be in pushing a point on which he felt strongly—calling the same official five or ten times on the telephone in a single night to make sure he knew what the mayor wanted—would have found his gentle, almost reticent personality in sharp contrast with the job of cutting the city payroll by 20 percent. He got more help from career civil servants than from political commissioners.

The career administrators were as effective as Gogol's Pavel Chichikov in finding dead souls. While Chichikov bought and sold nonexistent serfs, the civil servants eliminated from the payroll people who had either already left the civil service or were about to. A seasoned professional could drop a hundred or more people from a department within forty-eight hours and yet touch only about ten people who really wanted to stay at work. He would find people who had already put in their retirement papers and talk them into withdrawing them, so they could be fired in place of a "live" person. He knew who was planning to drop out to become a full-time graduate student and would persuade him to let himself be fired instead. Bit by bit he would make up the list, allowing the political commissioner to bask in the admiration of his humane attitudes. If a poor, blundering commissioner used the mandated personnel cut in an effort to get rid of a particularly obnoxious provisional civil servant, he would find the same person back at his desk a week later, having simply dropped from his "provisional" to his "permanent" slot. One such disappointment persuaded any realistic commissioner to let his career assistant carry on unaided.

Humanely or not, the job got done. The payroll was reduced from 200,000 people to about 160,000. The city continued to function—not better than it had before, but not much worse, either.

Washington played the third important role. First, it helped out with temporary credits until the Municipal Assistance Corporation, the Rohatyn agency, was able to sell enough of its own paper to make retirement of temporary loans possible. Congress later passed a long-term loan package, under fairly stringent terms, that enabled the city to get on with its capital reconstruction program. The crisis took an awful toll of the streets, bridges, subways, schools, and sewers of the city. Everything was sacrificed to the immediate needs of paying workers and meeting other pressing operating expenses.

If only it were possible to blame the whole fiscal crisis on housing, how easy it would be to avoid a second fiscal crisis: don't build housing. The trouble with that formula is that it's almost as easy to spend similar amounts of money imprudently on other kinds of improvements. The true problem that New York City faces—and how similar it is to the problems faced by the nation as a whole—is to separate prudent and essential government expenditures from those that merely look desirable to politically potent groups. Although it is difficult to arrive at figures, New York should certainly be able to keep its indigent, nonworking population from starving, living without shelter, or dying prematurely because its diseases go untreated. Certainly those are modest goals, compared with the hope for persuading or nudging the indigents to become part of the work force. And yet, if they do not become part of the work force, it is not at all clear that New York City, even with the cooperation of the state and federal governments, can protect itself against the costs that the indigent indirectly impose on the city.

In any case, the expenses that must be paid by all other citizens to give help to the poor become a galling tax when the poor are helped because they do not meet standards of behavior demanded by others. The basic failure, political as well as human, of the welfare system is that it makes no useful effort to change the habits of those indigents whose plight is partly of their own making. Instead, the system rewards teenage women for having illegitimate children, pays women for having been deserted (in fact or theory) by the men who supported them, supports others at public expense for their failure to prepare themselves to earn a living, and relieves convicted criminal offenders of the responsibility for caring for their legal dependents, to name only a few of the antisocial activities that are rewarded—another way of saying "encouraged"—by the welfare system.

It is not easy to suggest changes in the system without running into the problem of hardship during a transition period. And so the system goes on. But, politically, it continues only because reparations are being paid to other citizens of relatively modest means who do conform to specific standards of conduct. It can be correctly presumed that many of these citizens object strongly to government rewarding those who disobey the commandments which they themselves adhere to, however reluctantly. Therefore the moderate-income families get college loans, Medicare when they age, new school buildings for their children, favorable tax valuations on their New York City homes, a highly subsidized fare schedule on the city-owned transportation system (and on much of the privately owned sectors of the transportation system as well). In the long run, the sums given to the middle class to tranquilize them about the sums given to the unworthy poor, to use a currently abhorrent term, probably cost the city more than the grants to the poor themselves. Nevertheless, between the two of these and the costs of public education, the city's income is quite fully committed. Embarking on any large-scale capital program, even though its purpose may well be economic development to increase municipal government's income and reduce its expenses, might put the city back in precisely the same mess it fell into in 1975 through housing.

There is a logical stand-in for housing's melancholy role: the subway system. By the spring of 1984, Robert Kiley, successor to Richard Ravitch as head of the Metropolitan Transportation Authority, cruelly told the public that the capital program that Ravitch had brilliantly designed and encouraged the state legislature to adopt, would not be nearly sufficient to return the subways to an acceptable level of safety, cleanliness, and timely performance. No one really knows how much deterioration has undermined the operating rolling stock of the system, or the underground and under-river rights-of-way. It is perhaps unfair to hypothesize without expensive factual surveys. Yet, looking at the decay of vehicular bridges, water mains, concrete-based asphalt streets, and major highways within the city limits, the cautious observer should certainly dare to consider that the conditions of the system may be worse than anyone knows, and that the labor relations in the system and its resultant management weakness are so bad that any new capital equipment will deteriorate at least as quickly as it has in the past.

If one combines these awesome possibilities with the reluctance of passengers to pay ever-higher fares for unimproved, or only marginally improved, service much as the residents of city-aided apartment houses refused to pay higher rents for unchanged accommodations, one sees the prospect of a repeat of the 1975 fiscal disaster. The M.T.A. can be forced to borrow more and more money, the better to replace newer equipment that is deteriorating as fast as older equipment. Fares cannot be raised. The state has stretched to the breaking point the willingness of out-of-town taxpayers to contribute to a city transportation problem. The city, terrified that further breakdowns in subway service will accelerate the emigration of business firms, borrows money on its own, using its short-term borrowing power once again for an illicit purpose. Here we go again. Worst of all, the cure for such a train of events is not at hand. The power to reform the M.T.A.'s management system so that its unionized work force will cooperate with a speed-up campaign does not exist. The power to improve matters without management reform is illusory. Saving by cutting back money-losing services at light travel times and by closing lines that are grossly underutilized and merely duplicate bus service would be quickly deemed a racist plot to deprive blacks and Hispanics access to their jobs, as we have already noted. Where will a change in the attitudes of citizens toward local government come from? How will this large employer, the City of New York, be able to get reasonable productivity from its employees, including the employees of its affiliated agencies like the city transit system?

It might have been possible to initiate changes in work practices in 1978, when the first election after the fiscal crisis brought Edward Irving Koch to Gracie Mansion as the new Mayor. During the crisis itself, union members and their leaders had been quite cooperative with city government in cutting labor costs and deferring the cash wage increases that had been agreed to before the crisis. Union members and their leaders doubtless expected not only that they had first call on available funds to pay the deferred increases but that their self-sacrifice was to be something of an investment in easy relations with the city government. Koch, moving away from whatever he may have said during the period between the 1977 primary elections and the runoff between him and Mario Cuomo, made it clear that the entire crisis was not actually over. The city was still strapped. That fact, coupled with Koch's unwillingness to settle matters by private negotiation with the union leaders, certainly made him less than a hero to Victor Gotbaum, head of District

37 of the Federation of State, County, and Municipal Employees, the largest of the bargaining entities. Other union leaders may have shared Gotbaum's sympathies, but they showed somewhat greater discretion in expressing them.

In retrospect it seems possible that Koch beat Cuomo in that run-off election because both men knew that the new mayor would spend his entire first term as an official Scrooge, sending the Bob Crachets of city government pigeons for Christmas when they felt they had earned turkeys. That was a role to which Mayor Koch took readily, while Mr. Cuomo could not have put his heart in it. The deficits in spending and the increased state borrowing after his first two years as governor confirm the impression that Cuomo is happier when he can be generous than when he cannot.

Koch, conversely, demonstrates that he positively enjoys being ornery, and of all forms of being ornery, the one he most enjoys is the impromptu and spontaneous orneriness that seems an uncalculated expression of his deepest feelings. The impression is somewhat misleading. It's a reasonable guess that like many other people who enjoy their own apparent lack of restraint, Mayor Koch believes fervently in what he is saying at the moment he says it. He's also likely to feel equally fervently about a different view the next time the subject comes up. On matters on which he *really* feels deeply, he never wavers at all, and he doesn't say much, either.

Mayor Koch is deeply committed to the importance of social class, and his natural sympathies go to members of the working class, or the "middle" class as matters now stand. He seems to have far more respect for the rank and file, who are simply following their natural interests in demanding better pay and working conditions, than for labor leaders, who intensify those demands even when they know that the city's situation is precarious. He is deeply suspicious of wealthy people, unless they have made their own money and thus can be regarded as examples of the truly successful middle-class person. Koch is sympathetic to the poor when he believes that they had no part of the responsibility for being poor. His feelings about poor black people probably reflect his impression that they blame much of their poverty on the acts of white oppressors. His problems with the black middle class arise from the apparent unwillingness of members of that group to place their class interest ahead of their racial identity. They insist on maintaining in public that they are blacks first and middle-class Americans second, sometimes adding that white America, not they, established that order of priority.

The curious anomaly in the Koch position with respect to social class is that he combines middle-class attitudes on economic issues and on the morality of working and personal responsibility with a rather upper-class or pseudo-Bohemian tolerance for unconventional personal conduct. He supports rights for homosexuals, without ever quite defining exactly what this means, or precisely how much discrimination against homosexuals exists in New York. He supports the death penalty, which leaders of the women's movement generally reject, but he also supports issues that the women's movement supports strongly, including a measure that would make it extremely difficult for men's clubs to exclude women and, one presumes, vice versa. It is interesting that his personal tolerance for unconventional behavior has not so far alienated him from the middle-class voters who have been the backbone of his political strength. Nor has it in any way undercut the opposition to him in the old and new left community and among blacks, all of whom are similarly tolerant of the new morality that he seems to share.

The outcry against Koch arises mainly from two groups. Among the blacks, opposition is based on the feeling of many that the mayor actually is prejudiced against them, that he is, in the word that has been used so often that its meaning has been exhausted, a racist. Doubtless this perception of the Mayor is based less on any overt deprecation, than on his obstinate refusal to use the rhetoric of reassurance and kindly interest that blacks have come to expect. The Koch answer to their criticism is that he is no racist, that he believes in treating everyone the same and talking to blacks in the same way that he talks to everyone else. In fact, of course, no one actually treats everyone alike, nor should one. Those who have been the victims of persecution expect to be talked to with a particular understanding.

Yet even as one points to curiosities of Koch's behavior that seem to explain the black reaction to him, the reality of their feeling is somewhat different. The probabilities are, though this theory remains beyond proof, that no matter how Koch behaved nor how he talked to black people, the political importance of hating him would override any ingratiating manner. The frustrations of blacks over having made less progress than they expected to make by this time expresses itself in strong, unrealistic political ambitions—manifestly in widespread support of Jesse Jackson's nomination for the presidency. Blacks share a desire to elect a black mayor in New York, as they already have in Chicago and Los Angeles, but this desire is not accompanied by an easy readiness to compromise on a single black candidate. And so the several kinds of frustration express themselves in a proposition that has been repeated so often that it is based on an axiom—Koch and we hate each other—rather than on facts.

The other group of Koch-haters is the reform Democrats, who feel that Koch, having once been on their side, is now against them. Their opposition is probably based on Koch's unwillingness to appoint to high office those whom the reform Democrats bless, on his obduracy with the labor unions, and on his refusal to use the right terms and make the right noises. His advocacy of capital punishment and his tough verbal stand on crime and narcotics addiction express attitudes that are, in fact, very popular with the Democratic rank and file, though not with the ideological leaders. They can never forgive him for this deviationism.

None of these explanations for the opposition to Koch should be taken as justifying the feeling that he has been a perfect mayor but misunderstood. His real flaws are very different from those perceived by his political enemies to the left. They accuse him of favoring the rich when, in fact, his anti-rich bias has made his economic development strategies far less effective than they should be. He has misled himself by thinking that tough talk in dealing with the city's employees is the equivalent of commanding action. It isn't. The most important fact of his administration has been his political daring in sticking to the principle that the city had to cut expenses and keep them cut in order to survive. His stiff-neckedness on the budget issue has perforce made him obstinate on all other issues. His fear of negotiating with his political adversaries on the Board of Estimate has prevented him from meeting any of the complicated and important developmental goals of his administration. He needed not only to improve the city's business and its tax receipts, but also to clean the city and install equipment that no one wanted but that would rid the city of waste. But perhaps if he had been able to accomplish all these tasks, the city would already have slid back into fiscal imbalance.

Under a less ornery mayor, the city might not have been accepted in the credit markets. It might already be running a cash deficit instead of a surplus. It is also arguable that if Koch runs again for mayor and loses, his opponent will seek to solidify his position by distancing himself from Koch. Such a mayor, basing his policy on more services for all and patronizing the black population, will stretch the city's credit for the second time, replaying the 1975 near-bankruptcy. After 1984, New York might not be so lucky.

What, then, if these gloomy predictions are to be contravened by the future, are the possible sources of hope? First the city's elites must recognize that they cannot afford—meaning that the city cannot afford—their laziness and cowardice in fleeing from the responsibility for setting up standards of private behavior and prudence. The elites in recent years have been too busy relaxing in the pursuit of values like understanding others, compassionate dedication to the plight of the less fortunate, and preservation of the natural environment, to retain the strength and will to impose discipline, or to insist that government impose discipline on those it means to help.

The older elites in New York City were once the Anglo-Saxon families who belonged to the Protestant denominations closest to the Anglican Church. Now the old elites include Catholic and Jewish families who have had money for several generations. They are in rebellion of a sort against previous generations of their families, who wanted to impose ritualized standards on all forms of behavior, from readiness to lay down one's life for one's country to raising forks and spoons in proper order. There is more hope of courage and energy from the newer elites. These include those who have made their own money and a small group of intellectuals who were once so far to the left of the organized left that they have no seductive memories of revolutionary comradeship to inhibit them from denouncing what they once firmly believed in.

The elites should be protesting the use of welfare funds to reward action that is grossly antisocial and that ultimately, because it seems freed from stultifying conventions, tends to corrupt many who do not receive government help. The older elites instead are standing quiet. They are afraid of alienating their own children. The same elite groups are unwilling to put the sergeant's stripes back on the sleeves of those informed but informal educators of the city who prepared new arrivals for urban life. The attitudes that sergeants promulgate now strike the older elites as foolish, if not downright evil. The sergeants believe in action rather than consciousness as the crucial human state of being. They are crass, money-grubbing, anti-artistic, Philistine, when the older elites have come to believe that such traits are the problem of the modern world rather than signs of a toughness of mind and an imperviousness to mode that may just help to save it. The older elites consider themselves so entrenched and at the same time so besieged that they are able and willing to offer money to buy off their enemies. They do not relish the prospect of a fight, even if the odds on their side are favorable. There are younger elites who do not feel the same way; they are, in a word, vulgar.

The older elites want a government that does not recognize the wisdom, indeed the duty, of saying "no" to supplicants or strong enemies. To say "no" means to stimulate opposition among one's own people; to say "no" to one's enemies is to misapprehend their peaceful intentions. Unless the newer elites are willing to fight for a curtailment of private appetites to eat from public hands, there is little hope for the city's ability to cut down the demand for vast capital expenditures whose connection with an increase of revenue is tenuous at best. It's on the new elites that the city must depend for a stiffening of its ability to say "no." Part of the new elite will probably be a black elite.

The older elites are showing themselves unable to talk constructively with the new black elites, or the new whites, for that matter. They understood very well the quasi-aristocratic mien of the older black elites, who imitated faithfully the mores of the families they served; the imitators were even more stylized than the originals. The new blacks have fought their way forward; they don't know whom to imitate. What they are first to need, and last to admit the need of, is recognition by whites. It's only this new black elite whose members are close enough to the poor and yet sufficiently powerful to develop institutions that might save at least some of the children of households in which they are the third or fourth dependent generation.

Finally, the old elites have shown themselves incapable of working with church leadership in what had been its main interest, the call for an individually moral life. The elites are wholly irreligious; they applaud the clergy that has turned from its traditional preoccupation with morality to become a social service institution, running little theater groups for singles and sponsoring workshops on the operations of the Peace Corps and on South African history. The older elites are more interested in some of the buildings the churches meet in than in the churches themselves. If they can save the buildings by turning the churches out and converting the sanctuaries to post offices, libraries, information centers, or even discotheques, they would be happy. Once stripped of hymnals and clerics, churches are able to remind the old elites of St. Michel and Chartres, leaving the visitor serene in the knowledge that no religious service will disturb his mood.

Whatever religion's inadequacies, and they are many—sectarian strife, bungling stupidity of dogma—it is the institutional expression of an idea: that in the face of life, a sense of awe is not irrelevant. Whether worldly or religious, civic leadership that treats its problems with a sense of wonder is the city's need. Such leadership will take pride in the skill with which it measures gaps and possibilities, seizes opportunities, gauges the chances of opposing courses. The city's hope is that new elites will emerge, making the city's rise and fall a cyclical process as regular as the tides. Without a cycle of new elites still fresh enough to sustain their sense of awe, New York—having had one rise and fall—may be destined to diminish until it disappears as one of the world's great cities. It would not have been the first.

Epilogue

Cross-Country: Cross-Town

ENCUMBERED with shopping bags, straw bags, camera bags, paper bags, newspapers, magazines, make-up boxes, tennis rackets, the airline passengers who have already checked in wait at the gate for the voice on the loudspeaker to welcome them to their flight to the Pacific coast. It is eight o'clock in the morning, New York time. Some passengers who have a hand free of magazines try to set their watches back three hours. In six hours they will be in California, a trip that once took months, then days. Sixty years ago, the army air corps staged a magnificent feat, flying military planes from the East Coast to the West between the dawn and dusk of a single day. Within a lifetime it has become possible to cross the continent in a commercial plane in one third that time, every day, in less time than it took to go from Boston to Washington, D.C. The crowd fidgets, shifts position, complains, wonders aloud what the delay is. Restlessness has become the pandemic of the time; the only cure is movement until the next onset of restlessness.

When the passengers are kindly invited to board and make

themselves as comfortable as possible in their narrow seats, squeezing their hand luggage beneath the narrow seat in front of them, latching their seat belts, trying to avoid listening to the procedure they must follow if something goes wrong with the oxygen equipment, the terminal passageway moves away from the plane. Backward, the monstrous aircraft rolls away from the terminal building and, after some barely comprehensible words over the speaker system, begins to move forward.

Speed condensed the nation, until its length in time was no greater than the distance between two similar cities on the East Coast. But natural differences persist, when the clouds are sparse enough so that one can see the ground: the green of the eastern countryside, the quadrangular quilt patches of middle-western farmland, the browns of the desert, the blues and pur-ples of the mountains, the mottled browns and greens of the California valleys. Despite the physical differences, what one senses as one tries to look down at the land below is that the differences have been made banal.

Years before, flying lower, one passed over Buffalo, where the midwest once began, sensing that the people who had been unable to make a living on the Coast had found a niche for themselves here, a few hundred miles inland. The Western Reserve, Ohio and Indiana, once farmland that welcomed those who had broken their hands and backs on the stone-studded soil of Vermont, had become the industrial heartland, welcom-ing its second wave, the miners and steel workers, the rubber workers, the crane-builders from eastern Europe. Across the Mississippi are the newer farms, peopled by those who gave up in Kentucky, or Chicago, or St. Louis. And soaring over the Great Plains states, the grain-growing belt of the country, one imagines now the abandoned sod houses, the amalgamated farms, the vanished hired men and girls, the army of migrant workers and tank battalions of machinery that now bring in harvests that are the envy of the world and a danger to the producers through their very size.

And finally, the plane passes over the states with their remaining stands of wilderness, into which are infiltrating the newest national playgrounds, the ski resorts, the gambling resorts, the golfing resorts, the time-sharing A-frame second and third homes, the proliferating cities, the interstate highway systems, the dams and power plants that provide water and electricity for producing goods that are very different from the products of what was the industrial heartland of the past.

And yet, if one could see in detail beyond the general differences apparent from the sky, what one would find would be a mammoth dilution of differences between the geographies that seem so distinct from the sky. The same kinds of food, the same clothes, the same songs, the same entertainments, the same addictions pervade the continent, no longer spreading always from east to west with the pattern of settlement but also from west to east. New cities produce new styles, new foods, new furniture, new clothes, and they find their way back east. The nation becomes homogenized to an extent that would have been impossible before transport became so swift and communication so effortless.

What an eagle eye would see on the ground of America is a surcharge of human energy, a turbulent restlessness, the same restlessness that fills the airplane with passengers. For some Americans it is highly directional in its motion: the generation of new ideas, new enterprises, new causes, new matters of supreme importance, new perspectives on the obligations of a just, a full, a perfected society. For others it remains mere restlessness. On the drugstore window of a town in Idaho (Elevation 5,534 feet; Population 1,263 people) the sign reads: "Here for Parents' Info on Drug Abuse." It is no longer the large cities alone that must cope with the restlessness that leads to addiction.

New enterprises spring up while others die, fortunes are made in all parts of the country by those clever enough to divine what people will want, new services to bring them information that may or may not be of use to them, services to cook for them, bring food to them, accomplish for them with minimal effort the simpler and simpler tasks that once were necessary to maintain a household. And then, having made all muscular activity unnecessary, they find their inspirations supplemented by another group of geniuses who have found new ways to put muscles back to work again, on condition that they produce nothing useful but the body to which they were attached by nature. Running shoes and walking weights, machines of which the human body is the engine and the point of which is not to make or build or unite or separate but merely to keep the engine working, skis and tennis racquets, bicycles that by design go nowhere, pools in which one can swim for hours without changing place.

What is all this frenzied activity, this burning desire to restore to the body a semblance of what it was designed to accomplish, but a search for meaning, so much of which has been lost, not alone by the technical accomplishments that have eased the burden of life over the years, but by the restless intellects that have denigrated that accomplishment into something meaningless? It is meaningless because, they tell the youth and the leaders, anything that is imperfect is meaningless. Having conquered the natural world, we are left without any excuse for not having created a new and perfect human world. Not with our own efforts alone, but through government; it must save the whales, save the grizzlies, save the butterflies, save the deer, save the old buildings, save the new buildings, save the air, save the water, save the poor, the weak, the disabled. And it must manage all this without imposing standards of conduct on anyone except those who do not recognize the significance of salvation without souls.

The glorious contrasts spread below the plane as it covers the country in its flight, a set of contrasts as vivid as the city contrasts left behind on the East Coast, and nearly as compressed in time as they are compressed in space. The ordered energy of human intelligence and the disordered energy of human emotions struggle for mastery in a world in which everyone knows what the collective whole should do, but no one is quite clear what he or she is expected to do. Can order be replaced without superstition? Can new superstitions produce order without trammeling either intelligence or spontaneity?

Long before the questions can be answered, the lights flash on, and just in case the passengers did not notice them, a voice over the speaker tells us that the captain has turned them on. He tells us what to do: fasten our seat belts. In a moment he will tell us again what to do: to stop smoking. What a relief it is to be told what to do, and to know that obedience must be maintained for only a very short time. We must sit quietly until the light that just went on goes out. Then we can release our belts, and the ordered ranks will melt into a restless crowd. Somewhere forward, the door is opened by hands outside the world we have been in. With hands too full of shopping bags and hats and tennis racquets, relieved but unenlightened, we make our way slowly, in our imaginations pawing the carpeted airplane deck, toward the door.

Index

Abzug, Bella, 57
Adams, James Ring, 225
advertising, 217
affirmative action, 143–45
Aid to Families with Dependent Children, 78, 152
airports, 55, 59, 189
Algonquin Hotel, 204
aliens, undocumented, 76–77
Allegheny Mountains, 48, 49
almshouses, 189
Alphabet City, 61
Altman's, 134
Alvarez, Anita, 136
American Federation of Teachers (AFT), 39, 172–74
anti-Semitism, 145
apartment houses, 4, 8, 84–90; assessed value of, 194; condominium, 100; cooperative, 29, 31, 100; luxury, 39; postwar quality of, 86–87; rent controlled, 93, 98–104, 194, 198, 225, 226; rent stabilized, 99; segregated, 137; substandard, 89–90; tenement, 17, 39, 71, 87–88; welfare tenants in, 96–98; see also housing
Appalachian Mountains, 47
armed forces, segregated, 138, 214
Armstrong, Louis, 137
Army Corps of Engineers, U.S., 4
arson, 95–96
art world, 204–6, 218–19
Astor, Vincent, 15
Atlanta, Ga., 186–87
Auden, W. H., 206

automats, 8
automobiles: air pollution from, 57; fatalities from, 161–62; traffic congestion from, 57, 70
aviation, 55, 59, 189, 242, 245–46

Balanchine, George, 206
Baltimore, Md., 36, 50
Banfield, Edward, 105–6
bars: topless, 5; waterfront, 4
Bartok, Bela, 206
Baruch College, 31–32
Beame, Abraham, 23, 80; fiscal crisis and, 63–64, 229–30
Bell, Stephen, 181
Bensonhurst, 34
Berlin, 14–15
Best's, 134
Bethlehem shipyard, 50
Beyond the Melting Pot (Glazer and Moynihan), 130
Billy the Kid, 151
blackouts, 13
blacks, 13, 31–33, 38, 136–46, 192–93; affirmative action and, 143–45, crime and, 114–15, 140, 178–80; cultural differences of, 141–42, 148; in "dead-end" jobs, 193–94; dependency among, 146–47; education of, 41–42, 136, 168, 170, 172–74, 177, 220; 1863 draft riots and, 106; election of, 43–44, 139, 199; elite among, 240; employment of, 64, 138, 139, 143–45; higher education

blacks *(continued)*
of, 168, 220; housing and, 88–89,
137; immigrants vs., 140–142, 177;
Jews vs., 145, 173; in judiciary, 139;
Koch and, 236–37; middle-class, 40,
138, 142, 236; northward migration
of, 136; in police force, 133, 143,
179–80, 220–21; population of, in
New York, 129, 136; as portrayed in
theater, 210–15; segregation and,
41–42, 136–40, 168, 170; subway
service and, 65–66; voting rights of,
42–43
Blitzstein, Mark, 112
block associations, 37
blocks, arrangement of, in Manhattan, 187
Board of Aldermen, 190
Board of Education, 33, 173–74
Board of Estimate, 62, 72, 73, 74, 171,
190–91, 238
Board of Regents, New York State,
167–68
bootlegging, 110–11
borough presidents: Board of Education appointments by, 173–74;
mayor and, 191–92; responsibilities
of, 191
Boston, Mass., 36, 49, 186–87, 204
Boyer, Paul, 107–8, 149–51, 153, 164
bridges, 24, 28, 49–50, 59, 60, 61, 65
Broadway, 5, 61, 137, 187, 204,
210–16
Bronx, the: gentrification in, 35–36;
housing in, 23, 30–31, 35–36, 90, 93;
as part of New York, 61; waterfront
in, 60
Brooklyn: Democratic party in, 17,
192; gentrification in, 36; housing
in, 23, 34, 36, 203; manufacturing
in, 72–73; as separate city, 61–62,
87; waterfront in, 34, 60
Brooklyn Bridge, 49–50, 60, 61
Brooklyn Dodgers, 137–38
Brooklyn Marine Terminal, 54
Brooklyn Navy Yard (New York
Naval Shipyard), 50, 124–25

brownstoners, 37
Bryant, William Cullen, 6
Bryant Park, 6
Buffalo, N.Y., 243
building codes, 197, 224
building inspectors, graft paid to, 197
Bundy, McGeorge, 171–72
Bureau of Labor Statistics, U.S., 68
buses: express, 37; Forty-second
street crosstown, 3–8
Business Week, 15
bus shelters, 79–80
bus terminals, 4, 5
Byrne, Brendan, 56

cable TV, 80
Cagney, James, 111
Call Me Mister (Rome), 213–14
capital punishment, 120–21, 126, 236
Carey, Hugh, 12, 63, 64; fiscal crisis
and, 228–29; Westway and, 201;
World Trade Center sale supported
by, 186
Carl Schurz Park, 28
Carnegie Hill Association, 30
Caro, Robert, 203
Catholics, 106, 133, 239
Central Park, 11, 108, 209
Chanin Building, 8
charities, 106, 153, 156
Chelsea, 201
chemical industry, 70
Chicago, Ill., 243
Chinatown, 77, 116, 137
Chinese-Americans, 116
Chrysler Building, 7–8
Citizens Union, 191
City Council, 102, 190; apportionment of, 43, 190–91; at-large members of, 190; J-51 tax exemptions
and, 74–75; president of, 171
City Fusion party, 190
City Planning Commission, 20
City University of New York, 6,
31–32

Civilian Complaint Review Board, 180–81
Civil Liberties Union, 155–56
civil rights movement, 42–44
Civil War, U.S., 105–6
Clinton, DeWitt, 47–49, 52, 55, 187, 194
clipper ships, 49
Coffin, William Sloane, 182
cogeneration, 82
Columbia University, 47–48
Commission on Human Rights, 21
Commodore Hotel, 7
Communism, as theme in *They Shall Not Die*, 212–13
comptroller, 171, 230
condominiums, 100
Coney Island, 61
Congress, U.S.: Enterprise Zones and, 81; fiscal crisis and, 231; public housing and, 89; representation in, 190
Conquering the Wilderness (Columbia University), 47–48
Consolidated Edison, 70, 82–83
Constitution, U.S., 123, 190
Constitutional Convention, U.S., 48, 204
Coolidge, Calvin, 181
Co-Op City, 31
cooperative apartments, 29, 31, 100
Correction, Department of, 26
corruption, municipal, 18, 106, 107, 195–97
Costello, Frank, 18, 196
Cost of Good Intentions, The (Morris), 224
Cradle Will Rock, The (Blitzstein), 112
credit industry, 16
crime, 5, 13, 105–27, 162; blacks and, 114–15, 140, 178–80; drug-related, 164; in early 1900s, 108–9; by gangs, 113–14, 116; incidence of, 114; organized, 111–12, 195–96; police force size and, 117; in Prohibition era, 110–12; and quality of life, 116–17; random, 115, 125; redlining

and, 95–96; social cost of, 110; in subways, 66, 67, 114, 115, 116; on waterfront, 51
Criminal Court, 125
criminal justice system, 26, 117–27; federal judiciary and, 119, 123–25; indeterminate sentencing in, 120, 122; plea bargaining in, 118; youthful offenders in, 120, 122; *see also* prisons and jails
Cuomo, Mario, 128; Koch vs., 234–35; Long Island prison closed by, 124
Customs House, 49

Daily News Building, 8
Dead End (Kingsley), 38–39
death rates, 157–62
Deep Are the Roots (D'Usseau and Gow), 214–15
Democratic party, 18, 21, 23, 139, 189–190, 191–92; in Brooklyn, 17, 192; Lindsay in, 12, 23; reform movement in, 195–99, 201, 237
department stores, 7, 11, 134, 137
dependency, ethic of, 146–47
Depression, Great, 40, 84, 85, 86, 152
deputy mayor, 79
DeSapio, Carmine, 201
Detroit, Mich., 25
diamond cutting, 25
diplomatic immunity, 207
diseases, 157–61, 162–63, 164–66
divorce, 168–69
Doctors Hospital, 28–29
domestic help, 29–30, 36, 138
Dominicans, 136
draft riots (1863), 105–6
drug abuse, 140, 157, 164–66, 244
drug trade, 5, 6, 114, 116, 125, 164
Dudley, Edward, 139
Duffy, John, 159–60
d'Usseau, Arnaud, 214
Dutchess County, 124
Dutch traders, 46–47

Eakins, Thomas, 204
East River, 3, 49
East Tremont Road, 31
Ecology of Housing Destruction, The (Salins), 96–97
Education, Board of, 33, 173–74
education, higher: blacks in, 168, 220; city-run, 6, 27, 31–32, 168, 189; private, 6, 27, 168; segregation in, 168; state-run, 167–68
education, parochial, aid to, 170
education, public, 23, 25, 168–77, 189; blacks and, 41–42, 136, 170, 172–74, 177; control over, 169–74; expenditures for, 170, 175; immigrant assimilation and, 131, 176–77; as panacea, 169; performance of students in, 174–75; school prayer issue and, 169–70; segregation in, 41–42, 136, 170; teacher's role in, 175–78
Eighth Avenue, 5
Eisenhower, Dwight D., 198
elderly: as crime victims, 115; public housing for, 198
electrical power, 79, 82–83, 98, 101; cogeneration of, 82; Moses and, 199; municipal use of, 82–83; nuclear generation of, 147–48
Ellington, Duke, 137
Ellison, Ralph, 177
eminent domain, 73, 187
Enterprise Zones, 80–82
entrepreneurship, 244; city attitudes toward, 82–83, 186–87
environment, 147–48, 245; air pollution and, 57, 70, 73, 147; litter and, 6; nuclear energy and, 147–48; solid waste disposal and, 37, 147–48; unemployment vs., 70; Westway and, 4
Environmental Protection Agency, 73
Erie, Lake, 47
Erie Canal, 47–49, 50, 51, 187
Esposito, Meade, 192
express buses, 37

fast food, 6, 7
Fay, Frank, 10
Ferber, Edna, 211
ferries, 24
Fifth Avenue, 6–7, 30
financial institutions, 25, 32, 49, 94–95, 225
Fire Department, 14; formation of, 189; women in, 44, 221
fire insurance, 95–96
First Avenue, 34, 137
fiscal crisis (1975), 63–64, 78, 225–31, 233, 238
Fisher, Harold, 63
Flexner, James Thomas, 48
food stamps, 153
Ford Foundation, 171–72
Foreman, Carl, 216
Forest Hills, 66
Forty-second street: crosstown bus on, 3–8; proposed reconstruction of, 69
Franklin, Benjamin, 204
frontier, lure of, 150–51
fur industry, 69

gambling, 5, 112, 196
gangs, 113–14, 116
gangsters, 110–12
garment industry, 25, 61, 134; exodus of, 70; labor conditions in, 71, 77; proposed relocation of, 69; unions in, 71, 76–77
General Sessions Court, New York County, 125
gentrification, 35–37, 93
George, Henry, 181
George Washington and The New Nation (Flexner), 48
George Washington High School, 31
German-Americans, 20, 61, 107, 133, 136
Gershwin, George, 111, 212
Gershwin, Ira, 111, 212
G.I. Bill of Rights, 167

Glass Menagerie, The (Williams), 10
Glazer, Nathan, 130
Glendale, 136
Gogol, Nikolai, 230
Golden, Howard, 192
Goldmark, Peter, 59
Gotbaum, Victor, 234–35
Gow, James, 214
Grace, W. R., Building, 6
Grace Line, 53, 54
Gracie Mansion, 28
Graduate Center, City University, 6
graffiti, 7
graft, 196–97
Grand Central Station, 7
Grand Concourse, 61, 90, 93
Grand Hyatt Hotel, 7
Grapes of Wrath (Steinbeck), 151
Gravesend Bay, 34
Great Lakes, 24
Great Society, 22–23, 32
Greek-Americans, 132
Green Pastures, The (Connelly), 210–11
Greenpoint, 72–73
Greenwich Village, 35, 201
Gulick, Luther, 22
Gun Hill Road, 31

Hall, Peter, 80–81
handicapped persons, mass transit for, 66
Handlin, Oscar, 130
Harlem, 137, 138, 160
Harley Hotel, 8
Harris, Elisha, 159
Harvey (Chase), 10
Hassam, Childe, 7
Health Department, 162
health services, municipal, 17, 23, 26–27, 148; moral order and, 163–66
Hell Gate Bridge, 28
Hell's Kitchen, 151
Heyward, DuBose, 211–12
Himmelfarb, Gertrude, 152
Hispanics, 36, 43, 64; crime and, 114–

15, 116; immigration of, 136; population of, in New York, 129, 136; subway service and, 65–66
History of Public Health in New York City, 1866–1966, A (Duffy), 159–60
Hoboken, N.J., 52
Hoffman, Hans, 206
homeless persons, 5, 38, 91, 155–57, 189
Home of the Brave, The (Laurents), 215–16
homicide rate, 162
homosexuals, 5; rights of, 44, 45, 183, 236; as teachers, 45, 169
hospitals: Doctors, 28–29; municipal, 23, 26–27, 148; voluntary and proprietary, 27
Hotel Theresa, 137
hotels: segregated, 136–37; as temporary housing, 91
House of Representatives, U.S., representation in, 190
housing, 84–90; in the Bronx, 23, 30–31, 35–36, 84, 90, 93; in Brooklyn, 23, 34, 36, 203; deterioration of, 90–93; discrimination in, 21, 88, 92, 137, 139; ethnic groups and, 97, 98; gentrification and, 35–37, 93; location, effects of, 93–96; luxury, 39, 58; middle-class, 26, 41, 137, 222, 226; postwar, 17, 26, 84–93; prewar, 26, 84, 86; in Queens, 23, 194; rehabilitation, 36, 37, 87, 91, 92; and rent control, 98–104; shortage of, 90, 92; Staten Island, 23, 35; suburban, 15, 58, 194; subsidies, 45, 91; and taxation, 40, 87; temporary, 91; on upper East Side, 29, 30; for veterans, 17, 85, 87; welfare tenants, effects of, 96–98; *see also* apartment houses, rent control
housing, public, 88–90, 187; Democratic party and, 198; federally funded, 89, 91–93; overcrowding in, 92; state and city, 90; temporary hotel quarters for, 91; U.D.C. and, 224–25

Housing Authority, 31, 32, 89, 92
housing construction, 84–90
Howe, Irving, 130
Hudson River, 4, 14, 24, 47, 49, 50, 201
Hudson Tubes, 56
Human Rights Commission, 21

Iceman Cometh, The (O'Neill), 217
Idea of Poverty, The (Himmelfarb), 152
illegitimacy, 160, 168–69, 232
immigrants, 25, 31, 129–36; blacks vs., 140–42, 177; denounced as criminals, 107; illegal, 76–77, 136; intermarriage and, 132–33; nativist attitudes toward, 106, 131, 134; in politics, 132; in public school system, 131, 176–77; quotas on, 134–35, 149; return to native lands by, 140; settlement houses for, 106, 150
Impelliteri, Vincent R., 19
infant mortality, 159–61
insurance: against crime, 110; fire, 95–96; health, 41, 78, 153, 160, 163, 232
integration, 41–42, 92
International Ladies' Garment Workers Union (ILGWU), 71, 76–77
Invisible Man (Ellison), 177
Irish-Americans, 18, 20, 61, 64, 107, 130, 133, 134
Israel, 206
Italian-Americans, 31, 107, 130, 133, 134

Jack, Hulan, 139, 199
Jackson, Jesse, 237
Jacobi, Abraham, 159–60
Jacobs, Jane, 35
jails, see prisons and jails
Jamaica, 66
Jamaica Bay, 17
Jews, 20, 61, 107, 132, 133, 134, 200;

blacks vs., 145, 173; elite among, 239; as portrayed in theater, 215–16
J-51 tax exemptions, 74–75, 87; see also housing
Jones, J. Raymond, 139, 199
Jones Beach, 199
judiciary: blacks in, 139; in criminal justice system, 119, 120, 123–26; federal, 119, 123–25; racial and sex discrimination examined by, 44, 220–21
Juilliard School of Music, 209
Junior League, 30
Justice Department, U.S., 43

Kanawha River, 48
Kefauver, Estes, 18
Kefauver hearings (1948), 195
Kennedy International Airport, 18, 55
Kerner commission report, 193
Kew Gardens, 66
kidnapping, 111
Kiley, Robert, 65, 233
Kingsley, Sidney, 38–39
Koch, Edward I., 12–13, 23, 79–80, 179, 200–201, 234–38; anti-rich bias of, 235, 238; blacks and, 236–37; Consolidated Edison and, 82–83; Lasker criticized by, 124; middle class and, 40–41, 45, 235, 236; reform Democrats and, 201, 237; unions and, 12, 234–35; Westway and, 201; World Trade Center sale supported by, 186
Korean-Americans, 39

Labor party, 190
LaGuardia, Fiorello, 61, 189–90, 199
LaGuardia Airport, 55
landmark preservation, 30, 205
Landmarks Conservancy, 30
Lasker, Morris, 123–24
Laurents, Arthur, 215

Lawson, John Howard, 212–13
lawyers, 29, 49, 118
Lefrak, Samuel J., 69
Legal Aid Society, 118
Lehman, Herbert H., 200
L'Enfant, Pierre Charles, 187
Levitt, Arthur, 21
Lexington Avenue, 7–8
Liberal party, 21, 23
life expectancy, 157–59, 163
Lincoln Center for the Performing Arts, 205, 209
Lindsay, John, 21–23, 54, 62, 99, 125; as Democrat, 12, 23; police force and, 117, 179, 180; transit strike and, 12
litter, 6
Little Italy, 61
Lombard, Carole, 112
Lombroso, Cesare, 109
London, 14, 26, 109
Long Island, 15; assessed property values on, 194; rail service to, 57–58; state prison on, 124
Long Island Expressway, 199
Long Island Rail Road, 63, 73
longshoremen, 51, 55
looting, 13
Louis, Joe, 136–37
Lower Bay, 24, 34
lower East Side, 61

McCoy, Rhody A., 172–73
McGlynn, Edward, 181
McGraw-Hill Building, 4–5
Macy's, 63
Madison Avenue, 7, 30
Magistrate's Court, 125
Manes, Donald, 192
Manhattan: automobiles in, 57; cable TV in, 80; as New York City, 49
manufacturing, 25, 68–83; chemical, 70; in Enterprise Zones, 80–82; factory obsolescence in, 70, 75; garment, 26, 61, 69, 70, 71, 76–77, 134;

neighborhood groups vs., 72, 73, 74; reasons for exodus of, 78; zoning restrictions on, 71, 74
Marshall Plan, 51–52
Mayor's Committee on Management Survey, 22
Mayor's Committee on Slum Clearance, 202
Medicaid, 78, 153, 160, 163
Medicare, 41, 232
melting pot, 130–34
mental institutions, persons released from, 38, 91, 116, 155–57
Merton, Robert, 94
Metropolitan Life Insurance Company, 84, 137
Metropolitan Museum of Art, 204–5, 209
Metropolitan Opera Company, 204–5, 209
Metropolitan Transit Authority, 12, 63–67, 233–34
middle class: blacks in, 40, 138, 142, 236; future as viewed by, 39–40, 45; housing for, 26, 41, 137, 222, 226; Koch and, 40–41, 45, 235, 236; occupations of, 39; programs of benefit to, 232–33; taxation of, 40, 232; visibility of, 38–39
Mobil Building, 8
Mohawk River, 47
Monitor, 49
moral order, restoration of, 163–66
Morris, Charles R., 225–26
mortgages, 86, 94–95, 224, 225, 227–28
Moscow, 15
Moses, Robert, 199–203; as candidate for governor, 199–200; fall from power, 201–3; Westway and, 201
Motley, Constance Baker, 139
Moynihan, Daniel Patrick, 130
muggers, 109, 115, 164
Mulberry Street, 34
Municipal Assistance Corporation, 231

municipal bond ratings, 13–14
municipal buildings, 17
municipal employees, 17, 33–35; during fiscal crisis, 230–31; wages and benefits of, 78
My Man Godfrey (film), 112

Nadler, Jerrold, 58
Narrows, the, 24, 34, 46
Nassau County, 194, 199
National Association for the Advancement of Colored People (NAACP), 137
National Council of Churches, 183–84
National Origins Immigration Act (1921), 134–35, 136, 149
Native Son (Wright), 213
nativism, 106, 131, 134
neighborhood associations, 37
Newark, N.J., 52, 56
Newburyport, Mass., 49
New Jersey, 5, 51, 52–53, 58; industry moving to, 72–73
New York Central Railroad, 50
New York City Charter, 180–81
New Yorker, 11, 27
New York Herald, 6
New York Herald Tribune, 20
New York Magazine, 105–6
New York Naval Shipyard, 50, 124–25
New York Philharmonic orchestra, 209
New York Post, 136
New York Public Library, 6–7
New York State Power Authority, 199
New York Times, 10, 11, 20, 33, 52, 220, 224
New York University, 6
Norfolk, Va., 50
Normandie, S.S., 14
nuclear power generation, 147–48

Oak Ridge, Tenn., 85
Ocean Hill-Brownsville school district, 171–74
O'Dwyer, William, 9–11, 14, 16–19, 28, 61–62, 113
Office of Price Administration, 99
Of Thee I Sing (Gershwin and Gershwin), 111
"Ol' Man River," 211
Olmsted, Frederick Law, 108
opera, 27, 204–5, 209, 212
operating costs, municipal, 21
Operation Bootstrap, 81

Paris, 15
Park Avenue, 7, 30, 37–38
parks, 189, 199; Bryant, 6; Carl Schurz, 28; Central, 11, 108, 209
parole, 120, 122
Partisan Review, 204
PATH trains, 56
Patrolmen's Benevolent Association, 180–81
peep shows, 6
Peter Cooper Village, 84
Petrified Forest, The (film), 111
Philadelphia, Pa., 36, 48, 49, 50, 204
piers, 4, 14, 52–54, 58, 186, 188
Pittsburgh, Pa., 25
plea bargaining, 118
Pleydell, Albert, 10
police brutality, 23, 178
Police Department, 5, 13, 117–18, 150, 175, 178–81; blacks in, 133, 143, 179–80, 220–21; civilian complaints against, 180–81; corruption in, 107, 108, 196; ethnic composition of, 130, 133; formation of, 188–89; priorities of, 116; professionalism of, 26; racism in, 178; size of, in Lindsay administration, 117; size of, in 1945, 26; transit, 66, 116; women in, 179
Pollock, Jackson, 218

Pope, Generoso, 18
population: aggregate, 160; in jails and prisons, 113; land resources for growth in, 27; in manufacturing jobs, 69; nonwhite, 129, 136; in public housing, 89; in rental units, 79, 84, 100; on welfare, 154
Porgy (Heyward), 211–12
Porgy and Bess (Gershwin and Gershwin), 212
pornography, 5, 6
Port Authority of New York and New Jersey, 5, 52–59, 63; office space owned by, 59, 185–86; port facilities of, 52–55; transportation facilities of, 5, 55–56, 59, 189
port of New York, 24, 34, 46–47, 48, 49, 55–59
Potomac River, 48
Powell, William, 112
Power Broker, The (Caro), 203
prayer in school, 169–70
preparatory schools, 29
press: foreign-language, 135; immigrants' assimilation aided by, 132
Prison Association, 106
prisons and jails, 26, 106, 118–26, 179; conditions in, 119, 123–24; construction of, 122, 123, 124, 125; cost of, 121, 123, 125; property values and, 123; purpose of, 119–20
private clubs, 45, 236
probation, 120, 122, 126
professionals, 35–36
Progress and Poverty (George), 181
Progresso, Il, 18
Prohibition, 110–12, 134
Project Finance Agency, 225
prostitution, 5, 107, 112, 196
Public Enemy (film), 111
publishing, 217
Puerto Ricans: election of, 43; population of, in New York, 129, 136; *see also* Hispanics
Puerto Rico, 81

Quakers, 119
quality of life: crime and, 116–17; manufacturing and, 72, 74
Queens: Democratic party in, 192; housing in, 23, 194; manufacturing in, 73–74; as part of New York, 61; proposed garment district in, 69; subway service in, 66, 195; undervalued property in, 194; waterfront in, 60
Quick Roll Leaf Manufacturing Company, 73–74

railroads, 50–51, 57–58; commuter, 63, 73; elevated, 60; *see also* subways
Ravitch, Richard, 12, 64–65, 229, 233
Reagan, Ronald, 81
real estate development: by Port Authority, 185–86; on waterfront, 58–59
Rebel, Priest, and Prophet (Bell), 181
Red Hook, 34, 54
redlining, 95–96
Reles, Abe, 18
religious organizations, 106, 119, 149, 181–84, 240–41
rent control, 93, 98–104, 194, 225, 226; alternatives to, 103–4; arguments for, 100–101; costs of, 102–3; Democratic support for, 198; *see also* housing
rent stabilization, 99
Republican party, 21, 22, 23, 189–90
restaurants: Greek, 132; inspection of, 162; Italian, 31, 32–33; segregated, 137
Revolutionary War, 49
Riis, Jacob, 155
Riis Park, 199
Riker's Island, 124, 200
River Club, 30
Riverdale, 61
Riverside Baptist Church, 182
Riverton Houses, 137

Robeson, Paul, 211
Robinson, Jackie, 137–38
Rockefeller, Nelson A., 62, 63, 224
Roebling, John A., 50, 60
Roebling, Washington A., 50, 60
Rohatyn, Felix, 229, 231
Ronan, William J., 63
Rosencrantz and Guildenstern Are Dead (Stoppard), 217
Rumsey, James, 48
Ryskind, Morrie, 111

St. Lawrence Seaway, 52, 199
St. Louis, Mo., 243
Salins, Peter, 96–97
S. & S. Corrugated Box Machinery Manufacturing Company, 72–73
Sanitation Department, 27, 37; salaries in, 33–34; unionization in, 35
school boards, local, 171–74
Schrafft's, 130
Scottsboro case, 212–13
Second Avenue, 8, 34
Second Avenue subway, 62
segregation, 136–40; in armed forces, 138, 214; in education, 41–42, 136, 168, 170; in housing, 137; in public accommodations, 136–37
self-amortizing mortgages, 94
Selkirk, N.Y., 58
Senate, U.S., representation in, 190
Serkin, Rudolf, 206
settlement houses, 106, 150
Seventh Avenue, 5, 70, 93
sewage disposal, 186, 188
sex education, 168–69
Shanker, Albert, 173
Sharkey, Joseph, 198
shipping, 4, 14, 49, 52–55
shipyards, 49–50, 85
shopping bag ladies, 5
Show Boat (Hammerstein and Kern), 211, 213

Simpson, Sloan, 18
Single-Room Occupancy (S.R.O.) buildings, 91–92, 155, 156
Sixth Avenue, 6, 93
Smith, Alfred E., 199
smuggling, 110
social security, 41
solid waste disposal, 37, 147–48
Soviet Union, religious freedom in, 183–84
Staten Island: housing in, 23, 35; as part of New York, 61; waterfront in, 60
Steinbeck, John, 151
Stevenson, Adlai, 195, 197–98
stock market, 16, 61
street vendors, 6, 7
strikes: in construction trades, 108; fuel supplies jeopardized by (1946), 9–11, 13, 14; by teachers (1967), 172–74; by transit workers (1966, 1980), 12–13
Stuyvesant Town, 84, 137
suburbs, 5, 16, 189; black exodus to, 33
subways, 24–25, 60–67; during blackouts, 13; city unified by, 60–61; crime in, 66, 67, 114, 115, 116; deteriorating condition of, 64, 66, 233; fares for, 56, 61–62, 64, 198, 201, 232; maintenance of, 66–67; new equipment for, 64–65; proposed elimination of lines and stations, 65–66; ridership of, 64, 65, 66; Second Avenue line, 62; strikes shutting down, 12; unified system of, 61
Suffolk County, 199
suicides, 162
Sunnyside, 69
"sunshine" laws, 191
superblocks, 187
Supreme Court, U.S., 41–42, 123, 163
Sutton, Percy, 139

Tammany Hall, 18, 139, 196, 198–99, 201
taxation: of businesses, 78–79, 81; on industrial property, 74–76, 193; J-51 exemptions on, 74–75, 87; of middle class, 40, 232; organizations exempted from, 189
taxicabs, 39, 194
Taylor, Laurette, 10
Taylor Law, 62–63
television industry, 80, 217
tenements, 17, 39, 71, 85, 87–88
theaters: Broadway, 137, 204, 210–16; foreign-language, 132, 135; on Forty-second street, 4, 5; in Lincoln Center, 209; movie, 5, 6; off-off-off Broadway, 4; pornographic, 6; portrayal of blacks in, 210–15; segregated, 137
They Shall Not Die (Lawson), 212–13
three-card monte, 5
Times Square, 3, 5, 61, 65; proposed reconstruction of, 69
Tobey, Charles, 195–96
Tobin, Austin J., 52
Tocqueville, Alexis de, 149
Todd shipyard, 50
Tokyo, 15
Tombs jail, 123–24
topless bars, 5
Toscanini, Arturo, 206
tourism, 4, 5–6
traffic congestion, 57, 70
Transit Authority, 62, 63
transit police, 66, 116
transit system, 233–34; city's reliance on, 65; postwar middle class served by, 26; strikes shutting down, 12–13; *see also* subways
Transportation, Board of, 62
Triangle Shirtwaist fire, 71, 77
Triborough Bridge and Tunnel Authority, 200
Troy, N.Y., 47
trucking, 52
Tudor City, 8

tunnels, 24, 57–58, 59, 65
Turner, Frederick, 151
Twelfth Avenue, 4

unemployment, 70; from overseas competition, 77
unions, 39, 51, 53, 55, 149; in construction trades, 108; garment, 71, 76–77; Koch and, 12, 234–35; municipal, 35, 62–63, 234–35; paper, 108; police, 180–81; secondary wage scale permitted by, 76–77; teachers, 39, 172–74; theater, 206; transit, 12, 234
United Nations, 8, 105, 206–7
United States Steel Company, 128
universities, 6, 27, 31–32, 47–48
Upper Bay, 24, 34, 46
upper East Side, 28–30, 61
Urban Development Corporation (U.D.C.), 224–25, 227
Urban Masses and Moral Order in America, 1820–1920 (Boyer), 107–8, 149–51
urban renewal, 69, 73, 187–88, 203, 209–10

Vanderbilt, Commodore, 50
Venus Observed (Fry), 217
Vermont, 83
Vernon, Raymond, 70
veterans: educational benefits for, 167; housing for, 17, 85
violence, 6
visiting nurse societies, 106
Voting Rights Act (1965), 42–43, 190

Wagner, Robert F., Jr., 19–21, 23, 125
Wagner, Susan, 20
Wagner Act (1935), 77

Waiting for Godot (Beckett), 217
Wall Street, 16, 61, 65, 108
Wall Street Journal, 225–26
Walter, Bruno, 206
Ward, Benjamin, 179
Ward's Island, 160
Washington, D.C., 187
Washington, George, 48
Washington Heights, 31
water supply system, 27, 148, 162, 186, 188
Weisman, Steven, 224
welfare, 22, 41, 140, 148, 151–55; basic failure of, 232; city expenditures for, 154; housing and, 91, 96–98; population on, 154
West Indians, 142
West Side, 57
West Virginia, 48
Westway, 4, 201

Whitney Museum of American Art, 206
Williams, Tennessee, 10
women: rights of, 44, 45, 183, 221, 236; in work force, 145, 179
World of Our Fathers (Howe), 130
World Trade Center, 59, 185–86
Wright, Richard, 213

Yorkville, 136
Youth Board, 113–14, 150
youthful offenders, 120, 122
youth services, 17, 113–14, 149–50
Yunich, David, 63

zoning, 37, 71, 74, 136, 224